ISLAM IN
CONTEXT

ISLAM IN
CONTEXT

PAST, PRESENT, AND FUTURE

PETER G. RIDDELL
AND PETER COTTERELL

Baker Academic
A Division of Baker Book House Co
Grand Rapids, Michigan 49516

©2003 by Peter G. Riddell and Peter Cotterell

Published by Baker Academic
a division of Baker Book House Company
P.O. Box 6287, Grand Rapids, MI 49516-6287
www.bakeracademic.com

Printed in the United States of America

Library of Congress Cataloging-in-Publication Data

Riddell, Peter G.
    Islam in context : past, present, and future / Peter G. Riddell and Peter Cotterell.
      p. cm.
    Includes bibliographical references and index.
    ISBN 0-8010-2627-X (pbk.)
    1. Islam. 2. Islam—Essence, genius, nature. 3. Islam—Doctrines. 4. Islam—History.
  5. Civilization, Islamic. I. Cotterell, Peter, 1930– II. Title.
BP161.3 .R53 2003
297—dc21   2002154564

CONTENTS

ILLUSTRATIONS

INTRODUCTION

This book has been written with three aims in mind. First, we wish to help the reader to understand Islam. Wherever possible we have tried to look at the history and theology of Islam from the perspective of Muslims.

Second, we have sought to present an understanding of the ongoing interaction between the Islamic world and the rest of the world. We believe that it is impossible to understand present-day tensions, still less to resolve them, without identifying their underlying causes. In identifying those causes it is not sufficient to look at events in the immediate past. Rather, we need to go further back, to the root causes, which frequently are to be found in seeds sown by early history and sacred texts.

Our third aim is to take the next logical step and to attempt to identify a viable way forward that might help to resolve present tensions and conflict. In our view it is not the non-Muslim world that stands at the crossroads, but the Muslim world. Islam has, throughout its history, contained within itself a channel of violence, legitimized by certain passages of the Qur'an, though put in question by other passages.

The two streams within Islam, the violent stream and the stream advocating a more moderate approach to the non-Muslim world, have existed through the centuries but in constant tension. That tension has irrupted from time to time in internal conflicts, and sometimes in conflicts with surrounding nations. These have usually been relatively localized conflicts. But in the twenty-first century the situation has changed in a radical and potentially catastrophic way. It is now possible for relatively small but determined and well-financed groups to make use of sophisticated modern technology to threaten destruction on an unprecedented scale. Recent research by both Muslims and non-Muslims shows that these extremist groups have a strong attraction, especially among idealistic youth.

As President George W. Bush has attempted to do with the al-Qa'ida network, so other political leaders may be able to deal with the *acts* of such radical groups. But ultimately it is only the Muslim world that can deal with the roots of the problem, which, in our view, do *not* lie in Western materialism or nineteenth-century colonialism or American imperialism, but in Islam's own history, both distant and recent. Some moderate Muslim scholars agree. In the words of the Pakistani writer Izzat Majeed,

> We Muslims cannot keep blaming the West for all our ills. We have to first get our own house in order before we can even make any credible struggle possible to rid us of ignorance, living-in-the-past chest thumping and intolerance of the modern world. . . . Without a reformation in the practice of Islam that makes it move forward and not backward, there is no hope for us Muslims anywhere.[1]

This view stands in contrast to the current view that places the burden of blame on the non-Muslim world in general and on the United States of America in particular.

Our hope is that this book will appeal to readers raised in the broad Judeo-Christian tradition, though perhaps not actively practicing a particular faith. But we also hope that the book will find readers among those who do seriously practice their faith, whether Christianity, Islam, or Judaism.

The book is divided into three parts. The first focuses on the distant past, the period in which the foundations of Islam were laid, with an emphasis on the lifetime of Muhammad and his immediate successors. Here, although we have looked at the development of Islamic theologies, this has not been a major concern.

The second part of the book deals with the medium past, that period characterized by the clash of empires, a clash that has contributed so much to the present-day relationship between Islam and the non-Muslim world. We have included a consideration of the Crusades, Muslim empires, European colonialism, and the contentious Christian missionary movement.

Part 3 considers the more recent past and the present. This period is obviously marked both by ongoing and largely unresolved tensions and by actual conflict. Here we have offered tentative suggestions for appropriate responses of governments and of Christianity, but also responses that might be appropriate for the majority moderate Muslim world.

There are several features of this book that might be considered distinctive. First, we have attempted to penetrate beyond the many

---

1. Izzat Majeed, "Open Letter to Osama bin Laden," *The Nation*, November 9, 2001.

stereotypes that have circulated concerning the person of Muhammad, both negative stereotypes from non-Muslim writers and idealized stereotypes from Muslim writers.

Again, we have argued against the myth that empire is a one-sided thing, insisting instead that Western colonialism is only one chapter in the saga of empires, and that the ongoing clash between Muslim and largely "Christian" empires has sown seeds that have grown to the harvest we see today.

And we have tried to maintain a balance between academic rigor and readability. We have assured rigor by making critical reference to original sources such as the Qur'an, the collection of Traditions by Bukhari, the biography of Muhammad written by Ibn Ishaq, and other works by Muslims down the centuries. We also refer to original Western and Christian sources, such as the various chronicles of the Crusades. We strive to achieve readability by avoiding the esoteric and the obscure.

Finally, we address some of the hard questions. We challenge the non-Muslim world to attempt to understand Islam from the perspective of Muslims and to acknowledge past mistakes. At the same time, we challenge the Muslim world by suggesting that Islam stands today at a vital crossroads, and the way forward is for them alone to decide. As with all religious movements, Islam has, in its long history, faced many such crossroads: obvious examples are the one that inevitably confronted it at the death of Muhammad and the one following the massacre at Karbala.

The crossroads analogy is helpful if it is properly understood: the decision taken at the crossroads determined on each occasion whether Islam would advance along a single road (as it largely did after the death of Muhammad) or along several distinct roads (as it did after Karbala). At the beginning of the twenty-first century Islam advances to the crossroads along several routes, among them the road of violence. The question of significance to the future history of the world is whether, after negotiating the crossroads, the highway of violence will have been closed off, leaving Islam to advance peacefully, albeit along more than one road.

Peter G. Riddell
Peter Cotterell
London, June 2002

PART 1

LOOKING BACK

1

BEGINNINGS

When Muhammad was born in Mecca, more than five centuries after the birth of Christ, a movement was initiated that would utterly transform Arabia and the fortunes of the Arab peoples in the space of a mere twenty years. Few men have had a greater impact on world affairs, lasting century after century, than this man Muhammad.

Muhammad ibn Abdullah was born in Mecca, probably in the year 570. By the time of his death at the age of sixty-two he had brought into existence a dynamic movement that would carry Islam through the centuries and across the continents, birthing empires, transforming the sciences, and challenging economic, cultural, and political systems. At the twenty-first century, as occurred frequently in its past history, the Islamic faith that sprang out of Muhammad finds itself at a crossroads, facing a choice between a radical identity willing to use violence to achieve its goals, and a moderation that could accept and even welcome coexistence with other cultures; a choice between moving ahead along a single highway or pursuing separate roads, with travelers on each nervously eyeing the others.

ARABIA BEFORE MUHAMMAD

Muhammad came to a no-people. The Arabs were largely ignored by the two great empires of the sixth century: the Christian empire centered on Byzantium (Constantinople, the modern Istanbul), over to the west; and the Zoroastrian Sassanian empire to the east, in Persia. It is, perhaps, not surprising that Arabia was ignored. The great Empty Quarter held no attraction for the traveler, and the sea route to India had made the old overland caravan trail obsolete. The Arabs were peoples, not a people. The main thing that united them was their language, and even that was fragmented into a score of dialects.

The peoples of the Arabian peninsula had for centuries been largely nomadic, moving from one oasis to another, from one patch of scant

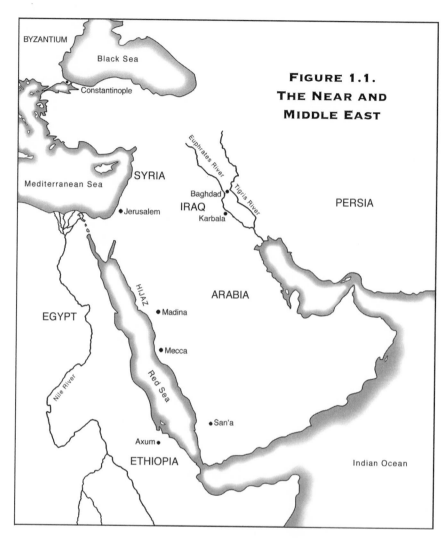

FIGURE 1.1.
THE NEAR AND
MIDDLE EAST

pasture to another, as water or vegetation failed.[1] Mecca had long been a center for trade, but through the years more and more people moved from the arid desert wastes to this new and fascinating city, with its Zamzam well, reputed to have healing properties.[2] But urban-

1. For a concise introduction to the historical and cultural milieu into which Islam was born, chapter 1 of Alfred Guillaume's *Islam,* 2d ed. (Harmondsworth: Penguin, 1956), is still invaluable. But see also the first chapter of Michael Nazir-Ali, *Islam: A Christian Perspective* (Exeter: Paternoster, 1983).

2. But for an alternative, revisionist approach to Mecca's history, cf. Patricia Crone, *Meccan Trade and the Rise of Islam* (Princeton: Princeton University Press, 1987).

ization, as always, brought with it problems. Out in the desert the rules were clear: look after your own clan. An attack on one is an attack on all. The need of one is the need of all. Fighting is unavoidable and noble. Death in fighting for the clan is an honorable death. If you are fortunate enough to live into old age, the clan will care for you, provide for you. Orphans, too, will be cared for. Every member of the clan of a few hundred people knew everyone else.

In the city all this was changed. Now there were the anonymous poor, with no one to care for them. There were fortunes to be made and lost, and with the fortunes went power. Beggars roamed the streets, orphans looked for help, the aged needed care. As always, the rich got richer but were never rich enough.

They had no religion in common. What they had was a confusing mixture: the worship of sun and moon, and stars, probably borrowed in part from the Zoroastrians, the worship of strangely shaped or unusually large stones, the worship of the spirits of trees and wells and springs. And providing it all with some kind of unity was the worship of idols, several hundred of them. The focal point for that unity was Mecca, where stood the Ka'ba, that cube-shaped storehouse for more than three hundred idols, kept by the Quraysh tribe and presided over by an official guardian.[3]

The term *Ka'ba* is related to the English word *cube,* and the building was just that, a cube-shaped building. It was not the only cube-shaped storehouse for idols in Arabia, but it was the most important. From time to time it had been destroyed by some accident and had to be rebuilt. At the time of Muhammad's birth, the Meccan Ka'ba was distinguished by a large stone built into one wall, the Black Stone. Later tradition maintained that the stone was originally white and had been given to Adam, some said to Abraham, as the foundation stone for the first House of Worship. But that was later tradition: at the time it was simply part of the stone worship of Arabia. Here, unexpectedly, is one of the important and perhaps surprising links of modern Islam to those early days, for the Ka'ba in Mecca in the twenty-first century contains that same Black Stone. It is certainly surprising that in such a strongly monotheistic religion as Islam a stone should play such a central role.

South of Mecca lay the great city of San'a, home to a good many Christians. Across the Red Sea lay the Christian kingdom of Ethiopia, founded on the lives of two Syrian Christian young men, Edesius and Frumentius, who had been shipwrecked on the Red Sea coast some-

---

3. See the article "Ka'ba," *The Encyclopaedia of Islam,* ed. J. H. Kramers et al., new ed. (Leiden: Brill, 1960–), 4:317–22.

time in the fourth century. It was probably Ethiopian influence that was responsible for that Christian presence in San'a. In the years ahead, the histories of Islam and Ethiopia would impact on each other many times.

MUHAMMAD: A PROPHET DISDAINED

When Muhammad was born in 570, his father, Abdullah, was already dead. This meant that his mother, Amina, was robbed of a husband in a strongly patriarchal society. The name Abdullah, *Abdu-llah*, Servant of Allah, is a reminder that his son did not invent the name of the One High God whom millions of Muslims through the coming centuries would worship.

For any account of the life of Muhammad we have three obvious sources: the Qur'an, the Traditions (*Hadith*), and the earliest biography of Muhammad that has survived, the *Sira* by Ibn Ishaq, translated into English by Alfred Guillaume and published as *The Life of Muhammad*.[4]

A Life of Muhammad?

The following attempt at a brief biography of Muhammad generally follows Ibn Ishaq and the Qur'an, but a quite different biography can be put together by playing down these obvious sources.[5] And that is possible, first, because there is no universal agreement among scholars as to the date when the Qur'an came to be written and assembled, and second, because Ibn Ishaq was writing more than one hundred years after Muhammad's death.[6] Not unconnected is, third, the fact that in the period after Muhammad's death traditions concerning his life and teaching began to accumulate, to multiply, some mere pious fabrications, some fabrications to support some disputed point of Muslim practice, some genuine memories. There is a good Muslim tradition saying that when Bukhari, one of six Muslim scholars who edited authoritative collections of these Traditions, came to assemble what he considered to be a reliable collection of them, he selected fewer than three thousand different Traditions from a total of six hundred thousand,[7] one half of 1 percent. And yet it must have been from these oral and written traditions that Ibn Ishaq compiled his *Sira*.

4. London and New York: Oxford University Press, 1955.
5. See, for example, Martin Lings, *Muhammad: His Life Based on the Earliest Sources* (New York: Inner Traditions International, 1983).
6. See W. Montgomery Watt, "The Reliability of Ibn Ishaq's Sources," in his *Early Islam* (Edinburgh: Edinburgh University Press, 1990), chap. 1.
7. See the article "Al-Bukhari," *Encyclopaedia of Islam*, 1:1296.

The position is summed up conservatively by Patricia Crone and Michael Cook:

> There is no hard evidence for the existence of the Koran in any form before the last decade of the seventh century, and the tradition which places this rather opaque revelation in its historical context is not attested before the middle of the eighth. The historicity of the Islamic tradition is thus to some degree problematic: while there are no cogent internal grounds for rejecting it, there are equally no cogent external grounds for accepting it.[8]

These two scholars proceed to set aside the traditional sources. Of the resulting biography Clinton Bennett says:

> According to these writers, Muhammad's life, as recorded in the *Sira*, is largely the invention of later generations; the real Muhammad was a Messianic-type figure who led a movement to re-possess Jerusalem; the Qur'an was posthumously composed sometime during the Khalifate of Abd al-Malik.[9]

The biography set out here takes a more positive view both of the Qur'an and of Ibn Ishaq's *Sira*, but at the same time recognizes that what we have in both is a redaction, a rewriting of events from the perspective of a period after Muhammad's death.

As usual in those days, the babe was put out to a wet nurse, a poor woman who would care for children until they were weaned, which might not be until they were three or even four years old. But this fact confirms other hints that the family was not a poor one. Indeed, it was an influential family. Muhammad's grandfather, Abd al-Muttalib, was guardian of the Ka'ba. His uncle, Abu Talib, was clan chief of the Hashimites, one of the ten or so clans that made up the Quraysh, the dominant tribe of Mecca.

The Year of the Elephant

Muslim tradition calls the year of Muhammad's birth The Year of the Elephant as a reminder of the attempt of the Ethiopian Regent in southern Arabia, the Yemen, to destroy the Ka'ba. In 523 there was a

8. Patricia Crone and Michael Cook, *Hagarism* (Cambridge and London: Cambridge University Press, 1977), 3.

9. Clinton Bennett, *In Search of Muhammad* (London and New York: Cassell, 1998), 110. John Wansbrough's alternative approach to the origins of Islam, presenting it as a movement that developed and came to fruition outside Arabia, is sympathetically considered by G. R. Hawting, "John Wansbrough, Islam, and Monotheism," in *The Quest for the Historical Muhammad* (New York: Prometheus, 2000), 520–23.

massacre of Christians in Yemen, and the Byzantine emperor, Justin, called on Ethiopia to go to the aid of the Christians there. This example of Christian solidarity in the face of non-Christian threats was to be repeated during the Crusades over five hundred years later.

Not only did the Ethiopians defeat the oppressors, they also annexed the Yemen to Ethiopia, whose emperor sent a man named Aryat as his viceroy. Aryat was soon displaced by the ambitious Abraha, defeated in single combat and killed. It was probably Abraha who built the big church in San'a. This church quickly established itself as a pilgrimage destination and was on track to eclipse the Ka'ba in Mecca. Rivalry between the Yemenis in the south and the Meccans to the north became more and more bitter, exploding when one of Abraha's allies in the Hijaz area between the two was assassinated. Abraha mounted a punitive expedition with the express intention of destroying the Ka'ba.

According to legend Abraha assembled an army of some twenty thousand men, and added to them thirteen elephants, headed by an enormous beast named Mahmud. The advance guard entered Mecca and took a certain amount of plunder, including two hundred camels belonging to Muhammad's grandfather, Abd al-Muttalib, guardian of the Ka'ba. He went out to meet Abraha and demanded the return of his camels. Abraha received him with respect but said: "You pleased me much when I saw you; then I was much displeased with you when I heard what you said. Do you wish to talk to me about two hundred camels . . . and say nothing about your religion and the religion of your forefathers, which I have come to destroy?" To that Abd al-Muttalib replied: "I am the owner of the camels, and the temple has an owner who will defend it."

The next day Abraha's army advanced on Mecca, led by Mahmud, the elephant. But once Mecca was in sight, the elephant refused to advance. Still facing Mecca it knelt down, and no amount of beating with iron bars or even with metal hooks could drive Mahmud to its feet. And now a strange cloud appeared in the west: great flocks of birds. As they came closer, it could be seen that each bird carried three stones, one in each claw and one in its beak. Some traditions said that the names of Abraha's soldiers were written on the stones. As the birds swooped over the soldiers, they dropped their stones on the named targets, killing any man hit by his stone.

Now came a further wonder: a roaring sound heralded a sudden flood of water, sweeping down from the mountains. It raged through Abraha's camp, sweeping away the bodies of Abraha's soldiers. The scattered remnant of the army fled southward, among them Abraha himself, stricken by some dreadful disease. When he reached San'a he died. There was only one survivor, Abu Yaksum, who took the melancholy story back to the Negus, the king, in Ethiopia,

> and going directly to the king told him the tragic story; and upon that Prince's asking him what sort of birds they were that had occasioned such a destruction the man pointed to one of them, which had followed him all the way, and was at this time hovering directly over his head, when immediately the bird let fall the stone, and struck him dead at the king's feet.[10]

That is the legend lying behind the history that scholars are trying to establish. The reference to the stones may allude to an outbreak of smallpox, which first appeared in Arabia about this time. The flood of water may well refer to a dam that burst its retaining wall at this time. In any case, the story cannot refer to the year of Muhammad's birth, 570; by then Abraha was already dead. The one reference to this event in the Qur'an is in Sura 105, but there is no suggestion there that the event coincided with the birth of Muhammad. According to J. S. Trimingham[11] the expedition occurred somewhere between 540 and 546, some thirty years before Muhammad's birth. Nevertheless, some significance can be found in this account since it provides early evidence of conflict between Christian empires and the religious authorities in Mecca. This rivalry and conflict was to intensify greatly in coming centuries.

Muhammad the Orphan

As an orphan Muhammad was of little importance in Meccan affairs, but he almost certainly suffered from the typical urban neglect of orphans, widows, the poor, and the aged. In later years he would remember his experiences. His mother died when he was six years old, and then his grandfather Abd al-Muttalib cared for him. And when his grandfather died, his uncle Abu Talib cared for him. As a young man he traveled with Abu Talib's trading caravan into Syria; on these journeys he probably heard some of the stories from the Old Testament and encountered the more powerful and developed world of the Christian Byzantine empire. He may have contrasted what he saw in Syria, a people united in the worship of one God, with the lot of the fragmented Arab peoples of his homeland, worshiping a multiplicity of idols.

10. See A. Guillaume's translation of Ibn Ishaq's biography of Muhammad, *The Life of Muhammad*, 25–30.
11. J. S. Trimingham, *Islam in Ethiopia* (London: Oxford University Press, 1952), 38–42.

FIGURE 1.2. LIFE OF MUHAMMAD

From His Birth to the First Visions: 570–610 (40 years)

?	Death of his father, Abdullah
570	Traditional date of Muhammad's birth at Mecca
576	Death of his mother; cared for by his grandfather Abd al-Muttalib, then by his uncle Abu Talib
582	Tradition of a journey to Syria with his uncle's caravan; prophecy of the Syrian monk Bahira
595	Marriage to Khadija

From the First Visions to the Hijra: 610–622 (12 years)

610	Muhammad as Warner; persecution begins
615	*Hijra* to Ethiopia
616	Quraysh boycott of the Hashimites
619	Death of Khadija and Abu Talib; Abu Lahab becomes clan leader
620	First contact with Yathrib, later known as Madina (Medina)
621	First oath of al-'Aqaba, the Oath of Women
622	Second oath of al-'Aqaba; Hijra to Madina

From the Hijra to the Submission of Mecca: 622–630 (8 years)

622*	Constitution of Madina promulgated; categories of emigrants and helpers emerge
624	Successful Nakhla raid; *razzia* becomes *jihad*; Battle of Badr
625	Battle of Uhud; paradise promised to those killed on jihad
627	Siege of Madina and Battle of the Ditch; men of Banu Qurayza executed
628	Attempted pilgrimage; Treaty of Hudaybiyya
630	Mecca entered; Ka'ba idols destroyed

From the Submission of Mecca to Muhammad's Death: 630–632 (2 years)

630	Battle of Hunayn; defeat of Hawazin
March 632	Muhammad performs Greater Pilgrimage
June 8, 632	Death of Muhammad

*Later became year 1 in the Muslim calendar.

Legend also has it that on one of the journeys into Syria Muhammad encountered a Christian monk named Bahira. Bahira had previously ignored these caravans, but after receiving a vision he prepared a feast for the travelers. Being just a boy, Muhammad was left behind to guard the baggage. Bahira, however, insisted that he be sent for, to join in the meal. Then Bahira questioned Muhammad about his lifestyle, examined the boy, and found between his shoulder blades the seal of prophethood. Abu Talib was then questioned about the boy and warned to take care of him: "Take your nephew back to his country and guard him carefully against the Jews, for by Allah! if they see him and know about him what I know, they will do him evil; a great future lies before this nephew of yours."[12] Even at this early stage of the account of the life of Muhammad, we can perceive a theme which would recur throughout his life and in later Islamic history: a deep suspicion of the Jews.

Back in Mecca the abilities of Muhammad and the swiftness of his mind were becoming apparent. After the Ka'ba had been accidentally destroyed on a particular occasion and was being rebuilt, the moment came for placing the Black Stone in position. The men could not agree on who should have that honor and decided to accept the advice of the next man to come into the court of the Ka'ba. The next man was Muhammad. His advice was Solomonic: place the Black Stone in a blanket, and each of you help to lift the blanket and carry the stone into position.[13]

Marriage to Khadija and a New Life

Khadija was a widow, an entrepreneur who ran her own trading caravans into Syria. She hired Muhammad to take charge of one of these caravans. The relationship developed, and despite the fact that she was fifteen years older than Muhammad, he married her. He remained faithful to her until her death, and she exercised a great influence on him, supporting him when he doubted himself, and through the marriage giving him a new and more influential position in Meccan society. Perhaps as important, she gave him leisure time. Muhammad took to retiring out to the desert, musing, pondering what he had seen in Syria and what that might mean for his Arab people. The cave

12. Guillaume, *Life of Muhammad*, 80f.

13. See the article "Ka'ba," *Encyclopaedia of Islam*, 4:317–22. This article notes the incident of the repositioning of the Black Stone at Muhammad's suggestion, but Maxime Rodinson (*Mohammed* [Harmondsworth: Penguin, 1971], 52) queries the historicity of the event. Ignaz Goldziher provides a rationale for the preservation of Ka'ba, Black Stone, and their related ceremonies: "The sacred memorial places of the Ka'ba associated with patriarchal times had their origin, like the whole Islamic cult of the Ka'ba, in the need to make acceptable to the new order pagan ceremonies that, because of the Arab character attached to ancestral tradition, were indispensable" (*Muslim Studies*, vol. 2 [London: Allen and Unwin, 1971], 279). See also Malise Ruthven, "Introductory: Pilgrimage to Mecca," chap. 1 of *Islam in the World*, 2d ed. (London: Penguin, 2000), esp. 13–17.

Hira was a favorite nighttime retreat for him. In that cave during his fortieth year Muhammad claimed to have received the first of the revelations that he would experience for the rest of his life. These would one day be written down and collected to become the Qur'an.

Muhammad himself was at first confused by his experiences. The Arabs believed in divinities, but they also believed in the *jinn,* spirits, especially spirits that inhabited the deserts. He wondered if his ideas were coming from them. Khadija, apparently, was the one who reassured him, and thus with new confidence Muhammad began to preach his message. It is all but impossible to assess this claim to revelation. Certainly the Qur'an itself details events at the cave Hira, and it is reasonably certain that Muhammad later claimed to have received further revelations, although never again in quite the way they had come in the cave. There, he said, the angel Gabriel had transmitted the revelations to him. Later it was claimed to be more subtle: the ideas were dropped into his mind as unconsciously as the bees learned how and where to construct their hives. It was *wahy,* inspiration, owing nothing to his own knowledge or volition.

For Muslims there can be no questioning the view that what Muhammad received was revelation from Allah, mediated by an angel. For the rationalist such as Maxime Rodinson, the Marxist writer on Islam, the question as to "what really happened" is less easily answered. His suggestion is that it was Muhammad's subconscious mind, working on all that he had learned from Jews and Christians, that produced the visions.[14] In any alternative explanation of the source of the "revelations," one must give due weight first to the fact that physical manifestations appear to have accompanied them, and second to the fact that either Muhammad or those who heard him or both were able to distinguish between his regular conversation and the "revelations," between what went into the Qur'an and what was reserved for the later collection of Prophetic Traditions.

Exactly what constituted the initial message is uncertain.[15] We do have the evidence of the Qur'an itself, but this is complicated by the manner in which the Qur'an has been assembled. The individual chapters, *suras,* are mostly composite, containing sections from different points in Muhammad's lifetime. And when the chapters were brought together, it was decided to have the longer chapters first and the shorter chapters last, a system that is almost exactly the opposite of their chronological order. The short chapters at the end represent

---

14. Rodinson, *Mohammed,* 77.

15. Most Muslims would accept Sura 96:1–5 as the first revelation to come to Muhammad.

some of Muhammad's earlier words, and those at the beginning his later words.

Muhammad as Warner

Even with this uncertainty we can at least suggest that Muhammad's early teaching had three strands to it. First was what would remain at the center of Islam, the statement that God is one and that there is but one God: the central doctrine of *tawhid*, oneness. Tawhid obviously implied an attack on the religion of the day, the worship of idols, and with it an attack on the prosperity that idolatry brought to Mecca. The second emphasis was a call to care for the aged, the widow, the orphan. As we have seen, Muhammad knew something of the experience of being a nobody, and now he spoke out against the heartlessness of the wealthy and the powerful. Third, he proclaimed himself a Warner, admonishing his listeners about the reality of hell awaiting those who ignored his call to believe in the one God.

Behind the Arabs were the years of ignorance, the age of *jahiliyya;* now an Arabic revelation had come for them, parallel to those already given to the Jews in Hebrew and to the Gentiles in Greek.

There was a ready response to this new teaching, both from among the poor, responding to his concern for them, and from the influential, responding rather to the intellectual appeal of the one God over against the absurdity of idolatry. Inevitably there was opposition, too. Bilal bin Ribah was a slave who became a follower of the new teaching and signified it by his continual repetition of what was obviously already a catchphrase of Muhammad's followers: "One, One." His owner, Umayya bin Khalaf, had Bilal dragged out into the desert and thrown on his back. A rock was placed on his chest, and Umayya threatened him: "You will stay here till you die or deny Muhammad and worship Al-Lat and Al-'Uzza."[16]

But Bilal's only response was the unvarying "One, One." Abu Bakr, an early follower of Muhammad and later his first successor, saw his sufferings and agreed to exchange one of his own slaves for Bilal, whom he immediately freed. Here we have evidence of the broad appeal of Muhammad's early message.

The persecution increased until in 615 Muhammad decided that it would be best for some, at least, of his followers to take refuge across the Red Sea in Christian Ethiopia (Abyssinia). This is sometimes called the first *hijra*, some seven years before the Hijra, the emigration to Madina (Medina), that now marks year one in the Muslim calendar.

16. The anecdote is recorded in some detail by Ibn Ishaq. See Guillaume, *Life of Muhammad*, 143–44, 303.

The Wicked, or "Satanic," Verses

In Mecca the persecution continued and even intensified, and Muhammad seems to have offered a compromise. While reciting what is now Sura 53, "The Star," he called out, "Have you thought of al-Lat and al-'Uzza and Manat the third, the other? . . . These are the exalted Gharaniq [birds?] whose intercession is approved."

These words, the so-called Wicked Verses, were taken by Salman Rushdie as the focus of *The Satanic Verses*, his book that caused enormous offense throughout the Muslim world. The event, Muhammad's supposed compromise, had been a matter of scholarly discussion for centuries, but it had never previously been brought to public attention. It is certainly not a Christian invention since all the evidence for it comes from Muslim sources. The classical Muslim writer Al-Tabari (who died in 923, three hundred years after the incident) says that Satan put the words onto Muhammad's tongue.[17] The Ahmadi text and translation of the Qur'an by Malik Ghulam Farid has an extended footnote on the matter that appears first of all to deny the incident altogether, and then to explain the offending words as being an interjection from an unbelieving Meccan bystander.[18] And yet Muhammad's action is entirely understandable: his followers were being tortured and persecuted, his movement would inevitably be threatened or even extinguished if the persecution worsened, and a wise man would make some concession to Meccan sensibilities. The recognition given to the three Meccan deities was limited: they were no longer deities but were *intercessors*. And the immediate results were gratifying: opposition ceased, and accessions to Islam multiplied.

But it seems that Muhammad soon realized that in giving some limited recognition to the three deities, he had compromised his central teaching, *tawhid*, the oneness of God. So the offending words relating to intercession were withdrawn, and the text that now stands at Sura 53:19–23 reads:

> Have ye seen Lat and Uzza and another, the third, Manat?
> What! For you the male sex, and for Him, the female?
> Behold, such would be indeed a division most unfair!
> These are nothing but names which ye have devised—ye and your
>   fathers—
> For which Allah has sent down no authority.

17. Guillaume, *Life of Muhammad*, 165f.
18. *The Holy Qur'an* (Rabwah, Pakistan: Oriental and Religious Publishing Corporation, 1969), 1138 n. 22, 882.

The news of the concession to the Meccan deities and the cessation of persecution seems to have reached the refugees in Ethiopia, indicating that it was now safe to return to Mecca. Many did so, but following Muhammad's about-face they found the persecution as bad or worse.

The Persecution Deepens

In 619 came the deaths of both Muhammad's wife Khadija and his uncle, the clan leader, who had protected him from personal attack. The new clan leader, Abd al-Uzza ibn Abd al-Muttalib, was nicknamed Abu Lahab, Father of Flames. He immediately withdrew all support from Muhammad. Abu Lahab's wife, Umm Jamil, is reputed to have crept out at night to lay bundles of thorns on the path where Muhammad was known to walk. By their actions they earned themselves a place in history, having a chapter of the Qur'an (Sura 111) devoted to them:

> Perish the hands of the Father of Flame! Perish he!
> No profit to him from all his wealth, and all his gains!
> Burnt soon will he be in a fire of blazing flame!
> His wife shall carry the wood—as fuel!—
> A twisted rope of palm leaf fibre round her neck!

But the following year a new option opened up before Muhammad. To the north of Mecca a new city, Yathrib, was evolving, yet doing so only with great difficulty. The nomadic peoples could coexist out in the deserts, but being brought together in the urban setting produced tensions and difficulties. After hearing of Muhammad and possibly being intrigued by the Qurayshi boycott of the Hashimites in general and Muhammad in particular, Yathrib sent a delegation to him. The meeting at al-'Aqaba, a hill just north of Mecca, resulted in 621 in the first Oath of al-'Aqaba, later known as the Oath of Women because it did not require the people of Yathrib to fight for Muhammad. In 622 this omission was remedied in the Second Oath of al-'Aqaba, committing the people of Yathrib to accept Muhammad's teaching and leadership and defend him if necessary.

In September 622 came the Emigration to Yathrib, the Hijra. And so closed the first, perhaps less impressive, part of the history of Islam. A new religion is announced, another religious leader climbs onto the stage of history, a few followers are gained, much suffering is nobly borne, but there is as yet little sign of what this infant movement might become.

Muhammad: In the Ascendant

The Hijra

Muhammad was aware of a plot to kill him. To avoid any blood feud afterward, the Quraysh tribe had agreed that one man chosen from each clan should carry out the assassination. Muhammad sent his followers ahead of him to Yathrib and then, accompanied only by Abu Bakr, he himself left Mecca. To avoid the inevitable pursuit, the two hid for three days in a cave; only when the Meccans had given up the pursuit and returned to the city did he and Abu Bakr make their way to Yathrib and safety. There he built a house for himself and shortly after that the first mosque. And now we may abandon the name Yathrib, and call the city by its new name, Madina al-Nabi, the City of the Prophet, or simply Madina (Medina).

At this point Muhammad's status was completely changed. He had a following of men and women from Mecca, from that time on known as the Emigrants, *Muhajirun*. He had the pledged support of the people of Madina, now to be known as the Helpers, the *Ansar*. He soon demonstrated his administrative ability, producing a written constitution for Madina, setting out a basic law code for the Arab and Jewish clans, incidentally allowing the Jewish clans freedom for their religion in return for their loyalty and acknowledgment of his authority.

The Beginnings of Jihad, *Holy War*

But he had a pressing problem: providing for the day-to-day needs of the Emigrants, who had lost their means of livelihood when they left Mecca. It was probably this that led to a succession of planned raids on the Meccan trading caravans, which had to pass near Madina on their way to and from Syria. The early raids were abortive; it seemed as though someone in Madina was reporting Muhammad's plans to the Meccans. In January 624 Muhammad sent out a small raiding party to Nakhla, with written instructions. They joined a Meccan trading caravan returning from Syria and awaited their opportunity. But time passed and the opportunity did not come. Now the success of their project was threatened by a peculiar Arab convention: the sacred months. The urban Arabs and the rural Arabs, the city dwellers and the nomads, lived in an uneasy symbiosis. Each needed the other. But fighting in general, and raiding caravans in particular, was part of Arab culture. To ban such practices would have been useless. The compromise was to ban attacks on the caravans during designated sacred months. When the raiders realized that a sacred month had begun, they considered the options: to return to Madina empty-handed or to attack in the sacred month. The caravan would soon be in sight of Mecca and safety. They decided to attack. One of the caravan guards was killed. The booty was carried off in triumph to Madina.

In Madina the rejoicing was muted: the attackers had desecrated the sacred month and thus broken with Arab tradition.[19] Muhammad announced a new revelation that justified the attack, reported in Sura 2:217:

> They ask thee concerning fighting in the Prohibited Month.
> Say: "Fighting therein is a grave (offence);
> but graver is it in the sight of Allah . . . to deny Him,
> to prevent access to the Sacred Mosque." [the Ka'ba in Mecca, banned to
> Muhammad's followers by the Meccans]

The revelation, if revelation it was, is clear enough. *Jihad* (struggle, holy war) ranks above Arab tradition. But Ibn Ishaq's account of the incident makes it clear that Muhammad at first disowned the raid and refused his share of the spoils. The Muslims at Madina denounced the attack. The Jews of Madina saw it as an omen against Muhammad. The Meccans made capital out of it.

The consequences of the successful raid were immediate. First, the raid polarized the two groups, the Meccans on the one hand and the Madinan Emigrants and Helpers on the other. Second, the traditional *razzia*, caravan raiding, became, for the Muslims, a religious duty, jihad, transcending traditional clan custom. And third, more Arabs were attracted to Muhammad and more Helpers made themselves available to Muhammad for future actions. These were not long in coming. In March 624 the Meccans sent out a strongly guarded caravan to Syria. Muhammad planned to attack it on its return journey, but his plans were once more made known to the Meccans. A force of some nine hundred Meccans was sent out to drive off Muhammad's three hundred. Muhammad ordered his force to take up positions at the well at Badr, thus denying water to the Meccans. This was more a battle than a caravan raid. The Meccans were driven off, but the caravan, by some swift traveling, escaped.

News of Muhammad's success against such odds spread quickly, and still more flocked to him. Their motives would soon be tested. A Meccan caravan was captured; the booty was enormous. The Meccans replied by assembling the largest force yet, some three thousand men. Muhammad again chose the ground for the battle, aware of the danger to his followers posed by the Meccan cavalry. At Uhud he estab-

---

19. See the discussion of the attack on Nakhla in Reuven Firestone, *Jihad: The Origin of Holy War in Islam* (Oxford and New York: Oxford University Press, 1999), 56ff., 86ff.

lished a strong position on a hill, warning his warriors not to leave the security of the hill. But when the Meccans broke under the first attack by Muhammad, the force on the hill, doubtless fearing that they would lose their share of the booty, abandoned their position and hurled themselves after the fleeing Meccans. At that point the Meccan cavalry charged, and now it was the Muslims who fled. It seems that Muhammad himself was wounded in the fighting.[20] This was defeat, but a defeat turned to good use by Muhammad, who reminded them of the cause: failure to follow the orders of the prophet.

This explanation of the calamity was to serve Islam throughout its history: if Muslims remained true to Islam, they would succeed; but failure, the loss of Allah's favor, would be attributed to disobedience to the prophet and to the teachings of the Qur'an.

The Promise of Paradise

Something else emerged at this point, a belief that would armor the more fanatical of Muhammad's followers through the centuries ahead: the belief that anyone who dies on jihad, struggling for Allah, is assured of an immediate place in paradise. Sura 3 moves into a consideration of the battle of Uhud at verse 140 and goes on to consider the situation of the archers who abandoned their position for the sake of plunder: "Allah did indeed fulfil His promise to you when ye with His permission were about to annihilate your enemy—until ye flinched and fell to disputing about the order, and disobeyed it." Sura 3:156 says of those who stayed out of the fight in fear of death: "Be not like the Unbelievers, who say of their brethren, when they are travelling through the earth or engaged in fighting: 'If they had stayed with us, they would not have died or been slain.'" Verse 169 goes on to promise: "Think not of those who are slain in Allah's way as dead. Nay, they live, finding their sustenance in the Presence of their Lord; They rejoice in the bounty provided by Allah."

So here we have the origin of a belief that would later strengthen the commitment of radical suicide bombers: the promise of paradise for all who die "in the way of Allah," on jihad.

Allied to the promise of paradise came a further promise, the forgiveness of sins. According to a Tradition recorded by the eminent theologian Muslim,

A man stood up and said, "Messenger of Allah, do you think that if I am killed in the way of Allah, my sins will be blotted out from me?" The

20. According to Abdullah Yusuf Ali, Muhammad was severely wounded, and in the heat of the battle word spread that he had been killed: *The Meaning of the Holy Qur'an*, 8th ed. (Beltsville, Md.: Amana, 1996), n. 460.

Messenger of Allah (may peace be upon him) said: "Yes, in case you are killed in the way of Allah, you were patient and sincere and you always fought facing the enemy, never turning your back on him."[21]

It may be that the near success of the Meccans emboldened them to make one further effort, this time to destroy Muhammad and his followers and to end the pretensions of the city of Madina. They put together a still larger army, some ten thousand men, larger than anything Muhammad could hope to field, and moved against Madina.

Mecca's Last Fling: The "Battle" of the Ditch

Once more Muhammad demonstrated his tactical skill. He saw that the city of Madina was open to attack from only one side, which faced the desert. Mountains guarded the other sides from cavalry assault. So he had a massive ditch dug between the city and the desert, and behind that ditch they waited.

The Meccans arrived, strong in cavalry but weak in water. The ditch denied the cavalry and cut off the Meccans from the only source of water, inside the city. The episode has been called the Battle of the Ditch, but in reality it was no battle at all, merely a few inconclusive skirmishes. After two weeks the siege ended and the Meccans withdrew, after accomplishing nothing beyond demonstrating once more the superior genius of Muhammad.

The Massacre of the Qurayza Jews

If the siege itself proved to be an anticlimax, the event had its climax in quite an unexpected way. The Jewish clan of Qurayza (Banu Qurayza) were accused of responsibility for leaking Muhammad's plans to the Meccans. According to Ibn Ishaq's account of these events, during the siege the Muslims had reason to believe that the Qurayza were preparing to stab their fellow Madinans in the back. But it is equally possible that Muhammad capitalized on his defeat of the Meccans by turning on the Jews, whose opposition had been a thorn in his side ever since the move to Madina.

At all events, when the siege was over, Muhammad turned his followers against the Qurayza Jews. In their turn the Jews were besieged in their quarter of the city. They surrendered. A meeting of the Muslims was held to decide what to do with them. Sa'd was appointed to pass judgment, but before he did so he asked if Muhammad would accept his decision. He would. Then, said Sa'd, "I give judgment that the

---

21. Muslim, *Sahih Muslim*, ed. Abdul Hamid Siddiqi (Lahore: Ashraf, 1980), III, Al-Imara, chap. 1285, no. 4646, 1046–47.

men should be killed, the property divided, and the women and children taken as captive."[22]

Muhammad then had trenches dug, and the men were led out in batches and beheaded.

> There were 600 or 700 in all, though some put the figure as high as 800 or 900. As they were being taken out in batches to the apostle they asked Ka'b what he thought would be done with them. He replied, "Will you never understand? Don't you see that the summoner never stops and those who are taken away do not return? By Allah it is death!" This went on until the apostle made an end of them.[23]

To the Jewish men was added one woman. The property was divided, the women taken as slaves, and among them was Rayhana, who became Muhammad's slave.

In terms of the ethics of the day, the outcome would have surprised few. Muhammad did not himself pass sentence, but Ibn Ishaq's account makes it clear that Muhammad could have refused to accept Sa'd's decision. For a man of his time Muhammad's role in the incident is scarcely noteworthy; for the man who is presented as the exemplar, the perfect example, the incident casts a bleak question mark over that assessment.[24]

Mecca Becomes Muslim

Now Muhammad's star was clearly in the ascendant. Gathering his people together, he marched on Mecca, ostensibly to make the pilgrimage. The advance of so many toward Mecca clearly frightened the Meccan rulers. They sat down to parley with Muhammad, and a compromise was reached and written into an agreement, the Treaty of Hudaybiyya. Muhammad and his people were to return to Madina. They would make the pilgrimage the following year. In the meantime there was a truce: no more fighting. Only one year later Muhammad made his delayed pilgrimage to Mecca, but being still unwelcome in Mecca, made his way back to Madina.

The peace was short-lived: Muhammad accused the Meccans of killing one of his people in a confusing series of tit-for-tat killings. He gathered his followers together again and marched on Mecca, this time determined to occupy the city. He promised safety to the Mec-

22. Guillaume, *Life of Muhammad*, 464.
23. Ibid.
24. For a full and fair appraisal of Muhammad's character, see W. Montgomery Watt, *Muhammad: Prophet and Statesman* (London: Oxford University Press, 1961), chap. 9.

cans who stayed inside their houses as he took the city, and consequently there was little loss of life. The Ka'ba was emptied of its idols: one tradition has it that Muhammad merely pointed his staff at the 360 idols, at which they fell down, one after the other.[25] Now Muhammad was apparently master of the most important city in Arabia, but he still doubted his safety there and returned to Madina, from where he continued to organize and even to participate in raids aimed at enforcing the submission of the remaining Arab clans.

Two years later, in 632, Muhammad died peacefully in Madina. He had appointed no successor; indeed, it is doubtful whether there could have been a successor. But the new religion, the new sociopolitical movement, needed leadership. At the closing of an era Islam reached a crossroads: with the death of its founder the movement might simply fade away, or those Muhammad had left behind, virtually leaderless, might find a new path to follow.

With amazing rapidity the fragmented and insignificant Arab tribes, the no-people, had been turned into a single powerful nation, united under a single religion, worshiping the one God. And it was done in the lifetime of just one man.

---

25. Guillaume, *Life of Muhammad*, 552. There is some slight similarity to the fate of the Philistine idol Dagon, recorded in 1 Sam. 5.

2

CALIPHS
AND CONFUSION

Muhammad made one last pilgrimage to Mecca, but he was desperately ill even before he set out. He returned, worn out, to Madina. On the morning of his death he made his way to the mosque for the prayers, being led by his friend Abu Bakr, who had been one of the earliest converts to Islam. He returned to his tent, and there at about midday, resting in the arms of his wife Aisha, he died. Abu Bakr went out to the people: "O men, if anyone worships Muhammad, Muhammad is dead: if anyone worships God, God is alive, immortal."[1] Muhammad was dead, and with him ended those poetic exhortations that would be collected to become the Qur'an.

Muslims now had two urgent matters to handle: Muhammad's burial and the succession.

CALIPHS

Islam now reached the first of several crossroads it had to negotiate through its history. Muhammad was dead, and there was no obvious successor. As the news of his death reached the Arab tribes, there began a return to the situation before he had come. The tide had come in with a roar, and now the tide was going out. It was vital that as Islam had reached the crossroads as a unity, so it should advance beyond them as a unity. That unity must be provided by the identification of an acceptable successor to Muhammad.

Muhammad had several wives, several more, indeed, than the Qur'an allowed to lesser Muslims.[2] Of course the extra provision for

---

1. Guillaume, *Life of Muhammad*, 683.
2. A carefully researched list of Muhammad's eleven (and possibly twelve) marriages is given in Bennett, *In Search of Muhammad*, appendix 2. With respect to Aisha there is a Tradition recorded by Bukhari that gives the details: "Khadija died three years before the Prophet departed to Madina. He stayed there for two years or so and then he married 'Aisha when she was a girl of six years of age, and he consumed [*sic*;

Muhammad would have been unexceptionable in contemporary Arab society for a leader such as Muhammad. He claimed to have received a revelation that regularized his position:

> O Prophet! We have made lawful to thee thy wives
> to whom thou hast paid their dowers,
> and those whom thy right hand possesses
> out of the prisoners of war whom Allah has assigned to thee;
> and daughters of thy paternal uncles and aunts,
> and daughters of thy maternal uncles and aunts,
> who migrated with thee;
> and any believing woman who dedicates her soul to the Prophet
> if the Prophet wishes to wed her—
> this only for thee, and not for the believers. . . . (Sura 33:50)

And yet he had no son to succeed him. Fatima was his favorite daughter, but the idea that she might become the leader of Islam and Arabia was not even considered. There were four obvious places to search for the new leader: in Muhammad's own family; among the Emigrants, those first disciples of his who had born the heat of oppression in Mecca and had gone with him to Madina; among the Helpers, who had given him refuge in Madina when he so desperately needed it; and among the traditional Meccan rulers. Muhammad died at Madina, so the Meccans were not in a position to argue their case. Muhammad had no sons, so the family option appeared to be ruled out. Leadership, then, lay between the Emigrants and the Helpers. But they had passed over one obvious possibility. Fatima was Muhammad's favorite daughter, and she had married Ali ibn Abu Talib. Ali was thus related to Muhammad by blood (Abu Talib was Muhammad's uncle), and through his marriage. From the beginning some pressed Ali's claims, but they were put aside. Here was a decision that later would have serious consequences.

The First of the Rightly Guided Caliphs

Inevitably for those closest to Muhammad, the priority was clear: his body must be prepared for burial. On the other side of the city of Madina, the priorities were different. It was obvious that Islam was a success, and with success went power and wealth: nothing less than the leadership of a united Arab people was at stake. The Emigrants were otherwise occupied, so the Helpers set about appointing a new

---

consummated] that marriage when she was nine years old" (Muhammad ibn Ismail Bukhari, *Sahih al-Bukhari*, ed. and trans. Muhammad Muhsin Khan [Gujranwala: Dar Ahya Us-Sunnah, 1973–], V, LVII, chap. 43, no. 236, 153).

leader, one of themselves. When the Emigrants heard about that, Umar and Abu Bakr, both to become future leaders of Islam, went to the place where the meeting was being held. Umar had quickly prepared a speech, but Abu Bakr told him to be quiet, and Abu Bakr spoke. Umar commented that Abu Bakr not only said what he (Umar) had prepared, but said it in a more appropriate spirit than he himself would have done:

> "No one can deny your merit in the faith or your great precedence in Islam. God was pleased to make you Helpers to His religion and His prophet and caused him to migrate to you, and the honour of sheltering his wives and his Companions is still yours, and after the first Emigrants there is no one we hold of equal standing with you. We are the amirs (the commanders) and you are the viziers (the advisers). We shall not act contrary to your advice. Here is Umar and here is Abu Ubayda. Swear allegiance to whichever of them you choose."
>
> The two of them said, "No, by God, we shall not accept this authority above you, for you are the worthiest of the Emigrants and the second of the two who were in the cave and the deputy of the Prophet of God in prayer."[3]

The argument went on all around the three. It was suggested that there should be two leaders, one from the Emigrants, a Qurayshi Meccan, and one from the Madinan Helpers. Umar sat silent, then reached out his hand, took the hand of Abu Bakr (a traditional Arab act marking the sealing of any agreement),[4] and acknowledged him as Muhammad's successor. His action ended the debate: one by one the rest followed Umar's example.

Muhammad died on a Monday and was buried the next day. Abu Bakr—father of Aisha (Muhammad's favorite wife), the companion of Muhammad during the withdrawal to Madina, and leader of the Friday mosque prayers during Muhammad's illness—did not actually become Muhammad's *successor.* Instead, he became the leader of the Muslims and so also of the Arab people, their caliph, the first of four caliphs who would come to be called the Four Rightly Guided Caliphs. But the apparent unity implied in this rationalized history ignores the fact that the election of a leader had already introduced division among Muhammad's followers. The supporters of Ali's claims to

3. Bernard Lewis, ed. and trans., *Islam from the Prophet Muhammad to the Capture of Constantinople* (New York: Harper and Row, 1974), 1:2–5. See also Bukhari, *Sahih,* IX, LXXXIX, chap. 37, no. 301, 228–30.

4. John Esposito, *Islam: The Straight Path,* 3d ed. (New York and Oxford: Oxford University Press, 1998), 36. The handclasp marks an oath, *bay'a.*

leadership would eventually bring about the major Shi'a division, and the seeds of that division were sown here.

Abu Bakr was an old man and led Islam for only two years. His first task was to convince the Arab peoples that their allegiance was to Islam, not merely to Muhammad. There was a real danger that the grand alliance built up under the charismatic leadership of Muhammad would simply disappear with his death. He succeeded not merely in consolidating Muhammad's work but actually in expanding it south into the Yemen and north into Iraq and Syria; this was largely due to the military genius of Khalid ibn al-Walid, who was sent first to subdue the Arab clans that had withdrawn from the grand alliance on the death of Muhammad. Then in short order Khalid turned his forces northward into Syria and in 634 captured Damascus.[5] Khalid was certainly a fine warrior, but his ferocity and cruelty to his defeated enemies led to protests even from his own followers, and he was even said to have been later dismissed from his command by Umar,[6] the successor of Abu Bakr.

The fighting introduced a new danger. Some of those who had heard Muhammad and could be relied on to remember his teaching were casualties; others were aging and dying. Firsthand testimony to the prophet was disappearing. Abu Bakr initiated the process of gathering together those pronouncements of Muhammad that would eventually constitute the Qur'an.

The Second Rightly Guided Caliph

Umar was one of the Muhajirun, those who had taken part in the Hijra to Madina. His daughter Hafsa had been one of Muhammad's wives. As the second caliph he initiated a strong process of putting Muslim affairs in order: the ferocious Khalid was dismissed; the times of prayer, the details of the pilgrimage, and the rules relating to the Ramadan fast were all formalized. Umar was also responsible for laying the foundations of Muslim *Shari'a* law, although he had little to work on. Within the Qur'an itself only five or six hundred out of a total of more than six thousand verses have any bearing on Shari'a, and the majority of those verses deal with matters relating to the Ka'ba rituals, the pilgrimage, and so on. In fact, only some eighty verses directly relate to the present Shari'a. As Fazlur Rahman has said of the Qur'an, "Besides the detailed pronouncement on the law of inheritance and laying down punishments for crimes such as theft and adultery, which are not defined legally, there is little in it that is, properly speaking, legislative."[7]

5. For a detailed study of the early clashes between the Byzantine Empire and the Muslims, see Walter E. Kaegi, *Byzantium and the Early Islamic Conquests* (Cambridge: Cambridge University Press, 1992).

6. See the article "Khalid b. al-Walid," *Encyclopaedia of Islam,* 4:928.

7. F. Rahman, *Islam* (London: Weidenfeld and Nicolson, 1966), 69.

Umar's ten-year rule saw a transformation of Islam into the holistic religion that Muhammad seemed to have intended. A new calendar was introduced, placing the Hijra to Madina in year 1 of the
calendar. Islam reached out far beyond the borders of the Arabian
peninsula: northward into Syria, eastward into Mesopotamia, and
westward across the North African coastlands beyond Alexandria.
Before the confident Muslims, the armies of the Christian Byzantine
and the Zoroastrian Persian empires gave way. The expanding Muslim empire was held together by Umar's imposition of a new doctrine, displacing mere tribal and clan loyalties by a more profound
loyalty to Allah. There might be a caliph, but Islam was to be seen as
a theocracy.

Umar was murdered. One account has it that his murderer was a
Christian slave, and another that he was killed by a Persian captive,[8]
but there is also a strong suspicion that the Alids, supporters of Ali ibn
Abu Talib, were behind the killing.

As the third Rightly Guided Caliph, Uthman succeeded Umar, and
this marked a break: though Uthman was from Mecca, he was not—
like Muhammad, Abu Bakr, and Umar—a Hashimite, but from the
Umayyads. At this point Ali was again passed over in the choice of a
leader, possibly because he recognized that Islam had taken a new
turning and had become primarily a political and military movement
rather than a religious one.[9]

CONFUSION: KHARIJI, SUNNI, SHI'A, AND SUFI

The Third Rightly Guided Caliph

The Muslim empire was expanding more rapidly than its topsy-
turvy finances could support. Occupied cities were plundered, but the
soldiers kept the proceeds. Uthman, the third caliph, stopped that and
decreed that revenues, and especially the land revenues, were to go to
the Islamic state and be used to pay the growing bureaucracy. That
meant that positions of authority became highly remunerative, and
that in turn encouraged the growth of nepotism. Uthman unknowingly
planted the seed of future divisions when he appointed his nephew
Mu'awiya as governor of Syria. This appointment sealed the dominance of the Meccans and was quickly followed by other appoint-
ments also favoring them. The Madinans saw their influence disap-

---

8. Ruthven, *Islam in the World*, 72.

9. Ruthven (ibid., 174–76) offers a concise but perceptive analysis of the focal role
played by Ali in the leadership debates that followed the death of Muhammad. He is
painted as an uncompromising idealist over against the pragmatism of Umar and Uthman.

pearing,[10] and whether it was for this reason or as a more general protest against the moral decline in Islam, there was a general rebellion, in which Uthman was murdered.

The Fourth Rightly Guided Caliph

And so we come to Ali ibn Abu Talib, the fourth and last of the Rightly Guided Caliphs, and to the great divisions that have troubled Islam ever since. Islam had maintained its essential unity since it successfully negotiated the crossroads reached at Muhammad's death. But now it advanced toward a more challenging crossroads, which it would leave following different ways, highways, and byways.

Ali ibn Abu Talib succeeded Uthman. His name is significant: he was the son of Abu Talib, Muhammad's uncle, and so was a blood relative of the prophet. Perhaps just as important, he was married to Fatima, Muhammad's daughter.[11] So he had a double relationship to Muhammad, and if Tradition is to be accepted, there were many who from the beginning had demanded that he and not Abu Bakr should be the first caliph. Moreover, Ali had other credentials. He strictly followed Muhammad's example (*sunna*), and, inevitably, had a profound knowledge of the Qur'an.

Uthman was dead and Ali was the new caliph, but he appears to have made no attempt to identify, still less to punish, the murderers. There were not a few who suspected that the explanation was obvious: he had engineered the murder himself. Up in Syria, Mu'awiya demanded vengeance for his uncle's death. Nearer to home, Aisha, too, demanded that Uthman's death be avenged. Ali gathered his supporters together, and Aisha gathered hers. As the two armies met, Aisha watched from a safe distance, seated on a camel, from which came the designation Battle of the Camel. Aisha's army was defeated, though she was treated respectfully as Muhammad's widow and allowed to return to Madina.

Ali seemed to have no plans to deal with the third Rightly Guided Caliph's assassins. Mu'awiya decided to act, put together an army, and marched against Ali. On paper, at least, Ali had little to fear, but Mu'awiya used paper to gain time: when the two armies met at Siffin, Ali was confronted by a sea of waving paper. Mu'awiya had ordered his followers to spear leaves of the Qur'an onto the tips of their lances. There was a pause: Mu'awiya's followers were not particularly anxious to start a bloody fight, and Ali's followers were unnerved at the

10. See Esposito, *Islam: The Straight Path*, 37: "Many of the Medinan elite, who had been among the early supporters of Muhammad, resented Uthman's accession to power and the increased prominence and wealth of his family."

11. Note the Tradition that Muhammad said, "Fatima is the chief mistress of the women in Paradise" (Bukhari, *Sahih*, V, LVII, chap. 29, no. 29, 74).

FIGURE 2.1. SUNNI AND SHI'A ISLAM

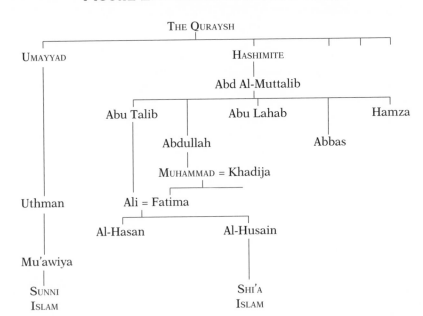

thought of attacking the Qur'an itself. Arbitration was proposed instead of confrontation. As it turned out, it was an arbitration, the outcome of which seems to have been already decided: it came down on the side of Mu'awiya. Ali was at fault for failing to take revenge on the assassins of Uthman. The battle of Siffin was avoided, but Islam was left with what amounted to two caliphs. On the death of Ali, Mu'awiya proclaimed himself caliph, and so initiated the Umayyad Caliphate, which would last for almost a hundred years.

The Kharijis

But the confrontation at Siffin had a further consequence. The appeal to arbitration outraged many of Ali's followers:

> When the arbitration was announced, the Kharijites shouted, "Only God can decide." It was not the job of human beings to counter God's command and sit as judge.[12]

In their view the true caliph had no need to submit to the humiliation of arbitration. Uthman had deserved that assassination. Mu'a-

12. Esposito, *Islam: The Straight Path,* 42.

wiya was a rebel, and the Qur'an laid it down that such rebels should be brought to heel.[13] They rejected both the outcome of the arbitration and Ali, and hence withdrew. It is not certain how their name *Khariji* (Arabic plural *khawarij*, "withdrawers") originated: they themselves trace it to the fact that they withdrew their support from Ali, but some Muslims apparently asserted that they had, in effect, withdrawn from orthodoxy: "It is to this episode of the exodus from Kufa that the Khawaridj owe their name ('those who went out'), more probably than to a general epithet expressing the idea that they had gone out of the community of the faithful, as it was later interpreted."[14]

The Kharijis now turned to fighting against Ali's followers, and in 658 this led to a devastating attack on them by Ali. Many of the Kharijis were killed. In revenge Ali was murdered in Kufa by a Khariji. But they survived as a dissident sect, a constant thorn in the side of orthodox Islam. They held to a tight morality: the Muslim would not attain paradise merely by being a Muslim, but must live strictly in accordance with the *sunna* (way, or example, of Muhammad). Those who did not were no longer Muslims. Here was a division in Muslim theology: serious sin separated the sinner from the Muslim community (*umma*).[15] And consistent with this principle, they rejected Ali as caliph and determined that any Muslim might lead Islam, provided only that he was living strictly according to the sunna.

They continued their often-violent opposition to the remainder of the Muslim world. Philip Hitti comments: "In endeavouring to maintain the primitive, democratic principles of Islam the puritanical Kharijites caused rivers of blood to flow in the first three Moslem centuries."[16] But the first three centuries did not see the end of Khariji violence: "Although defeated as a major force, Khariji doctrines continued to inspire revolts among oppressed or marginal groups throughout Islamic history."[17] In the tenth century, Abdullah ibn Ibad, in Algeria, began a movement that generally adopted Khariji ideas; the Ibadi movement has continued to the present, particularly in Oman.

The extremist al-Qa'ida group, responsible for the destruction of the twin towers of the World Trade Center in New York in September 2001,

13. Sura 49:9: "If two parties among the believers fall into a quarrel, make ye peace between them: but if one of them transgresses beyond bounds against the other, then fight ye against the one that transgresses until it complies with the command of Allah."

14. Article "Kharidjites," *Encyclopaedia of Islam*, 4:1074–75.

15. And note Malise Ruthven's comment: "Although a small minority in today's Muslim world, the Khariji attitude of treating Muslim sinners as infidels closely resembles that of some modern fundamentalist groups" (*Islam in the World*, 179).

16. Philip Hitti, *History of the Arabs*, 10th ed. (London: Macmillan, 1970), 247.

17. Ruthven, *Islam in the World*, 177.

has seemed to some, such as the American Muslim activist Hamza
Yusuf,[18] to be continuing the Khariji tradition. The Khariji philosophy
does not sit comfortably with the diversity of urbanized Islam, and this
might in some small measure explain the withdrawal of the al-Qa'ida
leader, Osama bin Laden, from life in urban Saudi Arabia to the rural
life of Afghanistan, where a community apart could be established.

Shi'a and the Battle of Karbala: The Great Divide

Ali had lasted as caliph for only five years. He had three sons: Muhammad bin al-Hanafiya; Al-Hasan, who seems to have refused to
challenge the Caliphate of Mu'awiya in favor of a quiet life; and Al-
Husain. In 680 Mu'awiya died and was succeeded by his son Yazid.
This seemed to be an opportune time for Al-Husain to end what he
and his followers saw as rebellion. The argument was simple: Al-Husain was the grandson of the Prophet; Yazid was nothing. With prophetic blood running through his veins, Al-Husain could not but succeed. The Muslims of Iraq assured him of their support. So Al-Husain
marched forth to confront Yazid's army at Karbala, some sixty miles
from Baghdad. It was to be a momentous confrontation, more in the
nature of a massacre than of a battle.

The promised support of the Iraqi Muslims failed to materialize. Al-
Husain refused to surrender to the overwhelming force of Yazid. The
story of the battle[19] is retold, embroidered, and enlarged every year as
the Shi'a Muslims (as they became known) act out their passion play to
celebrate Ashura on the tenth day of the month of Muharram. Tradition depicts Al-Husain as going into battle carrying his son in his arms:

> With his six-month-old son Ali Asghar in his arms the Imam cried out to
> the enemy that as this innocent babe had defiled none at least he should
> be spared and a little water given him to allay his thirst. But the reply
> was an arrow shot at the child's neck, which pinned it to his father's arm.
> After returning the cruelly murdered child to its sorrowing mother's
> arms (who then sang a mournful mother's lament over her dead child)
> the Imam returned to pay the last of the sacrifice with his own blood.[20]

Al-Husain was surrounded by Yazid's troops, beaten to the ground,
and killed; then his head was struck off and dispatched to Yazid in
Damascus, where it was put on public display. The enormity of this
event only gradually dawned on the Muslim world: the grandson of

18. Hamza Yusuf, "A Time for Introspection," Q News, October 2001, 14.
19. Some writers see this not so much as a battle but an ambush and massacre. But
the traditional Shi'a view supposes a battle, however one-sided.
20. Quoted in Ruthven, Islam in the World, 181.

the prophet, not merely killed by Muslims, but his body dishonored. Karbala created a breach in Islam that has never been healed and may never be healed. The remnant of Al-Husain's followers withdrew but only to a defiant stand against Yazid and the Umayyad Caliphate. So, with the passing of time, the *Shi'a*, Partisans of Ali, turned from being a mere dissident group to become a powerful sect.[21]

With Shi'ism came also a new interpretation of Islam. Al-Husain's death becomes martyrdom and Al-Husain himself an intercessor:

> Shi'ism places great value on the intercession of saints, the "friends" of God who mediate God's grace and blessings to the believers. As in Christianity, suffering and compassion, martyrdom and sacrifice, atonement and redemption are central motifs in salvation history. In contrast to the Sunni, Shii believe that the intercession of the Imams is a necessary part of history, from the redemptive death of Husayn to the return of the Hidden Imam at the end of time.[22]

The division was more than emotional: it found a theological underpinning. The Shi'a insisted that only a blood descendent of Muhammad could lead Islam. Yazid's caliphate was illegitimate, as were those of Mu'awiya and even those of the first three Rightly Guided Caliphs, Abu Bakr, Umar, and Uthman. Ali is the first caliph, Al-Husain the second. But certain consequences followed this new understanding of leadership. Traditions going back to those other caliphs were rejected as unreliable. And more. The leader of Shi'a Islam, by virtue of the prophetic blood flowing in him (linking him mystically not merely to Muhammad but back before him even to Adam), bore a divine light. When settling disputes about doctrine and practice, the Sunnis developed the doctrine of consensus, *ijma'*, but the Shi'a would have none of it: the Imam alone could make such decisions. The term *Imam* itself took on two different meanings: for Sunnis it meant primarily the leader of the congregational prayer in a mosque, but for the Shi'a it meant principally the leader of all the faithful, that is to say, all the Shi'a.

The Sufis

From its beginnings Islam has contained its mystical strain. The experiences claimed for Muhammad (e.g., his visions of angelic beings) provide a foundation for Muslim mysticism. People expect certain things of their religions: an explanation of the origins and meaning of life, an indication of what lies beyond death, and rules for living. All these are provided within orthodox doctrine. But there is a further expectation:

21. See Esposito, *Islam: The Straight Path*, 43–45.
22. Ibid., 110.

FIGURE 2.2. SHI'A ISLAM: THE TWELVE IMAMS

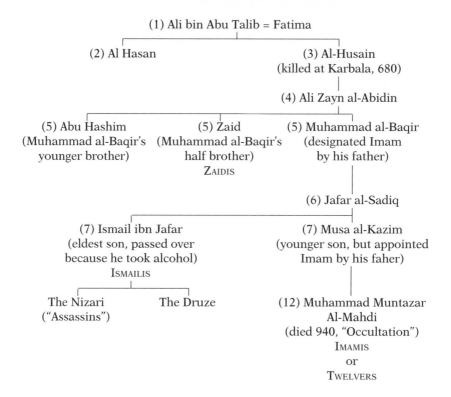

that religion will move the devotee beyond the mundane to the ineffable. In the years following the death of Muhammad, it seemed that the mundane had taken over to the exclusion of the ineffable.

The Sufi movement (from *suf,* wool, relating to the woolen cloak worn by the teachers of the would-be mystics) restores the mystical to Islam. The best known of the early Sufis was the Persian Mansur Al-Hallaj (858–922), who took as the starting point of his teaching the oneness of Allah. From *tawhid* he drew out the idea of the Muslim's oneness with Allah and set out a pathway, a *tariqa,* that would enable the seeker to go beyond the mere outside of Islam, the exoteric, to the esoteric meaning, to embrace Allah in the final mystical experience. On the positive side of all this, there tended to be an emphasis on love—the love of God and the believer's love for God—but on the negative side there developed an undoubted tendency to undervalue the religious forms, jealously guarded by the *ulama,* the religious scholars who claimed to be guardians of orthodoxy.

Almost inevitably the Sufis moved toward a perceived heresy: the Sufi emphasis on purity, abstinence, and piety contrasted with the laxity to be observed in the majority of the ulama. But it was specifically the search for some kind of union with Allah, *fana'*, in which, it was claimed, the difference between subject and Object, between me and Thee, is somehow transcended by an act of faith. The aim might have been orthodox, but the terminology did not appear to be. Al-Hallaj claimed that in this sense of total submission to Allah, he himself became the Truth, *al-haqq*. The consequences of this readily misunderstood assertion were catastrophic. He was executed with a horrifying ferocity, his hands and feet cut off, and his body exposed for two days, decapitated, and then burned.[23]

It was Abu Hamid Al-Ghazali (1058–1111) who returned Sufism to the fold of orthodoxy. A scholar of the Islamic sciences in Baghdad, he experienced a personal crisis through a sense that the academic world in which he labored was futile. He abandoned the academic world, left Baghdad, and moved to Syria, where he was initiated into a Sufi order. He traveled on, gathering knowledge and experience; the outcome was his book *The Revivification of the Religious Sciences*, which pulled together the spirituality of Sufism and orthodox theology. Love of God and the search for a personal experience of God achieved respectability. He was recognized as a *mujaddid*, a renewer of Islam.[24]

The somewhat arid nature of orthodox practice has apparently driven many Muslims into the practice of Sufism. The would-be Sufi is attached to a master, a teacher, a *sheikh* or *pir*, someone who is believed to have attained, at least in some measure, the sought-after experience of Allah. The sheikh would hold to a particular *tariqa*, an order of Sufis with a common practice, inherited from some illustrious founder, and would instruct his students in theology and in the practice of meditation. The methodology involved the *dhikr*, meditation on Allah, using a formula[25] revealed by the sheikh. Frequently resort is made to music and dance, especially among the *darwish*, the dervishes, the repetitive movements and music providing a stimulus to achieving a trance state and the desired experience of withdrawal from the world. The tomb of the sheikh frequently becomes a place of pilgrimage, a practice expressly anathematized by Muhammad, according to Tradition:

Narrated Aisha, when the Prophet became ill, some of his wives talked about a church which they had seen in Ethiopia and it was called Mariya.

23. Ruthven, *Islam in the World*, 226–29.
24. Esposito, *Islam: The Straight Path*, 104–5.
25. Note the similarity to the Hindu mantra.

Um Salma [*sic*] and Um Habiba had been to Ethiopia, and both of them narrated its beauty and the pictures it contained. The Prophet raised his head and said, "Those are the people who, whenever a pious man dies amongst them, make a place of worship at his grave and then they make pictures of it. Those are the worst creatures in the sight of Allah."[26]

It is ironic that despite this Tradition the *hajj* pilgrimage usually includes a journey to the tomb of Muhammad at Madina.

Sufism is, in a sense, a reinterpretation of the tenets of Islam, moving them from their surface meanings to something more profound. Just as *tawhid*, the oneness of Allah, is reinterpreted to signify oneness *with* Allah, so the pilgrimage is perceived not merely as a journey along the caravan trail to Mecca, but as following the tariqa of the sheikh to reach Allah, the ultimate reality. Almsgiving is not only giving *zakat* at the mosque, but a total giving of oneself to Allah and to the Sufi brotherhood. Of course the exoteric, or common, understanding of the Pillars is accepted as well, but it is the esoteric, the inside, that is the goal of the Sufi. Jihad is not the physical militaristic struggle on behalf of Allah, but it is a struggle with the self and its desires, the struggle to dismiss the earthy and to replace it with spiritual purity.

Islam had now advanced far beyond the boundaries of the Arabian peninsula, but while it entered the period of the Four Rightly Guided Caliphs along a single broad road, the rule of Ali and especially that of Al-Husain brought Islam to crossroads, which it left along different routes. The main highway was taken by the Sunnis. A lesser road, though not without its significance, was taken by the Shi'a. Along a third road, scarcely discernible as a road, traveled the Khariji. The Sufis, being adaptable, trod either the Sunni or the Shi'a road, though not the Khariji road. The Muslim travelers carried with them their Qur'an and would soon add to that the Traditions. Further along their respective routes, they all would encounter the philosopher-theologians, the *mu'tazila*, who would question not a few of the theological assumptions carried along so far without question by the Muslim peoples.

26. Bukhari, *Sahih*, II, XXIII, chap. 69, no. 425, 237.

3

BELIEFS
AND PRACTICES

It is now possible to see the gradual emergence of Muslim belief and practice. None of this is spelled out in any systematic way in the Qur'an, but it all developed more as a matter of consensus than as a response to a formal written code.

THE FIVE PILLARS

Although the Five Pillars are not given in any formal way in the Qur'an, there is an early Tradition that Muhammad had stipulated five:

> Narrated Ibn Umar: Allah's Apostle said: Islam is based on (the following) five (principles),
> 1. To testify that none has the right to be worshiped but Allah, and Muhammad is Allah's Apostle.
> 2. To offer the (compulsory congregational) prayers dutifully and perfectly.
> 3. To pay Zakat (i.e., obligatory charity).
> 4. To perform Hajj (i.e., Pilgrimage to Mecca).
> 5. To observe fast during the month of Ramadan.[1]

At the heart of Muslim belief is tawhid, the oneness of God, and this is reflected in the crucial act of the Muslim: the duty of *shahada*, repeating the affirmation "There is no God but God, and Muhammad is his *rasul*, messenger." This affirmation also defines the status of Muhammad: he is the messenger, not a deity to be worshiped. The affirmation is always repeated in Arabic, even by those for whom Arabic is a second or even an unknown language.

Second is prayer. Prayer is to be enacted five times each day. For Muslims prayer is more than a repetition of words since it involves

1. Bukhari, *Sahih*, I, II, chap. 2, no. 7, 17.

significant actions: kneeling, looking to left and right, touching the ear. Muslims have their own *qibla*, the direction to be faced when praying. Sura 2:144–50 makes the qibla plain: "From whencesoever thou startest forth, turn thy face in the direction of the Sacred Mosque." Earlier in the same sura there is reference to the fact that originally the qibla had been to Jerusalem, but the change was made to distinguish Jew and Christian from Muslim.

Third, Muslims are required to pay a proportion of wealth to the mosque as a tithe, *zakat*, although the actual tariff is somewhat complicated. In addition to zakat, which carries no merit since it is obligatory,[2] there is the possibility of giving additionally to the poor, *sadaqa*. As the word itself suggests (righteousness), there is merit to be acquired through such giving (merit to be set against the giver's sins), which, unlike zakat, may be directed to such acts of charity as the giver wishes.

Fourth is fasting, required during the month of Ramadan, the month in which tradition believes that the revelations first came to Muhammad. It seems that Muhammad introduced fasting into Islam in the second year of the hijra. Following the practice of Jewish fasting on the tenth day of the month Tishri, he imposed a fast on the tenth day of Muharram. But with his gradual disenchantment with the Jews of Madina, this was changed to a month-long fast in Ramadan ("The Scorcher"),[3] celebrating the first of his revelations. Tradition says that this took place on "The Night of Power" (*Laylat Al-Qadir;* Sura 97:1–5), though there is no agreement on which is the night of power.[4] During daylight hours no food is eaten and nothing is drunk, though once darkness has fallen Muslims are free to eat and drink at will. In the Muslim heartlands the beginning and ending of the times of fasting may still be determined by the traditional test of the ability to distinguish between a black thread and a white one, but

2. In fact a Tradition implies that Muslims who fail to pay their zakat will be tormented in hell: "They who hoard up gold and silver and spend them not in the way of Allah, announce to them a painful torment on the day when it all will be heated in the fire of hell, and their foreheads and their flanks and their backs will be branded with it: 'This is the treasure which you hoarded for yourself. Now taste of what you used to hoard!'" (Bukhari, *Sahih,* II, XXIV, chap. 2, no. 484, 275).

3. At that time, Ramadan fell in the hottest part of the year. The Arab calendar was divided into equal months, with an additional month intercalated as necessary to keep the calendar in step with the seasons. Later, Muhammad is believed to have introduced a simplified system of twelve equal lunar months without intercalation. Consequently, Ramadan is no longer necessarily a scorcher.

4. Yusuf Ali notes that the twenty-third, twenty-fifth, or twenty-seventh night of Ramadan has been suggested, as well as other nights, but he prefers to leave the matter open (*Meaning of the Holy Qur'an,* n. 6217).

with the geographical expansion of Islam the duration of each day's fast in most countries is simply determined by the clock. During Ramadan the Qur'an is publicly and privately read through, according to the thirty sections (*juz'*, pl. *ajza'*) of the sacred text.

The fifth Pillar is pilgrimage, *hajj*. Once in a lifetime Muslims are expected to make the greater pilgrimage to Mecca. The practices of the greater pilgrimage (which can only be performed in the annual month of pilgrimage) appear, in some cases, to reflect pagan origins. Perhaps the most evident is the central role of the Black Stone. Even Umar, the second Rightly Guided Caliph, is supposed to have said of the kissing of the Black Stone: "Had I not seen the Apostle kissing you, I would not have kissed you."[5] It is usual to assume that hajj today follows the pattern set by Muhammad on his last pilgrimage, but there is a Tradition that brings this into question. It appears that because of his physical weakness, and so that the people could see him, Muhammad performed the circumambulation of the Ka'ba while riding on a camel, and instead of kissing the Black Stone he merely touched it with his stick. It is also said that he rode his camel when he performed the "running" between the two hills of al-Safa and al-Marwa.[6]

The hajj concludes with the festival of completion, the Id al-Adha, and this is celebrated by Muslims throughout the world, not merely by those who have completed the pilgrimage. A sheep or goat or even a camel is slaughtered and the meat shared between the one offering the sacrifice and any needy neighbors.

THE SIX BELIEFS (IMAN)

The observance of the Five Pillars is what marks Muslims from non-Muslims, rather than a pattern of belief, and the most vital of these observances is the first. A Tradition attributed to Abu Dharr records a conversation with Muhammad. Abu Dharr recalled:

> The Prophet said, Gabriel came to me and gave me the glad tidings that anyone who died without worshipping anything beside Allah would enter Paradise. I asked "Even if he committed theft and even if he committed illegal sexual intercourse?" He said, "(Yes), even if he committed theft and even if he committed illegal sexual intercourse."[7]

5. Bukhari, *Sahih*, II, XXVI, chap. 49, no. 667, 390–91; and Muslim, *Sahih*, II, V, chap. 484, nos. 2912, 3, 4, 5, 642.

6. Muslim, *Sahih*, II, VII, chap. 485, no. 2918, 643.

7. Bukhari, *Sahih*, IX, XCIII, chap. 33, no. 579, 431.

This hadith (tradition) emphasizes the central role of the Affirmation and of the doctrine of tawhid. Allah, however, is almost unknowable and unapproachable. For Muslims, Allah is best known through his ninety-nine wonderful names.[8]

Muslims believe in angels, though there is no hierarchy among them, and no "archangels" as such. However, there are certain named angels. Gabriel, *Jibreel*, is the most prominent because of the role assigned to him in transmitting the revelations to Muhammad (Sura 53:5–10). Sura 81:20 describes him as one "endued with power, with rank before the Lord of the Throne," but it is the commentators who have identified the messenger as Gabriel; he is not named in either place.

There is belief in the prophets, most of them Old Testament prophets, although not necessarily designated as prophets in the Bible. The prophets are believed to have shared a common religious belief and practice, and each to have come to their communities with either a new revealed book or with an affirmation of previous revelations.

There is a belief in the books, and it is popularly believed that through history each nation has had its prophet and each nation its holy book, all originating in the Preserved Tablet in heaven. While there is a theoretical belief in both Old and New Testaments, or at least in the Jewish Torah and the Christian Gospel, Muslims do not generally accept either the extant versions of the Jewish or the Christian Scriptures (or even the Pentateuch and the Gospels) as being reliable. It appears that discrepancies between Muhammad's version of events and the Old Testament record of the same event[9] were early on noted by the Jews of Madina and explained by Muhammad as due to the Jews—and with respect to the New Testament, the Christians—having allowed their scriptures to become corrupt.

Inevitably there is belief in a Last Day, a Day of Reckoning, a Day of Resurrection, a Day of Upraising, more generally referred to as The Hour, *Al-Sa'a:* "They ask thee about the Hour—When will be its appointed time? Say: 'The knowledge thereof is with my Lord: None but He can reveal as to when it will occur'" (Sura 7:187). At that Hour

8. Bukhari, *Sahih*, IX, XCIII, chap. 11, no. 489, 363.

9. The story of the attempted seduction of Joseph by Potiphar's wife appears in Genesis 39 and Sura 12. The Qur'an account introduces the feature of Joseph's torn shirt. Since his shirt was torn at the back, this proved that he was attempting to escape from Potiphar's wife and not assaulting her. Consequently, he is not at that point imprisoned, and she is ordered to apologize to him. Imprisoned later, he interprets the Pharaoh's dream from prison, in the Qur'an account, whereas in Genesis he is brought before Pharaoh for that purpose. And in the Qur'an, it is Joseph, rather than Pharaoh, who suggests that he be made second ruler. For further discussion, see chap. 4 below, under "The Qur'an and the Bible."

there will be a general resurrection, and the books will be brought out, individual books recording the lives of every individual. For those whose good deeds have outweighed their bad deeds, their books will be given to them in their right hands; but for those whose evil deeds outweigh their good deeds, the books will be given in their left hands.

Paradise is the ultimate reward for Muslims. It is described in some detail in the Qur'an:

> As to the righteous, in a position of security. Among gardens and springs; dressed in fine silk and in rich brocade, they will face each other;
> Moreover we shall join them to Companions (*huri*) with beautiful, big and lustrous eyes.
> There can they call for every kind of fruit, in peace and security. (Sura 44:51–55)

> And Companions with beautiful, big, and lustrous eyes—like unto pearls well-guarded.
> A reward for the deeds of their past. (Sura 56:22–24)

The families of believers are there, too: "And those who believe and whose families follow them in faith—to them shall We join their families . . . and We shall bestow on them of fruit and meat, anything they shall desire" (Sura 52:21–2).

The "Companions" have attracted much attention from Western commentators on the Qur'an, who have tended to see them as celestial prostitutes.[10] Muslim commentators and Sufis tend rather to spiritualize the idea and point to the Qur'an's reference to their chastity (Sura 56:35–36).

Finally, there is belief in the decrees. The Qur'an seems to take a generally deterministic view of human life. Sura 74:31 states, "Thus doth Allah leave to stray whom He pleaseth, and guide whom He pleaseth." This finds an echo in Sura 35:8: "For Allah leaves to stray whom He wills, and guides whom He wills." In a somewhat confused passage Sura 4:78 puts it even more strongly: "If some good befalls them, they say, 'This is from Allah'; But if evil they say, 'This is from thee (O Prophet).' Say: 'All things are from Allah.'"[11] The question of free will and predestination, between the absolute omnipotence of God and the responsibility of humanity, divided Muslim theologians.

10. See, for example, Sir William Muir, *The Life of Muhammad*, ed. T. H. Weir (Edinburgh: Grant, 1923), 74–76, for a brief, unsubtle discussion of this aspect of the Qur'an.

11. The succeeding verse, however, seems to take a different view of evil: "Whatever good happens to thee is from Allah; But whatever evil happens to thee, is from thy (own) soul."

The determinists argued that to attribute free will to human beings limited an omnipotent God. The advocates of free will countered that to deny free will ran counter to the sense of human accountability implicit in the notion of the Last Day and Judgment. Both sides were able to use Qur'anic texts to justify their positions.[12]

THE MU'TAZILA

Calling themselves the people of divine justice, a group emerged, the Mu'tazila, who were ready to prioritize the use of logic and reason in determining the meaning of any Qur'anic passage. They rejected the idea of an eternal Qur'an and of a perception of omnipotence that led to determinism. Allah, they insisted, could only decree what is good. Evil is the consequence of human freedom and therefore rightly to be judged by Allah at the Hour. It was the Mu'tazila who produced a theodicy, a doctrine of divine justice holding that Allah *must* punish evil and reward good, but Allah being just *must* provide humanity with the means for doing good, whether through the Books or by sending prophets.[13] To conservative Muslim scholars this appeared to question Allah's omnipotence: freedom for humanity appeared to mean bondage for Allah.[14]

The Mu'tazila emerged at some time in the century after the death of Muhammad and brought into Islam both philosophical thinking and a rationalizing process. They labored at producing a systematic theology that was both Qur'anic and intellectually sound. Their name seems to come from a root meaning "separation," perhaps because they were in a sense schismatics, separating themselves from the main body of Muslims; perhaps because they distanced themselves from the dispute between Shi'a and Sunnis; and possibly because they separated out true believer from compromised believer:

> Whereas the Kharijites regarded a grave sinner as an outright infidel, and the main body of Muslims considered him a "sinner-Muslim," the Mu'tazila held that he was neither a Muslim nor a non-Muslim. This doctrine is known as that of the "intermediate state."[15]

The insistence by the Mu'tazila that the Qur'an was *created*, not eternal, may well have arisen from the realization that an eternal Qur'an came close to being a second deity, thus compromising tawhid, but also opened the way to an identification of an eternal Jesus, the

12. Esposito, *Islam: The Straight Path*, 70.
13. R. C. Martin, R. Woodward, and D. S. Atmaja, *Defenders of Reason in Islam* (Oxford: One World, 1997), 202.
14. Rahman, *Islam*, 89.
15. Ibid., 88.

Christian Word of God, with the eternal Qur'an, the Muslim Word of God. The Mu'tazila Caliph al-Ma'mun (813–33) expressed the danger rather clearly. He wrote of the "orthodox" Sunni teachers: "They are thus, like the Christians when they claim that Isa bin Maryam was not created because he was the word of God. But God says, 'Verily We have made it a Koran in the Arabic language,' and the explanation of that is, 'Verily We have created it.'"[16]

Three categories emerged: the believer (*mu'min*), the sinner (*fasiq*), and the infidel (*kafir*). To belief in the oneness of God they added the concept of the *justice* of God: that the omnipotence of Allah does not make him the cause of human wickedness, for which humanity, not Allah, is responsible.

In his celebrated work *Kitab al-Usul al-Khamsa* (Book of the Five Fundamentals), the Mu'tazila Qadi 'Abd al-Jabbar (935–1024) lists the five *Usul:*

- Tawhid, the oneness of Allah
- *'Adl*, Allah is just, and evil deeds originate in creation
- The promise (*al-wa'd*) and the threat (*al-wa'id*), reward for the good and punishment for the evil
- The intermediate position. The Khariji position is expressly rejected: the Muslim guilty of serious sin is still a Muslim, although he is neither a believer nor an unbeliever
- Allah's right to command the good and prohibit evil[17]

Although the Mu'tazila enjoyed a measure of official favor in the ninth century, it was short-lived, and their formulations never attracted mass support. An Allah who was unequivocally omnipotent and a Qur'an that was eternal proved to be more attractive than the rationally more coherent perceptions of the Mu'tazila. Here was a problem that would face Islam again at the beginning of the twenty-first century: how to turn Muslims away from an inherited tradition that involves emotionally exciting self-discipline and even sacrifice, and toward a new look in Islam, intellectually and rationally satisfying but lacking in emotional appeal.

SHARI'A

Since Islam is intended to relate to every part of human behavior, whether individually or corporately, it required the formulation of a

---

16. Quoted by Esposito, *Islam: The Straight Path*, 71–72.

17. Martin et al., *Defenders of Reason in Islam*. In chap. 5, 90–115, the *Kitab* is given in translation.

law system that could deal with theft, murder, inheritance, marriage, and divorce. All of this gradually emerged through the Law Schools of the eighth and ninth centuries. Although the detailed judgments of the four Law Schools differed in certain respects, there was agreement on the foundation of Shari'a law: Qur'an and Hadith (Tradition), Consensus (*ijma*), and Analogy (*qiyas*).

The expected consensus was theoretically that of the Muslim community, but since such a consensus could never be determined, it became rather the consensus of the *ulama*, the jurists, the legal experts.

It is a mistake to think that Muslims need only the Qur'an to determine belief and practice: the Traditions of the Prophet have an almost equal authority, especially in determining law. A useful distinction between Qur'an and Hadith is offered by Muhammad Abdul Rauf:

> It is important to bear in mind that the teachings given to Prophet Muhammad were of two types. One the Prophet conveyed to his followers in his own words. This category is called Hadith. The second category of revelations given to the Prophet Muhammad consisted not only of ideas but also of actual words. The Prophet was commanded to keep the words and to transmit them as they were to his followers. The total message revealed in this form is called the Qur'an.[18]

Any Tradition consisted of two parts: the *matn*, or text, the story itself; and the *isnad*, the chain of witnesses to the story, tracing it back authoritatively to Muhammad. When the Traditions came to be gathered together and classified, their reliability was made to depend strongly on the isnad. A short isnad was preferred to a long one, and the characters of the individual witnesses also came under consideration. Women were important in the study of Hadith. Fatima Bint Al-Hasan (who died in 1087) was famed for her piety, her calligraphy, and the quality of the many isnads that she knew.[19]

Shari'a is a path, and for Islam it is the path to be followed by Muslims. The law system has three aspects to it: the Laws of Inheritance, the *hadd* punishments (criminal law), and the Commandments and Prohibitions. Each system is called *fiqh*, and the same term is used for the general concept of law.

The Qur'an and the resultant fiqh permits but does not require polygamy. Sura 4:1–3 exhorts the Muslims at Madina, who were facing

18. Muhammad Abdul Rauf, *The Islamic Tradition* (Niles, Ill.: Argus, 1978), 18.

19. Muhammad Zubayr Siddiqi, *Hadith Literature* (Cambridge: Islamic Texts Society, 1993), 117–23. The same source describes Karima Al-Marwaziyya, a contemporary of Fatima, as an authority on Bukhari's *Sahih*. See also Ignaz Goldziher, "Women in the Hadith Literature," in *Muslim Studies*, vol. 2, chap. 5, 366–68.

the problem of the care of those women who had lost husbands, their natural protectors, in the fighting, possibly at Uhud:[20]

> To orphans restore their property, nor substitute worthless things for
>   good ones;
> and devour not their substance with your own.
> For this is indeed a great sin.
> If ye fear that ye shall not be able to deal justly with the orphans,
> marry women of your choice, two, or three, or four;
> but if ye fear that ye shall not be able to deal justly then only one. . . .

The Qur'an itself recognizes, "Ye are never able to be fair and just as between women, even if it is your ardent desire" (Sura 4:129); in recent times it has been argued that this observation means that Muslims should have only one wife. In the immediate context of fighting in which men died and women were left widowed, the provision of a limited polygamy is at least understandable. Whether it is equally appropriate in any other circumstance and in every other age is a matter for Islam to determine, and at the present time it seems that most ulama are not likely to give credence to a change in this matter.

Among the Shi'a the practice of *mut'a*, temporary marriage, is sometimes allowed. The practice is based on Sura 4:24: prohibited are "women already married, except those whom your right hands possess [i.e., women captured in jihad]. . . . Except for these, all other are lawful, provided ye seek them with gifts from your property. . . . Give them their dowers as prescribed."

Evidently temporary marriage was practiced in the early years of Islam. It originates, perhaps, in Islam's preoccupation with moral issues and its recognition of the strong sexual drive in the male. As the Muslim scholar Ayubi writes, "Islam is indeed a religion that stresses above all the collective enforcement of public morals; . . . with a certain fringe . . . the obsessions with sex, women, and the human body . . . borders on the pathological."[21] The sex drive is considered a potential source of sexual license and is met by the dual provision of polygamy and mut'a. Muslim writers contrast this with the Christian and Jewish respect for celibacy and monasticism, which have no equivalent in Islam. In fact, within Islam marriage is a duty, *wajib*, for a man and by some Muslims it is seen as a religious obligation, *fard*.

20. Abdur Rahman I. Doi, *Shari'ah: The Islamic Law* (London: Ta Ha Publishers, 1984), 145.

21. N. Ayubi, *Political Islam* (London: Routledge, 1991), 35, 44.

Divorce, *talaq*, is theoretically easy, at least for the man, under Shari'a law: the repetition of the formula of repudiation on three occasions. According to the Qur'an the three must be separated by three menstrual periods[22] to ascertain whether or not the woman is pregnant. If she is, the husband cannot proceed with the repudiation. The woman has only the right of legal separation, *faskh*, or the couple may agree to a halfway arrangement, conditional separation, or *khul*.

But divorce is seen in Islam as an evil, and Sura 4:39 suggests counseling for a couple considering divorce.

Shari'a commands beating as the punishment for immorality: one hundred stripes for man and woman (Sura 24:2). For theft the punishment is the amputation of the hands (Sura 5:38). Where practiced, this is usually limited to the amputation of one hand. This punishment is considered in a lengthy footnote in Muslim's collection of Traditions. Muhammad Asad is quoted as saying that "this severe punishment of Islam" is justified because in a true Muslim society everyone would be provided for adequately, and in proportion to the resources of the community. In such a situation theft could not be the result of need but of greed.[23] In view of this rationalization of the punishment (that Muslim society would be such that theft would simply be unnecessary), it has been argued that Muhammad himself is reported to have rejected suggestions that the punishment was too harsh: "By Him in whose hand is my life, even if Fatima, daughter of Muhammad, were to commit theft, I would have cut off her hand."[24]

Islamic law does not accept the Western economic system since the Qur'an forbids taking interest on loans: "Those who devour usury will not stand except as stands one whom the Evil One by his touch hath driven to madness. That is because they say: 'Trade is like usury.' But Allah hath permitted trade and forbidden usury" (Sura 2:275).

Despite claims that Sura 3:130 makes it clear that it is *extortionate* usury that is forbidden ("devour not usury, doubled and multiplied"), the Qur'an clearly forbids all usury, which might well have been reasonable in a society with zero levels of inflation, but is problematic in today's world. Since even Islamic banks, living in the modern world, cannot survive without some form of charge on loans or some kind of reward for deposits, what are often termed "service charges" or "operating costs" are levied against borrowers, and depositors are rewarded

22. Sura 2:228: "Divorced women shall wait concerning themselves for three monthly periods. Nor is it lawful for them to hide what Allah hath created in their wombs."

23. Muslim, *Sahih* III, chap. DCLXXVII, nos. 4175–86, 907–9.

24. Ibid., no. 4188, 910.

with shares in the bank.[25] Following the International Islamic Conference of 1976, the Islamic Council of Europe produced, in 1980, a Universal Declaration.[26] But this is not a declaration of human *rights*, since
rights are the preserve of Allah; humanity has *duties*. Section IV of the
Declaration affirms the ban on usury: "The procurement of wealth and
the production of goods must be lawful in terms of the Shari'a. Usury
(*riba*), gambling, hoarding, etc., are forbidden sources of income."[27]

The Shi'a inevitably had a problem with the Sunni concept of
Shari'a and developed their own system of law based on Qur'an and
Tradition (yet only those Traditions that went back to Muhammad
through Ali), but not using consensus.[28] The Shi'a Imam, the leader of
the Shi'a Muslims, had the authority to identify Shari'a law through
his authoritative interpretation of the Qur'an. In fact, the individual's
right or responsibility to interpret the Qur'an (*ijtihad*), denied in
Sunni Islam, was at least partially restored in Shi'a Islam. Later, when
there was no Shi'a Imam, this ijtihad authority tended to go to the
Ayatollahs, speaking on behalf of the Imam.

FOLK ISLAM[29]

As with every religion, many Muslims found that recognized orthodox
practice had its limitations and found its restrictions irksome. A more
practical system for dealing with the realities of daily life steadily
emerged. Religions, including Islam, are not fixed entities: they change in
response to new situations, new insights, and new contacts with competing religious, economic, and ethical systems. These changes tend to find
their source in the ordinary people's practices, to be initially resisted by
the leadership, who may eventually legitimize what cannot be displaced.

For many Muslims the worldview, the way in which the world is
perceived and understood, has five layers to it.[30] Apart from the rest is

25. "International Islam: Moslems and the Modern World," *The Economist*, January
3, 1981, 25. See also "Survey: Islam and the West," *The Economist*, August 6, 1994, 8–9,
for a more considered approach to the problem of *riba*.

26. Cf. Andrew Rippin and Jan Knappert, eds., *Textual Sources for the Study of Islam*
(Chicago: University of Chicago Press, 1986), 192–97.

27. See Salem Azzam, ed., *Islam and Contemporary Society* (London: Longmans,
1982). See also p. 129 n. 33 of the present work.

28. Andrew Rippin, *Muslims: Their Religious Beliefs and Practices*, 2d ed. (London:
Routledge, 2001), 116–21.

29. See Bill Musk, *The Unseen Face of Islam* (Eastbourne: MARC, 1989), for a full
discussion of the whole range of practices generally designated "Folk Islam."

30. The number of "layers" will obviously depend on the classification employed.
See Musk, *Unseen Face of Islam*, 176, for a diagrammatic analysis of the Muslim worldview; and Bruce Bradshaw, *Change across Cultures* (Grand Rapids: Baker, 2002), 112,
for a "three-zone" presentation attributed to the Hausa of West Africa.

Allah, below whom are first the angels and then the jinn, the spirits. Below them, again, is humanity, and finally comes the animal world. Communication across these layers is always possible: even Allah has revealed himself through Gabriel to humanity. The *shaman*, the "wise man," can invoke the spirits of the dead and the jinn. Communication in such ways may mean access to information otherwise unattainable, to resolve problems otherwise insoluble.

A crucial concern of all peoples is sickness and the threat of death. If orthodox medical treatment fails or is unavailable, then the ailing must have recourse to other treatments. In Folk Islam there is no mere accident: accidents and illnesses have causes, not merely physical causes but spiritual causes. Consequently they can be resolved by using spiritual methods. The Qur'an is a potent resource: recitation of the Qur'an and particularly repetition of the Ninety-Nine Wonderful Names of Allah may bring help. A passage of the Qur'an written down and tied round the wrist or neck may help. Sometimes people write a verse of the Qur'an on paper, place the paper in water so that the ink of the writing is dissolved, and then drink the solution. People seek help through dreams and visions, exorcism, and even astrology.

Running alongside this is the notion of *baraka*, blessing. Some people are blessed, lucky. Some days are more baraka-blessed than others: Friday is very much so, and Thursday nearly as much, being adjacent to Friday. The wise businessperson will defer important decisions from Wednesday at least to Thursday, and better still to Friday. The month of Ramadan is particularly laden with baraka. Places have it, too: the most auspicious of all places is Mecca, and there the most auspicious of all is the Ka'ba and its Black Stone. People returning from the pilgrimage carry with them baraka that can be passed on to those who encounter them.

The notion of the jinn, acknowledged by orthodoxy, is expanded in Folk Islam to include the idea of the *qarina*, the twin spirit, created when a child is born and attached to the child for life. The qarina is evil and its task is to undermine the faith of its human counterpart. The very act of sexual intercourse is, therefore, potentially dangerous, touching onto that other spirit world, and birth is usually accompanied by the repetition of Qur'anic verses (especially the invocation of Sura 1), and the *bismillah* ("In the name of Allah, most gracious, most merciful"). The prayer call may be whispered in the child's ear, and an amulet containing written Qur'an verses may be tied to the child's wrist or around the neck.

Spirit possession is, inevitably, part of Folk Islam. The *sar* or *zar* cults occur in many African countries that have a sizeable Muslim population. Ioan Lewis comments:

I refer to those anthropomorphic jinns that in Somalia, as in other Muslim lands, are held to lurk in every dark and empty corner, poised and ready to strike capriciously and without warning at the unwary passerby. These malevolent sprites are said to be consumed by envy and greed and to be particularly covetous of luxurious clothing, finery, perfume, and dainty goods. They are known generally as sar (Ethiopian zar), a word that describes both the sprites themselves and the symptoms attributed to them; the afflicted victim is described as having been "entered," "seized," or "possessed" by the sar.[31]

Sar possession may carry with it positive as well as negative overtones: the person with a sar is a person who is in touch with the other world, and may well be in a position to invoke that other world in solving some personal problem in this world—barrenness is a common example. Thus the woman with a sar (and it is most frequently a woman)[32] gains a status she might otherwise never have. This in turn leads to some women actively seeking sar-invasion by joining a group of those who already have the sar. On the other hand, sar invasion may also be linked with the concept of the evil eye, leading to the ostracism of the one with the sar. Among the Hausa people of Nigeria "the inability of the Hausa women to participate adequately in the ceremonial and public life of Islam leaves a gap which is filled by the spirit-possession cult."[33]

For many Muslims, Shari'a-based Islamic orthodoxy does not provide all that is needed by the religiously inclined, and between them Sufism and Folk Islam seek to provide what is missing. Such Muslims consider that orthodox practice does not adequately deal with sin, which must be accounted for at the inevitable day of judgment. Through greater devotion to Allah, through pilgrimage, and through devotion to men of great holiness, Muslims may hope to find both a lessening of their sin burden and an intercessor to plead for them.

31. I. M. Lewis, *Religion in Context* (London and New York: Cambridge University Press, 1986), 30–31. See also David Burnett, *Unearthly Powers* (Eastbourne: MARC, 1988), 169–74.

32. Lewis, *Religion in Context*, 32.

33. Mary Smith, *Baba of Karo* (London: Faber and Faber, 1954), quoted in Lewis, *Religion in Context*, 27.

4

QUR'AN
AND CHRISTIANITY

THE QUR'AN

It is all but certain that the Qur'an did not come together as a single volume in the lifetime of Muhammad. He made use of scribes to record some of his words in the Madina period, but most of his words were either memorized by his listeners or written down unsystematically as individual aides-mémoire.

Their importance was recognized shortly after Muhammad's death, and according to tradition Abu Bakr appointed Zaid ibn Thabit to prepare a written collection of the scattered texts: "Zaid continued: Abu Bakr said to me, 'You are a young man, intelligent, and we see no fault in you, and you have already written down the revelation for the Prophet of God, may God bless and save him. Therefore go and seek the Qur'an and assemble it.'"[1] In this Tradition Zaid goes on to describe his experiences in collecting the Qur'an:

> So I started looking for the Qur'an and collecting it from palm-leaf stalks, thin white stones and also from the men who knew it by heart, till I found the last Verse of Surat At-Tauba with Abi Khuzaima Al-Ansari, and I did not find it with anybody other than him. The Verse is:
> "Verily there has come unto you an Apostle from amongst yourselves. It grieves him that you should receive any injury or difficulty. . . ."[2]

Then the complete manuscripts of the Qur'an remained with Abu Bakr till he died, then with Umar till the end of his life, and then with Hafsa, the daughter of Umar.

1. Bernard Lewis, ed. and trans., *Islam: From the Prophet Muhammad to the Capture of Constantinople* (reprint, New York: Oxford University Press, 1987), 2:1–2. See also Bukhari, *Sahih*, VI, LXI, chap. 3, no. 509, 477.
2. Bukhari, *Sahih*, VI, LXI, chap. 3, no. 510, 478.

The Qur'an is only viewed as the Qur'an when it is in Arabic, but in fact it has been translated into many languages. English translations protect this understanding of the Arabic nature of the Qur'an by using a title such as *The Meaning of the Glorious Qur'an* (Pickthall's translation) or *The Meaning of the Holy Qur'an* (Yusuf Ali). The Qur'an was translated into Latin as early as 1143, at the order of Peter the Venerable, Abbot of Cluny. George Sale's translation into English, accompanied by an invaluable "Preliminary Discourse," appeared in 1734.

But in the first place the Qur'an was an occasional and oral message, preserved in the memories of those who had heard Muhammad, some of whom wrote down what they remembered.

The Uthmanic Recension

Variants of the Qur'anic texts began to circulate, as one would expect given the disparate forms in which elements of the Qur'an were recorded and the varied locations of these early records. Uthman took the manuscript that was in the care of Muhammad's widow Hafsa and returned it to Zaid with instructions that the collection was to be completed and three copies were to be made, eliminating any variants made in the interests of dialects of Arabic other than the Qurayshi dialect.[3] The original leaves went back to Hafsa, copies of the "official" text were widely distributed, and variant texts were ordered to be destroyed. None of the original copies of the Zaid text have survived.[4]

This is the outline of events as given by Bukhari. Other Traditions insist that the Qur'an was collected in Muhammad's own lifetime.[5] Bukhari's account is also brought into question by the assertion by Western scholars that the Qur'an is not, in fact, written in the Quraysh dialect, but in a common, or koine, dialect, which would have been widely understood among the Arab people.[6] A third question mark against Bukhari's account is the fact that divergent texts are known to have continued to circulate after they were supposedly suppressed. Hafsa had a codex that included at Sura 2:238 a reference to the afternoon prayer time. Abdullah ibn Mas'ud had a text that omitted the first sura and the last two suras. He is a particularly important witness

---

3. Bukhari, *Sahih*, IV, LVI, chap. 3, no. 709, 466.

4. Revisionist scholars question whether this collection ever existed.

5. Bell doubted that such a collection ever existed in Muhammad's lifetime, but he accepted the general outline of events as given by Ibn Ishaq (W. M. Watt, ed., *Bell's Introduction to the Qur'an* [Edinburgh: Edinburgh University Press, 1970], 40ff.). J. Wansbrough goes further and advocates the thesis that the Qur'an came together in its present form only in the third Islamic century (*Qur'anic Studies* [Oxford: Oxford University Press, 1977], 119ff.).

6. See the article "al-Kur'an," *Encyclopaedia of Islam*, vol. 5, section 6a, p. 419.

since Bukhari himself records a Tradition that Muhammad had com-
mended him as a faithful transmitter of the Qur'an, and he was said to
have memorized seventy suras.[7] Bukhari also records a Tradition going back to Aisha that Muhammad told his daughter Fatima that Gabriel came to him each year to "revise" the Qur'an, and that in the year
of his death Gabriel came to him twice.[8] The Tradition certainly implies that something like a Qur'an existed in Muhammad's lifetime,
and that there was some kind of ongoing review process. In other
words, even Tradition does not support the idea of a single and authoritative text of the Qur'an compiled by Muhammad himself or even
compiled in his lifetime.

The Uthmanic recension of the Qur'an was written in a consonantal
text, where the long vowels could be signaled but not the short vowels.
It was this ambiguity in Arabic orthography that was responsible for
most, though not all, of the variants in the early texts. Writing of the
codices of Ibn Mas'ud and Ibn Ka'b, Bell comments:

> No copies exist of any of the early codices, but the list of variant read-
> ings . . . is extensive, running to a thousand or more items in both
> cases. . . .

> The variant readings in the codices of both these men chiefly affect the
> vowels and punctuation, but occasionally there is a different consonan-
> tal text. For both, too, we have lists of the suras, and it is noteworthy
> that these differ from each other and also from the Uthmanic list in the
> order in which the suras are arranged.[9]

In fact, the claim often made that there is only a single version of
the text of the Qur'an is deceptive: textual variants do exist, and their
number is limited simply because records of earlier variant codices
have been more or less systematically destroyed.[10]

Contradictions within the Qur'an and Abrogation

Unlike the Bible, which has many authors, in Muslim tradition the
Qur'an owes its existence to just one man, Muhammad.[11] He claimed
to receive it as a revelation, piece by piece. He may even have had

---

7. John Gilchrist, *The Qur'an: The Scripture of Islam* (Mondeor, South Africa:
MERCSA, 1995).

8. Bukhari, *Sahih* IV, LVI, chap. 24, no. 819, 526–27.

9. Watt, *Bell's Introduction to the Qur'an*, 45.

10. Christianity, for its part, has carefully preserved the ancient manuscripts of biblical texts, so that by comparing them an authoritative text could be constructed.

11. But revisionist scholars would see the Qur'an as the product of a relatively
lengthy process and involving multiple authorship.

some of the later passages written down at once by a secretary, but mostly it was memorized by those who heard him, some of whom later wrote down what they remembered. Muhammad himself was not a systematic theologian, and the Qur'an is not a piece of sustained systematic theology.

There is a clear difference between many of the ideas of the early Meccan suras and the later Madinan suras. The theory of *naskh*, abrogation, canceling out one passage by a later passage where the two appear to be contradictory, seeks to resolve apparent conflicts and contradictions. A passage in a sura from the Madina period would abrogate a sura from the earlier Meccan period. But this brings a further problem with it: deciding which suras are earlier and which later, and which part of a sura is earlier and which part is later. Sura 5 tells Muslims: "Take not the Jews and the Christians for your friends," and yet in verse 82 of the same sura they are told, "Strongest among men in enmity to the believers you will find the Jews and pagans, but nearest to them in love you will find those who say 'We are Christians.'"

Some verses of the Qur'an counsel Muslims not to use force while others enjoin violence. Does the command to kill abrogate the command to be at peace, or does the command to be at peace abrogate the command to kill? Sura 9, which contains the Sword Verse, verse 5, is a Madina sura: "But when the forbidden months[12] are past, then fight and slay the pagans wherever ye find them, and seize them, beleaguer them, and lie in wait for them in every stratagem (of war)."

Yusuf Ali says that this verse dates to the ninth year after the Hijra. That would be 731, only a year before Muhammad's death.[13] It is this late dating that leads Muslim scholars such as Ibn Salama and Ibn al-'Ata'iqi to say that the Sword Verse abrogates some 124 earlier verses, many of which counseled patience and tolerance toward "pagan" people, including the pacific generalization:[14] "Let there be no compulsion in religion: truth stands out clear from error" (Sura 2:256).

12. The forbidden months referred to here are probably not to be taken as the sacred truce months, which obtained before the Muslim era, but the months granted by Muhammad to those pagan Arab tribes with whom he had concluded some kind of pact. During the specified months they would be left in peace, but if they had failed to embrace Islam by the conclusion of the months, then they would be counted as infidels and subjected to attack and subjugation. See Yusuf Ali, *Meaning of the Holy Qur'an*, 438, n. 1250.

13. Ibid., 435, in his introductory notes to Sura 9.

14. David S. Powers, "The Exegetical Genre Nasikh al-Qur'an wa Mansukhuhu," in *Approaches to the History of the Interpretation of the Qur'an*, ed. Andrew Rippin (Oxford: Clarendon, 1988), 130–31. Powers lists the verses abrogated by Sura 9:5.

The Order of the Chapters

In order to make sense of the Qur'an, a reader needs to know a good deal about Muhammad's life. Although the earlier suras are directed more at the warning message that Muhammad had for the people of Mecca, the later suras are much more concerned with various problems that confronted him as the leader of a successful political and religious movement in Madina. But the word *earlier* does not mean "first in the book." When the Qur'an was put together, the longer suras were placed first and the shorter suras last, but that is almost precisely the reverse of the chronological order: the short suras were proclaimed first, in Mecca, and the long suras last, in Madina. The principal exception is Sura 1, which has only 7 verses, compared with the 286 verses of Sura 2, the 200 verses of Sura 3, and the 176 verses of Sura 4. But Sura 1 is a prayer, and Abdullah ibn Mas'ud's collection of the Qur'an omitted it, which raises questions about its inclusion in any "original" Qur'an.

Qur'an and Inspiration

In Muslim thinking it is not Muhammad who was inspired, but the message he transmitted. Its origin is not in Muhammad, but in the Preserved Tablet kept in heaven and referred to in Sura 85:22. From this record there have been other revelations given: the Torah, the Old Testament Law, given to Moses; the Psalms, given to David; the Gospel, given to Jesus; and the Qur'an, given to Muhammad. The Torah is in Hebrew for Jews, the Gospel in Greek for Gentiles, the Qur'an in Arabic for Arabs and ultimately for all people.

The book itself is not seen as the product of Muhammad. It is inspired. The word used is *wahy* from the verb *awha*, used in the Qur'an more than seventy times. In Sura 16:68 the word is used of the bee. How does it know how to construct its hive and where to build it? The answer is wahy. The bee doesn't work it out logically: it is guided by God.

According to the Islamic scriptures, Muhammad's times of inspiration were accompanied by physical manifestations: perspiration, shaking, and even trance. An example is given by Bukhari:

> The Prophet waited for a while and then the Divine Inspiration descended upon him. Umar pointed out to Ya'la, telling him to come. Ya'la came and pushed his head (underneath the screen which was covering the Prophet) and behold! The Prophet's face was red and he kept on breathing heavily for a while, and then he was relieved.[15]

15. Bukhari, *Sahih*, VI, LXI, chap. 2, no. 508, 476.

Muhammad's own explanation was that the inspiration sometimes came

> ". . . like the ringing of a bell, this form of inspiration is the hardest of all and then this state passes off after I have grasped what is inspired. Sometimes the Angel comes in the form of a man and talks to me." Aisha added: "Verily I saw the prophet on a very cold day and noticed the sweat dropping from his forehead (as the inspiration was over)."[16]

It was this claim to inspiration that gave authority to Muhammad's teaching, although those who opposed him said that he was merely repeating what someone was telling him. Yet there is no denying that at least the earlier suras of the Qur'an are lively, highly imaginative, poetic, and in that sense inspired. The claim that the entire Qur'an is written in this same "inspired" form is debatable; the later suras can often seem labored (to non-Muslims, at least), giving the impression of being constructed to meet an immediate social or political need.

The Qur'an and the Bible

The Qur'an contains many references to the Old Testament, a good many to Jesus and Christianity, but little direct reference to the New Testament. The story of Joseph is given a whole sura (Sura 12), but it differs in many respects from the biblical account of Joseph's life. Joseph's brothers see their father's preference for Joseph and assume that he is out of his mind. The brothers then ask their father to let Joseph go with them to pasture the flocks. After throwing him into a pit, they go off and tell their father that a wolf killed him. Taken to Egypt, Joseph is sold to a rich man, whose wife tries to seduce him:

> But she in whose house he was, sought to seduce him from his true self: She fastened the doors, and said, "Now come, thou!"
> He said, "Allah forbid! Truly (thy husband) is my lord. He made my sojourn agreeable. Truly to no good come those who do wrong."
> And with passion did she desire him, and he would have desired her but that he saw the evidence of his Lord: Thus did We order that We might turn away from him all evil and shameful deeds. For he was one of Our servants, sincere and purified.
> So they both raced each other to the door, and she tore his shirt from the back. They both found her lord near the door. She said: "What is the (fitting) punishment for one who formed an evil design against thy wife?" (Sura 12:23–25)

16. Bukhari, *Sahih*, I, I, chap. 1, no. 2, 2.

The servants, however, intervened and said that she had tried to seduce him, and the proof could be seen in Joseph's shirt: torn from *behind*, when he was running away, not torn *in front*, as would be the
case if he was attacking her! But Joseph is imprisoned, interprets the
dreams of his fellow prisoners, the king's baker and cupbearer, and
when Pharaoh's restored cupbearer hears Pharaoh tell of *his* dream,
the cupbearer hurries back to the prison to get the interpretation from
Joseph. Pharaoh then sends to the prison and commands that Joseph
should come to him. But Joseph refuses until he has heard what has
happened to the woman who tried to seduce him. She was one of the
crowd surrounding Pharaoh, and at once she confessed her guilt and
Joseph's innocence.

This narrative is described here at some length to indicate the nature
of the Qur'anic references to Old Testament stories: a mixture of biblical
text and apocryphal additions. The differences and contradictions are as
surprising as the similarities, since the Jewish Torah, the Christian *Injil*
(Gospel), and the Qur'an are all supposed to have come from a heavenly
Preserved Tablet. The explanation given by Muslims is that the Torah is
not the same as the Pentateuch (the five books of Moses, called the Torah
by Jews), and the Injil is not the same as the Gospels. Yusuf Ali explains
the Muslim view that the first five books of the Old Testament contain "a
semi historical and legendary narrative of the history of the world from
the Creation to the time of the arrival of the Jews in the Promised Land.
There are in them some beautiful idylls but there are also stories of in-
cest, fraud, cruelty and treachery, not always disapproved."[17]

In part, of course, the accusation is true: the Old Testament depicts
people as they were and not as they should have been. And yet as we
have seen, the Qur'an itself contains an expanded and graphic account
of the attempted seduction of Joseph (Sura 12:21–35).

QUR'AN AND CHRISTIANITY

As we have already seen, one of the earliest significant contacts between the Arab peoples and Christianity occurred in the Ethiopian
occupation of the Yemen, and the subsequent Year of the Elephant,
when Abraha set out to destroy the Ka'ba. He was disastrously unsuccessful, and the Year of the Elephant came to be linked to the year of
Muhammad's birth.

Christians and Jews as Sources of the Qur'an

The question of the sources of the Qur'an is extremely important.
For Muslims there can be no such question: the Qur'an is a revelation

17. *Meaning of the Holy Qur'an*, 288.

out of the Preserved Tablet, a heavenly prototype, given to Muhammad through the angel, the "holy spirit," Gabriel. Muhammad is in no sense the author of the Qur'an; he provides the tongue to vocalize it, but it owes nothing to his knowledge of the events he describes: "From the standpoint of form it was his tongue that spoke; but he was not there at all, the speaker in reality was God."[18]

To Western minds accustomed to associating literary gift with formal education, it might appear surprising that a man such as Muhammad should be able to produce sustained poetic literature, often touching on ancient historical events, such as the imprisonment of Joseph in Egypt and his subsequent rise to power there. If the idea of divine transmission is rejected, then some alternative explanation must at least be attempted.

The nature of the Qur'an's passages that parallel texts from the Bible is itself indicative of a possible answer: that Muhammad's knowledge of these events came from oral traditions rather than from an acquaintance with the written Scriptures. For one thing Muhammad did not have access to an Arabic translation of any part of the Bible. For another thing there is a strong Muslim tradition that Muhammad was "functionally illiterate." By this is meant that while he could almost certainly read and write, he could not do so with any fluency. This tradition is based on a verse from the Qur'an: Sura 7:157 refers to him as "the unlettered prophet," the prophet of the umma, of the people, or of the *umiyya*, the illiterate. In either case the sense is that of a man who was no scholar, but simply a man of the masses, and like the masses, with only a limited education.[19] Chawkat Moucarry, quoting Ibn Abbas, offers a third possible interpretation of the verse, that Muhammad came from a people which had no scripture: the Arabs were an *ummi* people in the sense that they had no sacred writings, and Muhammad was one of those unscriptured people.[20]

The Journeys into Syria

But if not through revelation and not from actually reading the Scriptures, where did Muhammad's knowledge come from? First, there were the long journeys he took into Syria, initially with his uncle's trading caravans and later with Khadija's. On such journeys the travelers would relieve the boredom by repeating stories they had heard. These tales would inevitably be a mixture of an original story

18. Kenneth Cragg, *The Event of the Qur'an* (London: Allen and Unwin, 1971), 44, quoting Jalal al-Din Rumi.

19. See Chawkat Moucarry, *Faith to Faith* (Leicester: Inter-Varsity, 2001), 223–28, for a full discussion of the statement that Muhammad was *ummi*.

20. Ibid., 226.

and the pious fabrications and imaginative additions that had gathered around it.

Precisely this kind of embellished anecdote would be recited again and again on these long caravan journeys into Syria, with no opportunity for listeners to disentangle fact from legend. There would be a further consequence of learning in this way: the anecdotes would be like beads without their connecting chain or string, stories without important chronological links. It may well be this factor that explains the apparent confusion in Sura 19:28 between Old Testament Miriam and New Testament Mary, who is described as a "sister of Aaron." In Arabic the two names are the same, although centuries separated the two.

Christians and Jews in Mecca and Madina

There were some Christians and Jews even in Mecca, and even among Muhammad's immediate family. Fatima's cousin Waraqa ibn Qusayy is said to have been a Christian "who had studied the Scriptures and was a scholar." When Khadija told him about Muhammad, he is said to have replied: "If this is true, Khadija, verily Muhammad is the prophet of this people. I knew that a prophet of this people was to be expected. His time has come."[21] It seems also that when Muhammad began to experience his visions, he was troubled by them and uncertain of their source. It is said that while he was circumambulating the Ka'ba, he encountered Waraqa, who reassured him, telling him that the vision he had seen of some mighty figure was no other than Gabriel, who had appeared to Moses.[22]

After the Hijra, Muhammad lived in Madina, where there was a considerable community of Jews, and it appears that being near people who at least were familiar with the Old Testament caused Muhammad some embarrassment: "The standard against which the Madinan Jews judged the legends and sermons recited by Muhammad would have been their Hebrew Bible and Midrash, although they were undoubtedly familiar with the versions to which Muhammad referred as well."[23]

The real scandal, so far as the Madinan Jews were concerned, was that they considered Muhammad to be taking the legendary and apoc-

---

21. Guillaume, *Life of Muhammad*, 83.

22. Ibid., 107. Presumably Waraqa would have had in mind the appearance of the "angel of the Lord" to Moses in the burning bush (Exod. 3), but Gabriel is not named there nor anywhere else in the Pentateuch, though he is named in Daniel and in the nativity scenes in the New Testament.

23. Reuven Firestone, *Journeys in Holy Lands* (New York: New York State University Press, 1990), 157.

ryphal material, with which they were familiar, and turning it into authoritative scripture, which, for them, it was not.

Even in Mecca[24] the accusation had been made that the so-called revelations were merely tales told to him:

> The misbelievers say: "Naught is this but a lie which he has forged, and other have helped him at it." In truth it is they who have put forward an iniquity and a falsehood. . . . And they say: "Tales of the ancients, which he has caused to be written: and they are dictated before him morning and evening." (Sura 25:4–5)

In Madina the criticisms would have been more specific, focusing on the obvious conflict between the Qur'an's version of various events and what was written in the Old Testament. It may well have been these criticisms that caused Muhammad to break with both Jews and Christians in their *qibla*, the direction faced when praying. In Mecca and in Madina, Muhammad had prayed facing Jerusalem, to the north, but in the midst of his prayers on one occasion in Madina he is said to have turned through 180 degrees and completed his prayer facing Mecca (and the Ka'ba). The event was commemorated by the so-called Mosque of the Two Qiblas.

The proximity of an actual community of Jews, who would have some measure of familiarity with the Old Testament, might well explain why it is that the Qur'an is rich in references to Old Testament events, but beyond the birth narratives has little reference to specific events of the New Testament. There is one story about Jesus that is *not* in the New Testament. Sura 5:110 reads: "Behold! I taught thee the Book and wisdom, the Law and the Gospel. And behold! thou makest out of clay, as it were, the figure of a bird, by My leave, and thou breathest into it, and it becometh a bird by My leave."

The legend appears in more detail in chapter 2 of the apocryphal *Gospel of Thomas* and in the later Arabic *Infancy Gospel,* and it is one of the few stories that circulated about Jesus' childhood. He is supposed to have been playing in the street with other children on the Sabbath. They were making clay animals when a rabbi accused them of Sabbath-breaking. Jesus then breathed on his clay bird, and it immediately came to life and flew away, and with it disappeared the evidence of Sabbath-breaking. It is just the sort of story that might be expected to circulate orally among the credulous, and it might have come to Muhammad's attention through some itinerant storyteller.

24. Assuming with Yusuf Ali that Sura 25 is Meccan.

Islam's claim that Muhammad's pronouncements represented a direct and inspired revelation from God has inevitably carried in its train a long history of debate, sometimes acrimonious, not only between the respective theologians, Muslim, Jewish, and Christian (who *did* understand the issues), but also between what might be termed lay Muslims, Jews, and Christians (who did *not*). For the Jews the problem focused on the seeming confusion of inspired Scripture and uninspired accretions to it. For Christians the problem lay with the Qur'an's apparent denial of the crucifixion of Jesus. Well-intentioned dialogue has so far failed to resolve the problems arising from these seemingly irreconcilable views.

ISLAM AND THE CHURCH

The Christians of Ethiopia

Although in his early years Muhammad himself was sheltered from persecution by his uncle and guardian, Abu Talib, his followers were less fortunate. Eventually Muhammad encouraged them to leave. They might have gone south, to the Yemen, but doubtless Muhammad realized that almost certainly the Meccans would follow them there and drag them back to endure further suffering. It seems that he had heard of the Christian nation across the Red Sea, Abyssinia (modern Ethiopia), with a Christian *negus*, "king." There, he was sure, they would be well received and protected. Eventually some eighty-three men and eighteen women made the journey and were welcomed. The establishment of monotheism on the eastern coast of the Red Sea must have been welcome news to Christian Ethiopia, though the precise nature of that monotheism had yet to be determined.

Muhammad was clearly right in expecting pursuit: the Meccans sent two men after the emigrants, carrying gifts for the Negus.[25] The Meccans demanded that Muhammad's followers be sent back. The King hesitated, then questioned the refugees about their beliefs:

O king, we were an uncivilized people, worshipping idols, eating corpses, committing abominations, breaking natural ties, treating guests badly,

25. Trimingham, *Islam in Ethiopia*, 44–46, expresses some doubt about the historicity of this deputation to the Ethiopian *najashi*, "king."

It is interesting that in 2002 it was decided that there should be a Muslim university in the northern Ethiopian city of Mekele, to be called the Negashi University, commemorating the events of the first migration. Dr. Hassan Meki, Director of the Institute of Africa in Khartoum, suggested during an Ethio-Arab cultural week that the time when Ethiopia was viewed as an island of Christianity in a sea of Islam should end, and Ethiopia should join the Arab League (*The Daily Monitor*, Addis Ababa, June 19, 2002).

and our strong devoured our weak. Thus we were until God sent us an apostle, whose lineage, truth, trustworthiness and clemency we know. He summoned us to acknowledge God's unity and to worship him, and to renounce the stones and images which we and our fathers formerly worshipped.[26]

Their answer seemed to satisfy him, but the Meccans now accused them of concealing an important and, for the church, relevant and vital part of their beliefs: their teaching about Jesus. Again the king questioned them: "We say about him that which our prophet brought, saying, he is the slave of God, and his apostle, and his spirit, and his word, which he cast into Mary the blessed virgin." The negus is supposed to have replied, "By God, Jesus, son of Mary, does not exceed what you have said by the length of this stick."

Muhammad's biographer Ibn Ishaq comments that the king's *shums*, his counselors, "snorted" at this reply,[27] a good Muslim reply but a very inadequate Christian reply, and certainly they would have snorted had this been a genuine conversation! However, the Meccans returned home without the refugees but carrying with them the gifts they had brought for the Negus, who indignantly refused to accept them.

From time to time the refugees received news from Mecca, but meanwhile they were exposed to the form of Christianity practiced in Ethiopia. The ideas they encountered were clearly similar in many ways to those of Muhammad. The same concern for the poor, the same care for the aged and widows, the same emphasis on the one God, but this with a difference. They encountered the doctrine of the Trinity, the notion of God incarnate. Muhammad had never claimed or even hinted at such a role for himself: he was a prophet, neither more nor less. Some of the refugees found in this Christianity the completion of what they had learned from Muhammad. Among them was Ubaydullah bin Jahsh. His comment on his conversion is perceptive:

> "Our eyes are opened but yours veiled," i.e., We can see clearly but you are only trying to see: you can't yet see clearly, the metaphor being taken from a puppy who tries to open its eyes and flutters them before he can do so, i.e., We have opened our eyes and we see, but you have not opened your eyes though you are trying to do so.[28]

26. Guillaume, *Life of Muhammad*, 151.
27. Ibid., 152. The phrase "son of Mary," *ibn Maryam*, gives the game away. It was the regular Muslim designation of Jesus among Muslims, but one foreign to the Ethiopian church.
28. Ibid., 528.

Ubaydullah died in Ethiopia, and Muhammad eventually married his widow, Umm Habiba.

The Church in North Africa

The Christian church had expanded rapidly across North Africa, with Alexandria and Carthage as centers of administration and learning. The Berber people, however, were left largely untouched by this expansion: like the church in Ethiopia, other Christians concerned themselves more with the niceties of theological debate than with evangelism. Consequently the Berber people, who then as now stretched right across the North African coastal region, were marginalized and left to pursue their own animistic religion.

In A.D. 493 the Goth Theodoric ruled the Byzantine Empire, doing so from Rome. Unlike the majority of Goths he favored the preservation of Roman culture. But his rule was challenged by the Vandals, who marched through France and the Iberian peninsula (modern Portugal and Spain) and crossed into North Africa. They hated all things Roman, and before them the Romans and Greeks in North Africa fled, some to the Mediterranean islands, some to Rome, some to Athens. The exodus left the North African churches desperately weak, facing an overwhelmingly Berber population. The Vandals stayed only forty years and were driven out by Emperor Justinian.[29] But the damage to the church was done: their intellectuals scattered. And the Berbers, still unevangelized, remained there.

This was the situation across North Africa when Islam broke out of the confines of the Arabian peninsula and headed north and west. Only ten years after Muhammad's death Alexandria and all Egypt were in the hands of the Muslims. The church in Egypt greeted them with mixed feelings: because of its one-nature (monophysite) doctrine about Jesus, they had been treated roughly, as little better than heretics, by the rest of the churches that accepted the Chalcedonian doctrine of the two natures of Jesus, human and divine. The Muslims treated them rather better than the Byzantine Christians had done.

The Muslim advance across North Africa continued: in another fifty years Carthage fell, and the whole of North Africa was theirs. The Berbers needed little persuasion to accept Islam: their language was, after all, related to Arabic and not at all to Greek or Latin, the languages of the church. Their previous Christian overlords had done little to evangelize them and still less to advance their social conditions. The once-vibrant church of North Africa all but disappeared. As Latourette observes:

29. W. H. C. Frend, *The Rise of Christianity* (Philadelphia: Fortress, 1984), chap. 23.

In North Africa the Christian communities disappeared more quickly and completely than in any other of the major regions on the Mediterranean littoral. Probably the reason is to be found in their character. While some converts had been made among them, most of the Berbers seem to have remained non-Christian.[30]

The Muslim advance proceeded further, now strengthened by the accession of the Berbers. One of them, Tarik, led the leap across the Mediterranean to Gibraltar and even gave it the name *Jabal Tarik*. There is a lesson there for the church to learn: when it buries its head in monasteries and libraries, when it concerns itself primarily with philosophy and abstract theology, when it loses sight of the people, the consequences for both church and people are likely to be catastrophic.

The Four Letters: The Emperor Heraclius

There is a long and detailed passage in Ibn Ishaq's biography of Muhammad (though Guillaume is mainly giving al-Tabari's account) claiming that Muhammad sent letters to a number of rulers, calling them to submit to Islam. Muhammad is said to have turned to a legendary account of the beginnings of Christian missionary work, when Jesus sent Peter and Paul to Rome, Andrew and Matthew to "the land of the cannibals," Thomas east to "the land of Babel," Philip to Carthage in North Africa, John to Ephesus, James to Jerusalem, Bartholomew to Arabia, and Simon to the Berber people. According to Muhammad, some of Jesus' followers refused to go on these journeys, and Muhammad urged his messengers not to be swayed by their example.

Then follow details of the experiences of the messengers. In Alexandria the bishop is supposed to have given the messenger four slave girls to be taken to Muhammad. A long and somewhat confused section details the embassy to the Byzantine Christian Emperor Heraclius (575–641), who is supposed to have received Muhammad's letter with great respect. One version places this incident in 629, just after Heraclius's success in recovering the cross of Jesus from the Persians. The account concludes with a remarkable confession by Heraclius: "Alas, I know that your master is a prophet sent, and that it is he whom we expect and find in our book, but I go in fear of my life from the Romans; but for that I would follow him."[31]

30. Kenneth Latourette, "The First Great Losses of Territory," chap. 6 in *A History of the Expansion of Christianity*, vol. 2, *The Thousand Years of Uncertainty* (Grand Rapids: Zondervan, 1970), 304.

31. Guillaume, *Life of Muhammad*, 656. See the lengthy Tradition in Bukhari, *Sahih*, I, I, chap. 1, no. 6, 7–14.

There is no independent confirmation of these events, and the details given in Muslim sources serve only to make them more improbable. It would, of course, have been a major coup if Heraclius had become a Muslim or even acknowledged Muhammad as the prophet promised in Scripture (presumably a reference to the Muslim claim that the Paraclete, the "Comforter" promised in John's Gospel, was actually Muhammad, not the Holy Spirit). But it is debatable whether Muhammad himself ever thought of Islam as anything but a religion for the Arabs, and it is equally doubtful that he thought of himself as being in a position to send letters demanding the submission of rulers so much more powerful than himself.

Non-Muslims in Muslim States: The Start of Dhimmi Status[32]

In 628 Muhammad led an attack on the oasis of Khaybar, northwest of Madina, and after a lengthy siege the Jewish inhabitants surrendered and a *dhimma* treaty was accepted. The Muslims imposed a tax on them, the *jizya*, amounting to half their harvest, and promised them protection from any future attackers. This set the pattern for relations with non-Muslims.[33] Shortly before his death in A.D. 632 Muhammad led an army of some thirty thousand men to Tabuk, in the Gulf of Aqaba, and subdued the area, and again a dhimma treaty was imposed.

Although forcible conversion to Islam has not been the formal policy of Islam, it has happened repeatedly, especially during periods of Islamic expansion. It was certainly the norm during the campaign of Ahmad ibn Ibrahim, Muhammad "Grany," "The Left-Handed," in Ethiopia in the first half of the sixteenth century. According to Trimingham, the more fortunate Ethiopian Christians were allowed to submit to Ahmad and pay the jizya tax levied on them. Most were given the choice only between submission and death. Two Christian priests were captured and taken before Ahmad:

> He said, "What is the matter with you that you haven't become Muslims when the whole country has Islamized?" They replied, "We don't want to become Muslims." He said, "Our judgement is that your heads be cut off." They said "Welcome."[34] The Imam was surprised at their answer, and ordered them to be executed.[35]

32. See Bat Ye'or, *The Dhimmi: Jews and Christians under Islam* (London and Toronto: Associated University Presses, 1985), 44.

33. Bat Ye'or, *Islam and Dhimmitude: Where Civilizations Collide*, trans. Miriam Kochan and David Littman (Cranbury, N.J.: Associated University Presses; Lancaster, U.K.: Gazelle Book Services, 2002), 37.

34. It is likely that what they actually said would have been Amharic *yihun*, "So be it."

35. Trimingham, *Islam in Ethiopia*, 88f.

At Khaybar and again at Tabuk, Muhammad is said to have offered the people three options: conversion to Islam, submission to Islamic rule, or death. Submission to Islamic rule involved the payment of the jizya tax, and the acceptance of a reduced civic status, that of the dhimmi. According to Alfred Guillaume, the Tabuk community accepted the dhimmi status and the payment of the jizya tax, and the agreement was honored by both sides for more than a century.[36] The jizya requirement is set out in Sura 9:29:

> Fight those who believe not in Allah nor the Last Day,
> nor hold that forbidden which hath been forbidden by Allah and His Messenger,
> nor acknowledge the Religion of Truth,
> from among the People of the Book,
> until they pay the *Jizyah* with willing submission,
> and feel themselves subdued.

Through the centuries the dhimmi status has been variously interpreted, but it always involves some form of discrimination and diminution of rights. There was no stated amount for this tax: that was left to the discretion of the local Muslim rulers. Oddly enough, the imposition of the jizya tax had unexpected results. Since it brought in a not-inconsiderable revenue to the relevant authorities, mass conversion to Islam was often actively discouraged, although individual conversions were always accepted.

The tax had a special significance when Islam advanced westward across Egypt and northward into Syria and Asia Minor. In Egypt the Christians found their Muslim rulers no worse and in some ways better than their former Byzantine Christian rulers, who had harried them over their theology: they did not accept the formulations of the Council of Chalcedon on the relationship between the human and the divine in Jesus.

To the north (Syria, Asia Minor, and Iran), however, the situation was different, and Caliph Walid I (705–15) set about rooting out the churches and demanding that the Christians use Arabic instead of Greek. Emperor Heraclius, who was a contemporary of Muhammad, seems to have taken the view that the rise of Islam and the persecution of the church was some kind of divine punishment, not to be resisted, and a fulfillment of Old Testament prophecy in which God promised Abraham concerning Ishmael, "As for the son of the slave

36. Guillaume, *Islam*, 53.

woman, I will make a nation of him also, because he is your offspring"
(Gen. 21:13).[37]

ISLAM AND THE BIBLE: FIVE PROBLEMS

1. An Accusation: Jews and Christians Falsified Scripture

The Qur'an explains differences between Qur'an and Old Testament
and between Qur'an and New Testament as being due to Jews and
Christians in some sense falsifying the Scriptures.[38] This is odd, because the Qur'an also encourages Muslims to confirm Muhammad's
message by asking Jews and Christians what *their* message is:

> If thou wert in doubt as to what We have revealed unto thee, then ask those
> who have been reading the Book from before thee. (Sura 10:94)

> And before thee also the messengers We sent were but men, to whom We
> granted inspiration: if ye realize this not, then ask of those who possess
> the Message. (Sura 16:43)

But according to the Qur'an, the problem with both Jews and
Christians is their abuse of Scripture:

> They [the Jews] change the words from their places and forget a good part
> of the message that was sent them [Sura 5:13],
> From those, too, who call themselves Christians, We did take a covenant,
> but they forgot a good part of the message that was sent them. (Sura 5:14)

These verses are understood by commentators on the Qur'an as meaning either that the Jews willfully *misinterpreted* their Scriptures (and
knowingly passed over other parts) or that the text itself had been deliberately *altered*.

Sura 5 is a late sura, from the Madinan period, when Muhammad was
facing criticism from the Jews there: they knew their Bible well enough
to see the differences between Muhammad's version of certain events and
the Bible's version of the "same" events. So it is not surprising that the
same Sura tells Muslims *not* to take Jews and Christians as friends because "they are but friends and protectors to each other" (verse 51).

There is no agreement on just *how* or *when* the supposed alterations in the text or in the interpreting of the text took place. The

37. Clinton Bennett, *In Search of Muhammad* (London and New York: Cassell,
1998), 70–72.
38. See the very helpful chap. 2, "Have the Scriptures Been Falsified?" in *Faith to
Faith*, by Moucarry.

Jews, we know, took enormous care to ensure that the text of Scripture was preserved from corruption, and for the New Testament we have a wealth of ancient manuscripts from which to check the text. Thus it is difficult to see how any such alterations could be made.[39] Furthermore, it is a belief among Muslims that the text of the Message given by God, whether Torah, Gospel, or Qur'an, is given special protection by God to ensure that it should *not* be corrupted through its transmission: the doctrine of *tawatur*.[40]

2. The Suggestion That Jesus Foretold the Coming of Muhammad

Second, there is the suggestion made in the Qur'an that Jesus himself prophesied the coming of Muhammad. In Sura 61:6 Jesus is represented as saying: "O Children of Israel! I am the messenger of Allah to you, confirming the Law before me, and giving glad tidings of a Messenger to come after me, whose name shall be Ahmad." The alleged prophecy is said to come from John's Gospel and Jesus' promise to send "another Comforter" (John 14:16), another "Advocate." The Greek word used here, *paraklētos*, could be used in a legal sense as prosecuting counsel, as defending counsel, or more generally as one who is called to assist another. But some Muslims claim that this is a textual error: the text is corrupt and should read *periklytos*, meaning Praised. And Ahmad, one of Muhammad's names, also means Praised. Yusuf Ali comments on Sura 61:6: "Our doctors contend that Paracletos is a corrupt reading for Periclytos, and that in the original saying of Jesus there was a prophecy of our Holy Prophet Ahmad by name."[41] In fact there is no Greek manuscript that contains the word *periklytos* instead of *paraklētos* in John's Gospel. Moreover, the word *periklytos* does not occur anywhere in the New Testament.

3. The Trinity

Muhammad clearly knew something about Christianity. Since the very heart of his teaching was the oneness of God, what he seems to

39. But see M. A. Yusseff, *The Dead Sea Scrolls, the Gospel of Barnabas, and the New Testament* (Indianapolis: American Trust, 1985). He tries to explain when and how corruptions appeared in the biblical text but fails to distinguish between corruptions appearing in individual copies and the corruption of the authoritative text as a whole ("The Spurious Nature of the Greek Gospels").

40. See the article "Mutawatir," *Encyclopaedia of Islam*, 3:781: "The Kur'an is clearly transmitted by *tawatur*." However, the article notes that tawatur (multiply reported and certainly true) is claimed by Christians and Jews for events reported in their Scriptures, and quotes Al-Taftazani as saying that "the possibility that these reports should be *mutawatir* [genuine] is excluded," though no reason for this exclusion is given.

41. Yusuf Ali, *Meaning of the Holy Qur'an*, 1461 n. 5438.

have found most objectionable in Christianity was its doctrine of the Trinity, which looked to him like tritheism. It is, perhaps, not surprising: most Christians find the doctrine of the Holy Trinity difficult to understand and impossible to explain. But the problem is complicated in the case of Muhammad since it seems as though he thought of the Christian Trinity as Father, Mary, and their son Jesus. In Sura 5:116 we have Allah speaking to Jesus:

> "O Jesus the son of Mary! Did'st thou say unto men, 'Worship me and my mother as gods in derogation of Allah'?" He will say: "Glory to Thee! Never could I say what I had no right to say."

And similarly in Sura 4:171,

> O People of the Book! Commit no excesses in your religion: nor say of Allah aught but the truth. Christ Jesus the son of Mary was a Messenger of Allah and His Word which He bestowed on Mary, and a Spirit proceeding from Him: So believe in Allah and His Messengers. Say not "Trinity": desist.

On the question of the Trinity, Mohamed al-Nowaihi, Professor of Arabic Languages and Literature and Director of the Center for Arabic Studies in the American University, Cairo, admitted:

> It is true that many Muslims have mistakenly believed that Christians worship three Gods, and have not paid sufficient attention to the latter's protestations that their belief in the Trinity does not imply a multiplicity of Gods, that God is still one with them.[42]

4. The Virgin Birth of Jesus

The birth of Jesus from the Virgin Mary[43] is described twice in the Qur'an, each time presenting the story as the Gospels tell it plus elements from later legends. Sura 3:45–7 gives the story:

> Behold! the angels said:
> "O Mary! Allah giveth thee glad tidings of a Word from Him:
> his name will be Christ Jesus, the son of Mary,
> held in honour in this world and the hereafter,
> and of (the company of) those nearest to Allah;
> He shall speak to the people in childhood and in maturity.
> And he shall be (of the company) of the righteous."

42. Mohamed al-Nowaihi, "The Religion of Islam," *International Review of Mission* 65, issue 258 (April 1976): 216.
43. More correctly the virginal *conception* of Jesus.

She said:
"O my Lord! How shall I have a son when no man hath touched me?"
He said:
"Even so: Allah createth what He willeth:
When He hath decreed a plan, He but saith to it, 'Be,' and it is!"

Sura 19:22–30 continues the account:

So she conceived him, and she retired with him to a remote place.
And the pains of childbirth drove her to the trunk of a palm tree:
She cried (in her anguish) "Ah! would that I had died before this!
would that I had been a thing forgotten and out of sight!"
But (a voice) cried to her from beneath (the palm tree):
"Grieve not! for thy Lord hath provided a rivulet beneath thee;
And shake towards thyself the trunk of the palm tree;
It will let fall fresh ripe dates upon thee. . . ."
At length she brought the (babe) to her people, carrying him (in her arms).
They said: "O Mary! Truly an amazing thing hast thou brought!
O sister of Aaron! Thy father was not a man of evil,
nor thy mother a woman unchaste!"
But she pointed to the babe.
They said: "How can we talk to one who is a child in the cradle?"
He said: "I am indeed a servant of Allah:
He hath given me revelation and made me a prophet."

When Mary is called "sister of Aaron," there is an apparent confusion between Miriam in the Old Testament and Mary: the two
names are the same in Arabic. This confusion might well have
arisen from the fact that Muhammad had no chronological string
tying the elements of his knowledge into a meaningful sequence.
The probability of chronological confusion is strengthened by Sura
3:35, which describes Elizabeth as "a woman of Imran." However,
Yusuf Ali explains the words differently: "Aaron, the brother of
Moses, was the first in the line of Israelite priesthood. Mary and
her cousin Elisabeth . . . came of a priestly family, and were therefore 'sisters of Aaron' or daughters of Imran (who was Aaron's
father)."[44]

5. Qur'an and Crucifixion

Most intriguing is the one verse in the Qur'an which deals with
the crucifixion of Jesus. The Jews are being condemned in Sura
4:157 because

---

44. *Meaning of the Holy Qur'an*, n. 2481 to his translation of Sura 19:28.

they uttered against Mary a grave false charge (and) that they said "We killed Christ Jesus the son of Mary, the Messenger of Allah"—But they killed him not, nor crucified him, but so it was made to appear to them. And those who differ therein are full of doubts, with no (certain) knowledge, but only conjecture to follow, for of a surety they killed him not. (Sura 4:157)

The "grave charge" directed against Mary is obviously the accusation that she had been unchaste and that her pregnancy was the result. The remainder of the verse is both intriguing and perplexing: intriguing because the actual meaning of the passage is not clear; and perplexing because there appears to be one certainty at least about Jesus, that he was "crucified under Pontius Pilate."[45]

The most obvious meaning is that given by the majority of Muslim scholars: Jesus was not crucified. This then gives rise to a further problem: then who was crucified? The Qur'an offers no answer to the question, simply asserting that it seemed to those responsible for the crucifixion that they had crucified Jesus. The sixteenth-century *Gospel of Barnabas,* written in Italian by Father Moreno, a Christian turned Muslim,[46] provides a detailed explanation: it was Judas who was crucified, because God snatched Jesus away to the third heaven and made Judas resemble Jesus in appearance:

When the soldiers with Judas drew near to the place where Jesus was, Jesus heard the approach of many people, wherefore in fear he withdrew into the house. And the eleven were sleeping. Then God, seeing the danger of his servant commanded Gabriel, Michael, Rafael and Uriel, his ministers, to take Jesus out of the world.

The holy angels came and took Jesus out by the window that looketh toward the south. They bare him and placed him in the third heaven in the company of angels, blessing God for evermore.

Judas entered impetuously before all into the chamber whence Jesus had been taken up. And the disciples were sleeping. Whereupon the wonderful God acted wonderfully, insomuch that Judas was so changed

---

45. As Geoffrey Parrinder comments, "No serious historian doubts that Jesus was a historical figure and that he was crucified, whatever he may think of the faith in the resurrection" (*Jesus in the Qur'an* [London: Sheldon, 1965], 116).

46. See David Sox, *The Gospel of Barnabas* (London: Allen and Unwin, 1984). This is a thorough examination of the many questions raised by the so-called Gospel of Barnabas and ought to have ended the claims by Muslims, and even by Muslim scholars, that this Gospel is the one and only first-century Gospel written by a disciple of Jesus; see Muhammad ur-Rahim, *Jesus: A Prophet of Islam,* 2d ed. (London: MWH Publishers, 1979), 39. See also the discussion of the Gospel of Barnabas in Moucarry, *Faith to Faith,* 247–51. For a spirited, if forlorn, defense of the authenticity of the *Gospel of Barnabas,* see Yusseff, *Dead Sea Scrolls, the Gospel of Barnabas, and the New Testament.*

in speech and in face to be like Jesus that we believed him to be Jesus. And he, having awakened us, was seeking where the master was. Whereupon we marvelled, and answered: "Thou, Lord, art our master; hast thou now forgotten us?"

And he, smiling, said: "Now are ye foolish, that know not me to be Judas Iscariot!"

And as he was saying this the soldiery entered, and laid their hands upon Judas, because he was in every way like to Jesus. . . .

The soldiers took Judas and bound him, not without derision. For he truthfully denied that he was Jesus.[47]

Certainly many Muslims find it hard to believe that a prophet like Jesus could be *crucified*. Muhammad himself was well aware of the fact that prophets could be rejected and even killed, but crucifixion was a death cursed in the Old Testament.[48] How could a prophet die an accursed death?

Muhammad's rejection of the crucifixion of Jesus may possibly be traced back to the Christian philosopher Basilides,[49] who seems to have taught that Jesus was not crucified but someone else took his place. Perhaps this happened in the scuffle and confusion of the arrest, or perhaps at the cross things became confused and Simon of Cyrene was crucified instead of Jesus.

Since it is widely accepted on the basis of the historical record that Jesus *was* in fact crucified, it has been suggested that the text could be understood as meaning "they," the Jews, did not crucify him. E. E. Elder made this suggestion, and this certainly has the advantage of leaving the question of just who crucified Jesus open. However, the Arabic text does not emphasize the pronoun "they" as might have been expected if that was the intended meaning; this interpretation is just, but only just, *barely* possible.[50]

A third option is that taught by the Ahmadis. They came into existence around the beginning of the twentieth century, led by Mirza Ghulam Ahmad (1839–1908), who was born in the Punjab. He claimed to have received revelations from Allah when he was forty years old. He asserted that Jesus *was* crucified but did *not* die on the cross. Accord-

47. Aisha Bawany Wakf, ed., *The Gospel of Barnabas* (Karachi: Ashram Publications, 1976). This is a new edition of the translation by Lonsdale and Laura Ragg (London: Oxford University Press, 1907); see also F. P. Cotterell, "The Gospel of Barnabas," *Vox Evangelica* 10 (1977): 43–47.

48. Deut. 21:23.

49. Gnosticism certainly flourished in neighboring Egypt: Hans Lietzmann, "Egypt," chap. 13 in *The Founding of the Church Universal*, 3d ed. (London: Lutterworth, 1953). Basilides claimed the authority of the apostle Peter for his system.

50. See Parrinder, *Jesus in the Qur'an*, 120.

ing to the Ahmadis, Jesus was taken down from the cross alive and was resuscitated in the tomb through the efforts of Nicodemus, who in this account becomes a skilled doctor:

> Joseph of Arimathaea and Nicodemus, an expert physician, now came and took charge of the body of Jesus, brought it down from the cross, wrapped him in a linen cloth, which was impregnated with spices, and laid him in a sepulchre. . . . There can be no doubt that Joseph and Nicodemus must have continued to minister unto Jesus in the strong hope of reviving him.[51]

Jesus is said to have completely recovered and subsequently to have gone eastward in search of the lost ten tribes, eventually dying and being buried in Kashmir.[52]

Seyyed Hossein Nasr recognizes the importance of the Qur'an's denial of the crucifixion: "The Qur'an does not accept that Jesus was crucified, but states that he was taken directly to heaven. This is the one irreducible 'fact' separating Christianity from Islam, a fact which is in reality placed there providentially to prevent a mingling of the two religions."[53] Similarly, but polemically, the Ahmadi writer Muhammad Zafrullah Khan claims: "Once it is established that Jesus did not die on the cross, there was no accursed death, no bearing of the sins of mankind, no resurrection, no ascension and no atonement. The entire structure of church theology is thereby demolished."[54]

In the twenty-first century the debates between Muslims and non-Muslims focus on the Jewish people and the State of Israel, on worldwide Christianity in its various manifestations, and on the economic and political system generally designated capitalism. In the thinking of many Muslims the latter two are in good measure conflated.

Nasr (rightly) sees the inescapable logic of the incompatibility of the two religions, Islam and Christianity. Meanwhile, Zafrullah Khan sees beyond that to the "demolishing" of the religious element of the principal alternative to Islam.

51. Muhammad Zafrulla Khan, *Deliverance from the Cross* (Southfields: London Mosque, 1978), 33.

52. See Khan, *Deliverance from the Cross;* and Kenneth Cragg, *Islamic Surveys 3: Counsels in Contemporary Islam* (Edinburgh: Edinburgh University Press, 1965), chap. 10.

53. Seyyed Hossein Nasr, *Islamic Life and Thought* (London: Allen and Unwin, 1981), 209.

54. Khan, *Deliverance from the Cross,* 89.

PART 2

IN BETWEEN: THE EBB AND FLOW OF EMPIRE

5

THE AGE
OF MUSLIM EMPIRE

As we have seen, the three decades following the death of Muhammad were characterized by expansion of the lands under Islamic rule. This came at the expense of the Eastern Christian Empire, which mourned the losses to Islamic armies: Jerusalem, the holy city, as well as other great centers of Eastern Christendom such as Damascus and Egypt.

However, the Christian losses during this early period would be dwarfed by the military expansion that took place under the first of the great Islamic empires, that of the Umayyads. As we undertake a journey through the history of the great Islamic empires, and the period that followed, we will keep our eyes firmly fixed upon the evolving relationship between Christians and Muslims. This will provide an anchor for our study.

THE UMAYYADS (661–750)

It is not easy to form a detailed picture of the Umayyad dynasty. As Stephen Humphreys says, "The bulk of our historical texts on early Islam are to be found in a body of compilations and digests composed roughly between 850 and 950 A.D."[1] In other words, we depend on relatively late sources for the period of the Umayyads. Furthermore, these later sources were often hostile to the earlier Umayyad dynasty, since they were produced by historians writing under the successor dynasty that evicted the Umayyads from power.

Nevertheless, while debate surrounds much of the detail around the internal workings of the Umayyad dynasty, certain facts are clear, especially those involving the military expansion that took place and the impact on Christian and Jewish communities that lived under Muslim conquerors.

1. R. Stephen Humphreys, *Islamic History*, rev. ed. (London: Tauris, 1991), 71.

Expansion

The accession of Mu'awiya to the caliphate in 661 brought about a lull in the bitter division and civil war among the Arabs. He was to serve as caliph for nineteen years and was able to turn much of his attention to expanding the Islamic realm. This was the period of the "Jihad State," as explained succinctly by the modern Muslim scholar Khalid Yahya Blankinship:

> Like all other multinational empires, the Muslim state reached its greatest extent through a series of military campaigns. . . . Expansion became an ideological imperative justified on moral grounds. In the case of the Muslim caliphate, this imperative was the establishment of God's rule in the earth, for that was the sole legitimate sovereignty. God's rule was to be established by those kinds of efforts that He had ordained, which included armed struggle in His path. Such armed struggle became known as jihad and remained the most salient policy of the caliphate down to the end of Umayyad rule in 132/750.[2]

Damascus became the administrative center of the Muslim Empire. It lay at a relatively short distance from the heartland of the Byzantine Christian Empire. Mu'awiya held great hopes for capturing the Byzantine capital of Constantinople, and from 672 to 680 his armies launched a series of attacks on the Byzantine domains, including a five-year siege of the capital itself.[3] Although these campaigns did not succeed in capturing the great prize of Constantinople, they did represent the beginning of frequent attempts by successive Muslim rulers to destroy the Eastern Christian Empire, including another devastating but unsuccessful siege of the capital in 717–18. It is not hard to imagine the sense of threat that must have been felt by the citizens of Constantinople and its surrounding areas. They had seen Damascus, Jerusalem, and Egypt fall to the Muslim armies, and now they saw these same forces encamped outside the very gates of Constantinople itself.

Meanwhile, the Muslim armies were not resting on their laurels elsewhere. In a series of stunning military campaigns, the Umayyad generals swept out of Egypt and destroyed Byzantine control in North Africa. Thus, although Constantinople and most of Asia Minor had not yet been lost, the rest of the Byzantine Empire had been relinquished to the dynamic new faith of Islam.

2. K. Y. Blankinship, *The End of the Jihad State* (New York: State University of New York Press, 1994), 1.

3. John Julian Norwich, *Byzantium: The Early Centuries* (London: Viking, 1988), 323–24.

Nor could Western Christianity, centered on Rome, rest easy in the face of the rampant Islamic armies. After capturing all of North Africa, the Umayyad generals decided to strike north into Europe itself. In 711, Arab forces, led by a Berber general named Tarik ibn Ziyad, launched an invasion of the Iberian peninsular. Their landing and subsequent campaign was described by the Muslim historian Ibn 'Abd al-Hakim (d. 870/871), who provides the following account of a crucial battle with Visigothic forces under King Roderic on July 11, 711:

> When Tarik landed, soldiers from Cordova came to meet him; and seeing the small number of his companions they despised him on that account. They then fought. The battle with Tarik was severe. They were routed, and he did not cease from the slaughter of them till they reached the town of Cordova. When Roderic heard of this, he came to their rescue from Toledo. They then fought in a place of the name of Shedunia, in a valley which is called this day the valley of Umm-Hakim. They fought a severe battle; but God, mighty and great, killed Roderic and his companions.[4]

The Muslim victory was swift, and by 719 the Arabs controlled all the Iberian peninsula and called it *al-Andalus*.[5]

Thus Western Christianity had also suffered a major direct setback at the hands of the Muslim armies. But more was to come. The Muslims continued into France, conquering and plundering as they went. Contemporary accounts by an anonymous Arab chronicler testify to the methods of the invading army:

> The Moslems smote their enemies, and passed the river Garonne, and laid waste the country, and took captives without number. And that army went through all places like a desolating storm. Prosperity made those warriors insatiable. At the passage of the river, Abderrahman [Ibn Abdillah Alghafeki] overthrew the count,[6] and the count retired into his stronghold, but the Moslems fought against it, and entered it by force, and slew the count; for everything gave way to their scymetars [scimitars], which were the robbers of lives. All the nations of the Franks trembled at that terrible army. . . . Abderrahman and his host attacked Tours to gain still more spoil, and they fought against it so fiercely that they stormed the city almost before the eyes of the army that came to

4. Ibn 'Abd-el-Hakem, *History of the Conquest of Spain*, trans. John Harris Jones (Göttingen: W. Fr. Kaestner, 1858), 20.

5. This term is most likely a corruption of the Latin term for the Vandals, the occupants of the Iberian peninsula before the Muslims arrived.

6. Cf. the article "'Abd al-Rahman b. 'Abd Allah al-Ghafiki," *Encyclopaedia of Islam*, 1:86.

save it; and the fury and the cruelty of the Moslems towards the inhabitants of the city were like the fury and cruelty of raging tigers.[7]

The Muslim advance was finally stopped by Charles Martel at Poitiers in Central France in 732. Muslim armies were never to reach this point again. But their seeming invincibility resulting from decades of success had shattered the confidence of both Western and Eastern Christians. As a result, the Byzantines adopted essentially defensive strategies rather than engaging in frequent offensive campaigns, as was the case with the Muslim forces.[8] These ongoing conflicts had sown destructive seeds, ensuring that further conflict was to come.

Fragmentation

The Umayyads, like both predecessors and successors among rulers of the Islamic realm, were plagued by internal dissension and tendencies toward fragmentation. Among their adversaries were the Shi'a, those who looked to direct descendants of Muhammad as the only legitimate candidates to head the Islamic community.

With the assassination of Ali in 661, the Shi'a had lost their champion. However, Ali had three sons, and one, Al-Husain, came to be regarded as the great hope for Shi'a resurgence. As the grandson of the Prophet, Al-Husain seemed, to the Shi'a at least, to be far more deserving of the title of caliph than Mu'awiya or his successors.

However, Al-Husain also met a violent end, as we saw earlier. He was killed at Karbala in southern Iraq by an army led by the new Caliph Yazid in 681. With his death, and the desecration of his body by Yazid's troops, Shi'a despair reached a peak. Implacable opposition of the Shi'a to the Umayyads was to mark the remainder of the Umayyad period. The Shi'a cultivated contacts with Persian groups living under the Umayyads, waiting and hoping for their day to come.

The other offshoot that was to consolidate its separateness during this period was the Khariji. This was the first distinct radical sect in Islamic history. It declared those who did not follow them from among the Muslim community to be heretics or unbelievers. As the voice of extremist protest, their ideology was to reappear in various forms during subsequent centuries, right up to the present day.

Arabization and Islamization

The Umayyads were predominantly an Arab dynasty. The conquering armies were manned by Arab troops, especially in the early campaigns,

---

7. Edward Creasy, *The Fifteen Decisive Battles of the World*, 13th ed. (London: Richard Bentley, 1863), 251–52.

8. Blankinship, *End of the Jihad State*, 105.

and Arab troops remained in garrisons at different points of the newly established empire to ensure loyalty to the caliph in Damascus.

However, Arabness did not remain a thin veneer on the top of the conquered populations. Indeed, as Esposito comments, "In time, through a process of conversion and assimilation, language and culture, state and society were Arabized and Islamized."[9] Around A.D. 700 the conduct of administration throughout the Umayyad Empire came to be undertaken in Arabic rather than in the languages of the conquered peoples.[10] This had a profound effect over time, with conquered people groups gradually coming to redefine their own cultural identities.

This process was consolidated through the Islamization that, under the Umayyads, went hand in hand with Arabization. Although there were only a few instances of forced conversion to Islam, there were various incentives for the conquered peoples to change their faith. Not least of these was that becoming a Muslim meant that an individual could thereby avoid the special jizya tax levied by the Muslim authorities on non-Muslim subjects.

In speaking of Islamization, it should be noted that Islam at the time was still going through a process of formulation and fine-tuning. As Hawting comments:

> It seems clear that Islam as we know it [today] is largely the result of the interaction between the Arabs and the peoples they conquered during the first two centuries or so of the Islamic era which began in 622 A.D. During the Umayyad period, therefore, the spread of Islam and the development of Islam were taking place at the same time.[11]

Collapse

Great empires come and go, and like all others the Umayyads were to experience greatness and decline. An important reason for the Umayyad collapse was disenchantment among the considerable communities of non-Arab converts to Islam, known as the client peoples, or *mawali*. They resented the discrimination they suffered in social and economic domains. The mawali had to pay heavier taxes than Arab Muslims and were not permitted to marry Arab women. Client soldiers were paid less than Arab soldiers and received a smaller share of booty captured. All this was happening in a context where client peoples heavily outnumbered Arabs in con-

9. Esposito, *Islam: The Straight Path*, 40.
10. G. R. Hawting, *The First Dynasty of Islam*, 2d ed. (London: Routledge, 2000), 10.
11. Ibid., 1.

quered areas. As time passed, anti-Umayyad feelings boiled over throughout the empire.[12]

The collapse of the Umayyad dynasty in 750 was triggered by an intra-Arab power struggle. The family of the Abbasids, descendants of the prophet Muhammad's uncle al-'Abbas, successfully challenged the Umayyad ruling authorities. Military conflict erupted and civil war ensued. The last Umayyad caliph, Marwan II, was killed, and the Abbasid authorities took power in August 750.

THE ABBASIDS

The Abbasids at Their Peak

With their assumption of power, the Abbasid authorities moved the capital of the Islamic Empire to a new site at present-day Baghdad. The Abbasids were heavily critical of their Umayyad caliphal predecessors, portraying them as having slipped into decadence through the luxuries of conquest. They were also accused of not having sufficiently developed an effective Islamic legal system. The Abbasids thus presented themselves as the revivers of true faith.[13] The recurrence of this theme of revival has been a key feature throughout Islamic history, but it also points to recurring internal conflict between different elements competing to control the Islamic stage.

It is certainly true that the Abbasid period ushered in the fullest flowering of Islam. Arabic culture, arts, and knowledge were promoted during the first two centuries of Abbasid rule. The peak of Abbasid glory occurred under Caliph Harun al-Rashid (ruled 786–809) and his son al-Ma'mun (ruled 813–33). During this period Baghdad was a magnificent urban center, as described by the later Muslim geographer Yaqut al-Hamawi (1179–1229):

> The city of Baghdad formed two vast semi-circles on the right and left banks of the Tigris, twelve miles in diameter. The numerous suburbs, covered with parks, gardens, villas and beautiful promenades, and plentifully supplied with rich bazaars, and finely built mosques and baths, stretched for a considerable distance on both sides of the river. In the days of its prosperity the population of Baghdad and its suburbs amounted to over two millions![14]

12. Esposito, *Islam: The Straight Path,* 41; Guillaume, *Islam,* 82–83; W. Montgomery Watt, *The Majesty That Was Islam* (London: Sidgwick and Jackson, 1974), 27–28.
13. Esposito, *Islam: The Straight Path,* 41.
14. William Stearns Davis, ed., *Readings in Ancient History: Illustrative Extracts from the Sources,* vol. 2, *Rome and the West* (Boston: Allyn and Bacon, 1912–13), 366.

Caliph al-Ma'mun organized teams of scholars to translate into Arabic the works of ancient Greece, Rome, Egypt, and Persia. Through these translations much of the culture of the ancient world would later be rediscovered in Western Europe, which was wallowing in its own Dark Ages as the Abbasid civilization flourished.

Islamic philosophy thrived after borrowing heavily from earlier Hellenistic thought. There were major advances in medicine, and literacy expanded considerably under the early Abbasid caliphs. Furthermore, the new dynasty prioritized the formulation of an Islamic legal system. During the Umayyad period a class of religious scholars (*ulama*) had begun to emerge. Under the early Abbasid caliphs the ulama became a professional elite of religious leaders, and as such they served as key authorities in Sunni Islam. It was they who established that the sunna (way, example) of Muhammad should become the key reference point for determining what should and should not be sanctioned under Islam.[15] This led to the development and codification of *Shari'a* (Islamic law), as we saw in earlier discussion.

It is important to note that the Abbasids borrowed heavily from Persian culture. Whereas the Umayyads had clearly represented an empire of the Arabs, under the Abbasids the client peoples, or mawali, came into their own. Persians in particular played a major role in government and the military.[16]

Another fact that is of crucial importance to the notion of empire is the change in meaning of the word *Arab* during the Abbasid period. Previously it had signified the inhabitants of the Arabian peninsula, especially the desert regions. Under the Abbasids the concept of Arabness diversified considerably. Many of the client groups that had adopted Arabic as a result of earlier Umayyad legislation gradually became fully accepted as Arabs in their own right. Today the term *Arab* applies to the majority populations of countries stretching from Morocco to Oman. Almost two dozen countries are members of the Arab League; the understanding of Arab as merely those inhabitants of the Arabian desert has been long discarded. This process of enculturation brought about what is arguably the world's most successful case of imperial expansion.

Christians and Jews under the Abbasids

What of the Christians and Jews under the Abbasids? History records that their fortunes as protected minorities (dhimmi) fluctuated. Under the tolerant caliphs, such as al-Ma'mun, both Jews and

15. Hawting, *First Dynasty of Islam*, 1.
16. Esposito, *Islam: The Straight Path*, 51; Guillaume, *Islam*, 82.

Christians reached elevated positions within the Islamic Empire. A notable and often-cited example is Hunayn ibn Ishaq, a Nestorian Christian, who headed the empire's translation center.

But some later caliphs were not so enlightened. The Islamic legal codes that were appearing from around A.D. 800 included discriminatory legislation targeting non-Muslims. These legal provisions found their scriptural sustenance in Qur'anic verses such as 9:29:

> Fight those who believe not in Allah nor the Last Day,
> nor hold that forbidden which hath been forbidden by Allah and His Messenger,
> nor acknowledge the Religion of Truth,
> from among the People of the Book,
> until they pay the *Jizyah* with willing submission,
> and feel themselves subdued.

A number of specific discriminatory features emerged under Abbasid caliphs. At times Christians and Jews were not allowed to carry weapons or deliver war materials, were prohibited from riding horses at various periods, and were forbidden to wear their hair like Arabs. Some Abbasid authorities compelled the minority groups to wear badges or belts to facilitate their identification as non-Muslims. At times Jewish and Christian women were forced to wear two shoes of different colors.[17] Construction of new synagogues and churches was prohibited under certain caliphs, and repairs to existing houses of worship were often blocked.[18] Public displays of religion (such as blowing the shofar by Jews) were prohibited at times. The jizya poll tax prescribed for Jewish and Christian minorities reduced some communities to extreme poverty.[19]

Nevertheless, as Bernard Lewis states: "The Dhimmis were second-class citizens. . . . But by and large their position was infinitely superior to that of those communities who differed from the established church in western Europe in the same period."[20] This was especially so for the Jews; far better to be Jewish in the Islamic domains than in Europe during this period. As for Christians, the experience of dis-

17. This requirement was initiated under the oppressive Fatimid Caliph al-Hakim but was also in force under later Abbasid authorities.

18. This is still a complaint expressed in the modern day by some Christian minority groups in majority Muslim locations, such as Egypt.

19. Shlomo Dov Goitein, "The Jews under Islam 6th–16th centuries," in *The Jewish World: Revelation, Prophecy, and History,* ed. Elie Kedouri (London: Thames and Hudson, 1979), 180–81.

20. Bernard Lewis, *The Arabs in History,* 5th ed. (London: Hutchinson University Library, 1970), 94.

crimination and periodic persecution was one ingredient that, when added to other factors, increased the likelihood of a Christian military response in the future.

Rival Dynasties and Fragmentation of Empire

The Abbasids were dogged by rebellion and fragmentation. This was especially so from the middle of the tenth century, although it had been a feature of the earlier Abbasid period as well. For example, in 756 an independent Umayyad dynasty arose in Spain, paying allegiance to the first great dynasty of the Arabs and refusing to recognize the authority of the Abbasid caliphs in Baghdad.

From 945 Baghdad itself fell under the domination of the *Buwayhids*, a clan originating from southwest of the Caspian Sea, which gathered military forces and marched on Baghdad. They were the most influential force in the Abbasid dynasty for over a hundred years, though they paid nominal allegiance to the Abbasid caliphs, whom they placed on the throne and who became mere puppet rulers of a fragmenting empire.

The same period witnessed the emergence of the *Fatimids* in Egypt, who ruled there from 969 to 1171. They had previously been the dominant power in Tunisia (910–72). They were a Shi'a dynasty, claiming descent from Muhammad via his daughter Fatima. Among their notable achievements was the founding of Cairo as well as its al-Azhar mosque, which would become the center of Islamic orthodox Sunni teaching and includes the Muslim world's oldest university.

As with the Abbasids, the treatment of minorities by the Fatimids was rather enlightened for their age. However, there were difficult periods, particularly under the third Fatimid Caliph al-Hakim (ruled 996–1021). His despotic conduct is described by the fifteenth-century Muslim writer al-Makrisi:

> In the year 1009 the caliph of Egypt, Syria and Palestine, al-Hakim, ordered the Jews and Christians to wear sashes round their waists and distinguishing badges on their clothes. ... On 4 October al-Hakim wrote to Jerusalem ordering the destruction of the church of the Holy Sepulchre. ... He destroyed the monastery known as Dayr al-Qasr and strictly enforced the rule against Christians and Jews, requiring them to wear the special mark.[21]

An important factor to note in this period was the increasing dependence on (mainly Turkish) mercenaries to rule the empire. This

---

21. Elizabeth Hallam, ed., *Chronicles of the Crusades: Eye-Witness Accounts of the Wars between Christianity and Islam* (London: Weidenfeld and Nicolson, 1989), 22–23.

was to prove dangerous, as had been the case with the great empire of Rome in previous times.

THE SALJUQS (1055–1243)

The Saljuqs Encroach on Byzantine Domains

In the middle of the eleventh century, a new Islamic player emerged on the scene. This comprised the Turkish tribes, who were to drive the Byzantine Christians from most of present-day Turkey, known at the time as Asia Minor. The previous empires dominated or influenced by Arabs and Persians had failed to do this, despite countless attempts.

The first of the great Turkish tribes was that of the Saljuqs. Originating from Central Asia, many Saljuqid Turks had served for a long period as mercenaries to the Abbasids and had risen to prominent positions. The empowerment of individuals served to strengthen the whole Saljuqid community and would pay dividends in its confrontation with the Byzantines.

The migration of the Saljuqs across Central Asia had brought them into conflict with a number of Christian communities. A key community blocking their way was the Christian population of Armenia. In 1059 there was a fateful encounter between the two. A massacre of the Armenians by the Saljuqs was described in detail by an Armenian chronicler, Matthew of Edessa:

> A dreadful disaster befell the Christian faithful. . . . The Turkish people of Persia . . . launched attacks against the Christians of Armenia. . . . On 6 August 1059 the siege of Sebastea began, as did the slaughter. . . . At first, although Sebastea had no ramparts, the infidels had not dared to enter the city; they had mistaken the white domes of the churches which they saw rising over the horizon for their enemies' tents. But as soon as they realised their mistake, they gave vent to their rage in full. . . . They ruthlessly massacred an immense number of people, carried off a large amount of booty and took untold numbers of captives, men and women, young boys and girls, whom they sold into slavery.[22]

Twelve years later, Byzantine forces confronted this new Islamic threat at the Battle of Manzikert in Azerbaijan.[23] The Saljuq Turks led by Alp Arslan won a decisive victory. The writing was on the wall for the rump of land in Asia still controlled by the Eastern Christian Empire.

22. Ibid., 37.
23. For a graphic account of the battle, see ibid., 41–42.

Two years after defeating the Byzantines at Manzikert, the Saljuq Turks under Alp Arslan's son Malik Shah (ruled 1072–92) took control of Jerusalem by force from their fellow Muslims, the Cairo-based Fatimids.[24] This event was another cause of great concern to Byzantium and Rome.

Within Asia Minor, the Turks tended to settle on the high plains of Anatolia, leaving the rich coastal lands and ports to the Byzantines. There was a measure of cohabitation in periods when open conflict was not under way. But the increasing strength of the Saljuq Turks made a final showdown inevitable. After another century had elapsed, the year 1176 witnessed a major military clash between the Byzantines and the Saljuqs. On this occasion the Byzantines were again defeated and forced to acknowledge an independent Turkish state in Asia Minor.

Christians Living under the Saljuqs

The Greek minority living in the new Turkish kingdom was allowed to continue to practice their eastern Christian faith. In return, they had to pay the jizya tax. But Christianity in Asia Minor entered a period of terminal decline.

Many Greek priests fled to the safety of Constantinople, on the European side of the Bosporus. Many of the Christian faithful remaining in Asia Minor were drawn to convert to Islam because of various factors. First, the Turks changed a number of church buildings into mosques, including some of the most prominent houses of Christian worship. Allied to this was the fact that the Turkish rulers invested heavily in the development of new Islamic schools and mosques. Furthermore, the jizya tax paid by non-Muslims was higher than the zakat, which Muslims were required to pay, and this provided an additional incentive to convert to Islam.

Moreover, widespread nominalism came to characterize the Christian population living under Turkish rule. Hence, there was little attempt by local churches to evangelize Turks who settled among Christian populations. In times of economic and social difficulty, it is a relatively easy matter to replace one form of nominalism with another form of nominalism if such an action produces economic advantages. Thus little by little the religious profile of Asia Minor was altered.

The Saljuqid Empire expanded during the period that the Abbasid dynasty was declining. The Saljuqs paid nominal allegiance to the Abbasid dynasty, but real power lay outside the hands of the Baghdad-based caliphs. This gradual shift in power to Turkish forces within the

24. Watt, *Majesty That Was Islam*, 241.

world of Islam was to serve as a blueprint for the future, with Turkish groups coming to dominate the Islamic world for almost a millennium.

Thus Eastern Christianity, after centuries of setbacks and losses, had seen virtually all its territorial domains in Asia and the Middle East lost to successive Islamic empires: the Umayyads, the Abbasids, and the Saljuqs. Above all, we need to remind ourselves that this was the age of Muslim imperialism. Though empires came and went, from the perspective of Christian Europe the Muslim empires had been the principal factor in the erosion of vast domains that had previously belonged to Christendom. A Christian counterreaction was inevitable.

6

EMPIRES CRUMBLE

CHRISTIANITY STRIKES BACK: THE CRUSADES

In recent years Christian and Western scholars have engaged in much soul-searching about the Crusades and their legacy. Books have been written that have expressed far more sympathy for Muslim perspectives than was traditionally the case. Carole Hillenbrand's monumental volume *The Crusades: Islamic Perspectives* sets out to sensitize Western readers to Muslim views about the Crusades, in the belief that this will lead to greater understanding between the West and Islam.[1] In the late 1990s a "Reconciliation Walk" was organized by diverse Christian organizations and individuals. It consisted of thousands of Christians who marched along the route of the First Crusade all the way to Jerusalem, apologizing as they went for the actions of those early Crusaders some nine hundred years earlier.[2]

These new assessments of the Crusades by Western writers and Christians have proved controversial. The reconciliation walkers reported that "in towns and villages, people spilled out of their houses and applauded the team as they passed."[3] One walker reported the response from people in Beirut:

> If you did this in London or Sydney, you would expect a cynical response. The response from the people on the streets [of Beirut], particularly the Muslims, has been warm. The first word I have heard is "good." If there were such a word as "uncynical" that [would] be the way to describe it.[4]

1. Carole Hillenbrand, *The Crusades: Islamic Perspectives* (Edinburgh: Edinburgh University Press, 1999).

2. Cf. Lynn Green, *The Reconciliation Walk: Defusing the Bitter Legacy of the Crusades* (YWAM, Procla Media Productions, 1995), videocassette; Colin Chapman, "Living through the 900th Anniversary of the First Crusade: To Apologise or Not to Apologise?" *The Faith to Faith Newsletter* 1 (November 1998): 1–3.

3. "Christian Apology for the Crusades: The Reconciliation Walk." Available on the World Wide Web: http://www.religioustolerance.org/chr_cru1.htm.

4. Michael Karam, "Let's Forget the Crusades," *The Times* (London), September 19, 1998, 19.

In contrast Michael Karam, a Lebanese writer, commented:

> The Reconciliation Walkers are terribly sincere and terribly out of their
> depth. Their words tell us more about where they are from than where
> they are going. . . . We Lebanese see them as dabblers concerned with
> something that has been overtaken by many other, worse horrors during
> the past millennium. Yet in the best Lebanese tradition, they will be re-
> ceived with honour, listened to, offered coffee and sent on their way.[5]

In order to evaluate such approaches and indeed to assess the Crusades themselves, we have to consider the many factors that precipitated these military campaigns by Christians. History is like a chain,
with multiple links. We cannot lift one link from the chain of history
and examine it without taking account of the historical links that preceded it. It is not enough to examine and condemn the conduct of the
crusading knights without looking at the broader context of those
events.

Motives for the Crusades

The comprehensive Saljuq Turkish victory over the Byzantines at
Manzikert in 1071, with subsequent territorial gains in Asia Minor,
caused widespread consternation throughout the Christian world. The
Byzantines, who had long followed a defensive strategy in their conflicts with their Muslim adversaries,[6] looked for help to their co-
religionists. An urgent appeal for help was sent by the Byzantine Emperor to the Pope in Rome, the head of the Western Christian Empire.
It should be noted that relations between the Eastern and Western
Christian empires had long been strained, so such an appeal points to
the sense of panic felt within Christian ranks.

But there were other factors that contributed to the emergence of
the Crusades. The loss of the holy sites in Jerusalem centuries earlier
had been a bitter pill for Christian authorities to swallow, and they
had never given up hope of recapturing the city where Jesus was crucified. Indeed, despite the loss of Jerusalem to Muslims, Christian pilgrimages to the Holy Land had developed. However, in the middle of
the eleventh century Muslim harassment of, and attacks upon, Christian pilgrims had increased in frequency. Lambert, a chronicler of the
German pilgrimage of seven thousand people in 1064–65, recorded
the following account:

---

5. Ibid.
6. Blankinship, *End of the Jihad State,* 105.

When the pilgrims were just a short distance from Rama, . . . they were attacked by marauding Arabs. . . . Many of the Christians, thinking they might rely on their religion for assistance and salvation, had trusted in God's protection rather than in weapons. They were, as a result of the first attack, brought down by many wounds and robbed. . . . The other Christians did their best by throwing stones, . . . not so much to drive away danger as a desperate measure to escape imminent death.[7]

So piety was a motivating force for such pilgrimages, as well as for certain participants in the ensuing Crusades. A belief in eternal reward[8] justified a concept of holy war, and this proved to be a powerful attraction for many who joined the Crusades. Indeed, the twelfth-century writer Guibert of Nogent clearly believed the crusading motive was primarily a quest for eternal salvation: "What has driven our knights thither is not ambition for fame, for money, for extending the boundaries of their lands. . . . God has instituted in our time holy wars, so that the order of knights and the crowd running in their wake . . . might find a new way of gaining salvation."[9]

Some other motives had less of a spiritual dimension. Military campaigns always brought with them promises of wealth and plunder. Motives of personal ambition also came into play, as did hopes for trading opportunities. Hallam expresses well both the complexity and diversity of motives according to different participant groups:

> Complex though their motives were, it is easier to understand why knights joined the First Crusade than to explain the participation of hordes of peasant. . . . The theme of Jerusalem was all-important to them. They undertook the expedition not as a military campaign but as a pilgrimage, an important feature of 11th century life.[10]

The First Crusade (1096–99)

The First Crusade was precipitated by a statement by Pope Urban II in September 1096: "Anyone who sets out on that journey, not out of lust for worldly advantage but only for the salvation of his soul and for the liberation of the Church, is remitted in entirety all penance for his sins, if he has made a true and perfect act of confession."[11] Ironically, this promise of eternal reward for participating in

---

7. Elizabeth Hallam, ed., *Chronicles of the Crusades: Eye-Witness Accounts of the Wars between Christianity and Islam* (London: Weidenfeld and Nicolson, 1989), 35.

8. Cf. Pope Urban II's promise of sin forgiven, reported below.

9. Louise Riley-Smith and Jonathan Riley-Smith, *The Crusades: Idea and Reality, 1095–1274* (London: Edward Arnold, 1981), 55.

10. Hallam, *Chronicles of the Crusades*, 60.

11. Ibid., 63.

holy war is strongly reminiscent of a similar call in the Qur'an at Sura 3:158, mentioned in earlier discussion of the notion of jihad. There are two significant differences, of course. First, the Christian call for holy war was made by a human pope (albeit supposedly with divine sanction), and as such was subject to challenge by later theologians. The Muslim call to jihad, however, is cemented within the Qur'an for all time. Second, the doctrine of holy war has now largely fallen into disuse in Christian circles, whereas jihad as a military concept is still widely practiced by some Muslim groups (see chapter 11 for further discussion).

Several Christian armies set out, including a peasant mob led by Peter the Hermit. The chronicler Anna Comnena, daughter of Byzantine Emperor Alexius I Comnenus (ruled 1081–1118), described their fate:

> The Turkish sultan Qilij Arslan devised a plan: . . . he placed men in ambush at suitable places. . . . [Peter's group] fell into the Turkish ambushes near Drakon and were miserably wiped out. Such a large number of Franks became the victims of Turkish swords, that when the scattered remains of the slaughtered men were collected, they made not merely a hill or mound or peak, but a huge mountain, deep and wide, most remarkable, so great was the pile of bones.[12]

It was not only Muslim troops who slaughtered their adversaries. As they traveled through various routes in Europe, the crusading armies slaughtered whole communities of Jews whom they encountered. But the most bloody act was saved for the capture of Jerusalem on July 15, 1099. Numerous accounts, both Christian and Muslim, survive. We will draw on the record of the *Gesta Francorum*:

> Our pilgrims entered the city, and chased the Saracens, killing as they went, as far as the Temple of Solomon. . . . At last the pagans were overcome, and our men captured a good number of men and women in the Temple; they killed whomsoever they wished, and chose to keep others alive. . . . In the morning our men climbed up cautiously on to the roof of the Temple and attacked the Saracens, both male and female, and beheaded them with unsheathed swords. The other Saracens threw themselves from the Temple. . . . On the eighth day after the city was captured, they chose Godfrey of Bouillon as ruler of the city to subdue the pagans and protect the Christians.[13]

12. Ibid., 67–68.
13. Ibid., 93.

The language used in this account provides a window into attitudes of the time. The Crusaders are described as "pilgrims," their Muslim adversaries as "pagans." The thousands who were slaughtered by the Crusaders included Muslims, Jews, and some Eastern Christian residents of the city.

The outcome of this first Crusade, the most successful in terms of territory captured, was the establishment of a series of principalities in the region. These became Crusader states that were replenished from time to time from Western Europe. Jerusalem was the jewel in the Crusader crown. In the mind of the Christian authorities, the capture of Jerusalem vindicated the campaign and showed that God was on their side in their great counterattack against earlier Muslim expansion in the region.

Subsequent Crusades

Many crusading campaigns followed on from the first. We will only concern ourselves here with several key aspects of these campaigns, rather than discussing the detailed events surrounding them.

The Second Crusade lasted from 1147 to 1149 and was launched in response to the loss in 1146 of the Crusader principality of Edessa to Muslim attackers. Pope Eugene III called for a new crusade to recover the lost territory:

> We enjoin you in the name of the Lord and for the remission of your sins . . . that the faithful of God, and above all the most powerful and the nobles act vigorously to oppose the multitude of the infidel . . . and strive to liberate from their hands the many thousands of our brethren who are captives. . . . We accord them that same remission of sins that our predecessor Pope Urban instituted.[14]

Again we find a promise of forgiveness of sins associated with the campaign. This crusade ended in a failed attempt to capture Damascus.

The Third Crusade lasted from 1189 to 1192 and was launched after the fall of Jerusalem to the great Muslim warrior Salah al-Din (Saladin) on October 2, 1187. Saladin's armies had also captured Acre, Beirut, Sidon, and other prominent Christian strongholds.

Descriptions of Jerusalem's fall to the Muslims differ markedly between Christian and Muslim sources, though it seems that the brutality of the Christian capture of Jerusalem in 1099 was not repeated. One Christian account details the ransom terms laid down by Saladin:

---

14. Jean Richard, *The Crusades, c. 1071–c. 1291* (Cambridge: Cambridge University Press, 1999), 156–57.

Each person was to pay the price of their own head. A man paid ten bezants,[15] a woman five and a child one. Anyone who could not afford to pay was taken captive. So it happened that although many made the payment for their salvation, either from their own property or begged from elsewhere, 14,000 of the rest were left without a redeemer and were under the yoke of perpetual slavery.

This account provides a window into the disdain that Christians and Muslims felt for each other's faith at the time:

When the city had surrendered, a crier of the law of Muhammad ascended the height of the rock of Calvary and then loudly proclaimed their filthy law. . . . There was a cross fixed on top of the spire of the Hospitallers' church. They tied ropes around it and threw it down, spat contemptuously on it, hacked it into pieces, then dragged it through the city dungpits, as an insult to our faith.[16]

Pope Gregory VIII called for a crusade on October 29, 1187, in similar terms to the calls of his papal predecessors. Some land was recaptured, including Acre in July 1191 after a two-year siege, but not Jerusalem. It was to remain under Muslim control for over seven hundred years.

The loss of Jerusalem, and the comparative fragility of Christian control in the Crusader principalities, led to an increase in the frequency of subsequent Crusades. In 1198 Pope Innocent III issued a call for a crusade to consolidate Christian territory in the Holy Land and offered an indulgence: "All those who take the Cross and remain for one year in the service of God in the army shall obtain remission of any sins they have committed, provided they have confessed them."[17] The resulting Fourth Crusade lasted from 1202 to 1204. From a Christian perspective this was one of the most disastrous. Events took an unexpected turn due to political intrigue and power struggles. The crusading knights eventually directed their campaign not against Muslim adversaries but against the Byzantine Empire itself, because of Western suspicion at seeming Byzantine willingness to compromise with Muslims. Constantinople was attacked and cap-

---

15. The bezant was a gold coin that the Emperor Constantine introduced into the Roman Empire. It was the basis of trade in the Western world from the fourth to the twelfth centuries A.D.

16. Helen J. Nicholson, *Chronicle of the Third Crusade: A Translation of the Itinerarium Peregrinorum et Gesta Regis Ricardi* (Aldershot: Ashgate, 1997), 38–39.

17. Geoffrey de Villehardouin, "The Conquest of Constantinople," in *Chronicles of the Crusades,* trans. M. R. B. Shaw (Harmondsworth: Penguin, 1963), 29.

tured by Crusader forces, and a Western ruler was put on the Byzantine throne.

Pope Innocent III was furious at the conquest of Constantinople. He bitterly rebuked the papal legate who accompanied the Crusaders:

> It was your duty to attend to the business of your legation and to give careful thought not to the capture of the Empire of Constantinople, but rather to the defence of what is left of the Holy Land and, if the Lord so wills, the restoration of what has been lost. . . .

> How can we call upon the other Western peoples for aid to the Holy Land . . . when the crusaders having given up the proposed pilgrimage, return absolved to their homes; when those who plundered the aforesaid empire turn back and return with their spoils, free of guilt?[18]

After such a development, subsequent crusading campaigns were tainted. Further Crusades took place, but they were unsuccessful. Little by little the various Crusader strongholds fell to Muslim armies, often with great brutality. A chronicler described a Muslim raid on Sidon in 1253:

> When [the Saracens] heard the report (a true one) that the king had sent no more than a very small contingent of good men to fortify the city of Saida, they marched in that direction. . . . The Saracens poured into Saida and met with no resistance, for the town was not completely surrounded by walls. They killed more than two thousand of our people, and then went off to Damascus with the booty they had gained in the town.[19]

The year 1291 witnessed the end of the crusading venture with the fall of Acre, followed by the loss of the last remaining coastal towns.

An Assessment of the Crusades

In the preceding paragraphs we have recognized various motives behind each of the Crusades. One was a genuine desire to regain territory lost to invading Muslim armies in previous periods. In the process the Crusaders hoped to strengthen Christianity in the face of the Islamic threat.

The Crusades were notable for the absence of missionary concern. Taking the Gospel to Muslims was simply not a priority. Admittedly,

18. Elizabeth Siberry, *Criticism of Crusading, 1095–1274* (Oxford: Clarendon, 1985), 173–74.
19. Jean Joinville, "The Life of Saint Louis," in *Chronicles of the Crusades,* trans. M. R. B. Shaw (Harmondsworth: Penguin, 1963), 303.

during the Fifth Crusade in 1219 Francis of Assisi went to Egypt to preach among Muslims, was allowed to cross the battle lines to enter the Muslim military camp, and was treated with great courtesy. The sultan listened to Francis respectfully, then sent him back to the Christian camp. He was a pioneer of a new approach, and subsequently a number of friars entered Muslim lands to preach. A notable example was Ramon Lull (Llull), who became a Christian around 1260. He made repeated trips from his native Spain to North Africa to preach among Muslims, and he was eventually martyred there in 1316.[20]

Yet this more irenic Christian approach to Islam largely postdated the crusading campaigns. The Crusades themselves were rather characterized by savagery and intolerance. But it was mutual mistreatment, following on from centuries of bloody conflict, massacre, and Muslim imperial expansion. The victims of this recurring cycle of conflict were Muslims, Christians, and Jews. Likewise, the perpetrators were both Muslims and Christians.

Criticism of the Crusades among Christians is not a recent phenomenon. Indeed, there was a vigorous debate during the time of the Crusades, as recorded by Humbert of Romans, who wrote a response to critics of crusading in the late thirteenth century: "There are some . . . who say that it is not in accordance with the Christian religion to shed blood in this way, even that of wicked infidels. For Christ did not act thus. . . . [But Christianity] must be defended when necessary from its enemies by the sword."[21]

It should be remembered that the Crusades were a link in the chain of history. They represented the response of the Christian world to the earlier Islamic expansion and to the loss of the Byzantine territories in the Middle East and North Africa. They do, of course, raise substantial moral issues, but consideration of these should not be divorced from the historical context. If apologies are to be extended, it is important that this be done in a framework of mutual acknowledgement of error and excess, and shared repentance.

ISLAM IN SOUTHWESTERN EUROPE

After the Muslim invasion of Spain from 711, parts of the Iberian peninsula would remain under Muslim control until 1492, the year when Columbus sailed for the Americas. An Umayyad dynasty was in control, refusing to recognize the authority of the Abbasid caliphs in

20. See chap. 8, "The Missionaries."
21. Riley-Smith and Riley-Smith, *Crusades: Idea and Reality,* 105.

Baghdad and representing a living symbol of the gradual fragmentation of Islamic empire.

Just as Abbasid Baghdad served as a catalyst for the flowering of Islamic culture and knowledge in the ninth and tenth centuries, so Umayyad Spain became an important channel for the transmission of Islamic thought and for the flourishing of the arts and sciences. Under Caliph Abd al-Rahman III (ruled 912–61), the Umayyad dynasty centering on Cordova reached its zenith "as the most cultured city in Europe and, with Constantinople and Baghdad, as one of the three cultural centers of the world."[22] Agricultural techniques advanced dramatically; it is worth noting that most agricultural terms in modern Spanish are derived from Arabic.

Nevertheless, the period of Muslim dominance of the Iberian peninsula was characterized by rivalries and revolts from within. It was also dogged by regular outbreaks of warfare with neighboring Christian rulers. The Christian reconquest in Spain began to take effect in the middle of the eleventh century, and it precipitated fragmentation of the Muslim Umayyad Empire into multiple Muslim principalities. It made significant headway during the first half of the thirteenth century under Fernando III, king of Castille and Leon, when the Umayyad capital of Cordova, as well as Seville and other cities, was captured. Granada remained as the sole independent Muslim kingdom until its fall on January 2, 1492.

The modern Muslim scholar and diplomat Akhbar Ahmed writes with sorrow of the "permanent scar" the loss of Spain has left on the Muslim psyche.[23] The Christian world bore similar scars from earlier losses. Such scars have contributed profoundly to ongoing strains in the relationship between Christianity and Islam down through the ages.

THE MONGOLS, INVASION AND ABSORPTION

The decline and destruction of the Ummayad Empire in Spain was not the only setback suffered by Muslims in the medieval period. In the tenth century, the great Abbasid Empire based on Baghdad entered a period of gradual decline. It was destabilized by the Crusades from the West. But an even more destructive threat appeared from the East in the form of the Mongol invasions.

The Mongols posed a threat to both Christianity and Islam. But centuries of confrontation and conflict meant that there was no thought

22. Philip K. Hitti, *The Arabs: A Short History* (London: Macmillan, 1968), 129.
23. Akbar S. Ahmed, *Living Islam* (London: BBC Books, 1993), 70.

of joining forces to face the common Mongol foe. This is evident from the following comment by Davis, writing from a European perspective:

> It is easy to understand the horror which [the Mongols] inspired, for they were a threat not only to the frontier districts but to the whole Christian world, to Byzantium as well as Rome. The only encouragement to be gleaned was the fact that they were equally a threat to the existence of Islam.[24]

From a Muslim standpoint, the horror of the Mongol invasion is encapsulated by Ibn al-Athir, who laments

> the greatest catastrophe and the most dire calamity (of the like of which days and nights are innocent) which befell all men generally, and the Muslims in particular; so that, should one say that the world, since God Almighty created Adam until now, has not been afflicted with the like thereof, he would but speak the truth. For indeed history doth not contain aught which approaches or comes nigh unto it.[25]

In 1218 Genghis Khan, the Mongol leader dominant in China at the time, swept out of Central Asia into Islamic lands, rapidly overrunning Persia. Syria and Turkey submitted virtually without resistance.

Genghis Khan's devastating campaigns were not the last of the Mongol threat. His grandson Hulagu attacked Iraq itself in 1256. Two years later the Abbasid capital of Baghdad fell, amid carnage and massacre. This marked the end of the much decayed and fragmented Abbasid Caliphate. The last caliph was executed by being sewn up in a sack and trampled to death by Mongol horses.[26]

In 1260 both Damascus and Aleppo fell to Mongol armies. But that year the Mongol advance was finally stopped in Gaza by the army of the Mamluks, the dynasty based in Egypt, who had earlier overthrown many of the Crusader states. From that point on, Cairo became the effective center of the Islamic world.

As for the Mongols, it did not take long before the victors merged to become invisible among the vanquished. Ghazan, a descendent of Hulagu and subsequent ruler of the Mongol domains in the West, adopted Islam and restored Islamic law. The Mongol language and culture were gradually absorbed into the prevailing Per-

24. R. H. C. Davis, *A History of Medieval Europe* (London: Longman, 1957), 405.
25. Edward G. Browne, *A Literary History of Persia*, vol. 2 (London: Fisher, Unwin, 1906), 427–28.
26. Davis, *History of Medieval Europe*, 408.

sian/Islamic context. The Eastern Mongol Empire, in contrast, remained un-Islamized.

MAMLUKS

The Mamluks were to dominate the Islamic world in the Near East until the time of the Ottomans. They were mixed-race slave soldiers who took advantage of widespread political instability and opportunities to establish what Hitti refers to as "the last medieval dynasty of the Arab world."[27] The mid–thirteenth century marked their rise, and they were to dominate the Muslim world for over two hundred years.

The most famous Mamluk sultan was Baybars (ruled 1260–77). He cleared the region of most of the remaining Crusader strongholds and checked the advance of the Mongols. Baybars strengthened Mamluk military forces to make them powerful on the regional stage. He also devoted attention to domestic matters, instituting a significant building program and establishing a postal service between Cairo and Damascus.

INSTABILITY BREEDS RELIGIOUS EXTREMISM

However, this was a time of great political and social instability. Old certainties had been swept away with the fall of empires, and resulting power vacuums led to the kind of social turmoil that is commonplace in such circumstances. This was followed by a rise in religious fanaticism in the Muslim domains. Likewise, religious persecution flourished in Christendom at the same time, as it too struggled to establish political and social stability.

In this period of turmoil religious minorities suffered under both Muslim and Christian authority. In 1250 the final Abbasid authorities passed a decree specifying that Jews and Christians found in public without distinctive badges and belts were to be executed. In 1301 the color yellow was allocated to Jews and blue to Christians, to ensure that they were clearly identifiable while living in Muslim domains. This mirrored similar distinguishing marks required of Jews living in Christian Europe, including having them wear a yellow circle on outer garments, as well as caps with horns.[28]

Intense discrimination in the Islamic domains led to a large number of conversions to Islam. Sa'd b. Kammuna, the Jewish author of *Examination of the Three Faiths*, wrote in 1280: "We never saw anyone converting to Islam except when in fear, or out of quest for power, or

27. Hitti, *Arabs: A Short History*, 184.
28. Simon Dubnov, *History of the Jews* (London: Thomas Yoseloff, 1969), 3:28.

to avoid heavy taxation, or to escape humiliation, or because of infatuation with a Muslim woman."[29] In this period Jews suffered particularly. From 1335 to 1344 the Jews of Baghdad were exposed to brutal persecutions. There were Muslim attacks on property and person, synagogues were demolished, libraries destroyed, and many were forced to convert to Islam. The Jewish population of Baghdad was emasculated, only being replenished in due course by migrations of Jews expelled from Christian Europe.

---

29. Goitein, "Jews under Islam 6th–16th centuries," 185.

7

FROM MEDIEVAL TO MODERN

THE OTTOMANS PENETRATE EUROPE

Earlier we saw how the migration of Turkish tribes from Central Asia into the Near East was to add a significant new equation to Islamic history. The empire of the Saljuq Turks brought the Byzantine Christian Empire to its knees through military conquest and settlement in conquered areas. Under the Saljuqs, the demographic and religious profile of the region constituting present-day Turkey was to change forever. However, as great as the Saljuqs were, they would be outshone by another great Turkish empire, that of the Ottomans.

The Rise of the Ottomans

The Ottomans were a clan that settled in northeast Turkey in the thirteenth century, benefiting from earlier Saljuq successes in pushing back the boundaries of the Byzantine Empire. They gradually grew in strength, and in 1326 they conquered the city of Bursa and made it their capital. From this point on, their rise to prominence was steady and seemingly unstoppable.

In 1353 the Ottomans took Gallipoli. The significance of this event should not be underestimated. Gallipoli was on the European side of the Dardanelles. Its strategic value was underlined over 550 years later, when Allied forces tried unsuccessfully to capture it from the Ottomans in the First World War. By seizing Gallipoli, the early Ottomans had gained an important jumping-off point for further expansion into Europe. Both Eastern and Western Christians were well aware of this.

A period of great expansion followed. Over the three decades of the 1360s–80s Ottoman Sultan Murad conquered Bulgaria, Macedonia, and Serbia. Ira Lapidus captures the sense of panic felt in the Christian world: "The Ottoman conquests inspired a Europe-wide anxiety.

107

To check Ottoman expansion, the European states mobilized latter-day crusades."[1]

But worse would come. The year 1453 witnessed the fall of Constantinople to Ottoman Sultan Mehmet II. After centuries of unsuccessful sieges and attacks on the capital of the Byzantine Empire, Muslim forces finally overcame it. This represented the final collapse of Byzantium, which left deep scars in the psyche of Christian communities throughout Europe.

When one considers the attention given by scholars to the detail of the earlier conquest of Jerusalem by the Crusaders, and the sense of shame and apology surrounding that event as felt by many Westerners and Christians, it is striking that the fall of Constantinople to the Ottomans generally receives a much lighter touch. Some writers explain it away. The Turkish scholar Inalcik rationalizes the brutal methods of the Ottoman victors:

> When . . . his surrender terms had been rejected by the Byzantine Emperor, . . . Mehmed II ordered his army . . . to deliver a general assault and pillage the city. In any case the sultan could not prevent the pillaging of a city captured against resistance, and we know that he later allowed the return of those Greeks who, after the conquest paid ransom or who had left the city before the siege.[2]

Lapidus glides over the Ottoman methods of conquest without comment, referring to it merely as "a triumph which fulfilled an age-old Muslim ambition to inherit the domains of the Roman empire."[3] Similarly Jane Smith chooses not to mention details of the Ottoman brutality in victory.[4]

But the fact is that it paralleled that of the Crusaders in taking Jerusalem almost five hundred years earlier, with the population of Constantinople witnessing their city being pillaged and themselves being slaughtered or enslaved in large numbers. The following graphic eyewitness account by Makarios Melissenos captures the scene as the Ottoman forces achieved victory over the defenders of Constantinople:

1. Ira M. Lapidus, *A History of Islamic Societies* (Cambridge: Cambridge University Press, 1988), 306.

2. Halil Inalcik, "The Rise of the Ottoman Empire," in *The Cambridge History of Islam*, ed. P. M. Holt, Ann K. S. Lambton, and Bernard Lewis (Cambridge: Cambridge University Press, 1970), 1:295–96.

3. Lapidus, *History of Islamic Societies*, 307.

4. Jane Smith, "Islam and Christendom: Historical, Cultural, and Religious Interaction from the Seventh to the Fifteenth Centuries," in *The Oxford History of Islam*, ed. J. L. Esposito (Oxford: Oxford University Press, 1999), 342.

As soon as the Turks were inside the city, they began to seize and enslave every person who came their way; all those who tried to offer resistance were put to the sword. In many places the ground could not be seen, as it was covered by heaps of corpses. There were unprecedented events: all sorts of lamentations, countless rows of slaves consisting of noble ladies, virgins, and nuns who were being dragged by the Turks by their headgear, hair, and braids out of the shelter of churches, to the accompaniment of mourning. There was crying of children, the looting of our sacred and holy buildings. . . . There were lamentations and weeping in every house, screaming in the crossroads, and sorrow in all churches; the groaning of grown men and the shrieking of women accompanied looting, enslavement, separation, and rape.[5]

From Constantinople, the Ottomans pushed on to complete the conquest of the Balkans. In the late fifteenth century, the Ottomans absorbed Greece, Bosnia, Herzegovina, and Albania. The last three locations sprang into prominence in world news in the 1990s, when warfare broke out between Balkan Christian communities and Muslim communities that are descendants of those who converted to Islam during the period of Ottoman colonial rule in the region.

The issue of conversion is key. Before the Turkish migrations into Asia Minor, the vast majority of the population was Christian. By the fifteenth century, over 90 percent of the population was Muslim. Lapidus comments that "some of this change was due to the immigration of a large Muslim population, but in great part it was due to the conversion of Christians to Islam."[6] The great Byzantine Empire was in the process of disappearing from its very heartlands almost without living trace.

Ottoman expansion was not only at the expense of Eastern Christians. In 1517 the Ottoman Turks overthrew the Cairo-based Mamluk dynasty. The Ottoman Sultan Selim carried off the Mamluk Caliph Mutawakkil to Constantinople. Selim declared himself the new caliph, with his base in Turkey. From this point on, the Ottomans reigned as the supreme heads of the Muslim domains in the Near East. Sunni Muslims everywhere looked to the authority of the caliph in Muslim Istanbul, a city undergoing a metamorphosis from its former identity as Christian Constantinople.

The next and greatest sultan was Suleiman the Magnificent (ruled 1520–66). His period represented the height of the Ottoman Empire,

5. Makarios Melissenos, "The Chronicle of the Siege of Constantinople, April 2 to May 29, 1453," in *The Fall of the Byzantine Empire*, trans. Marios Philippides (Amherst: University of Massachusetts Press, 1980), 130–31.

6. Lapidus, *History of Islamic Societies*, 308.

both in terms of internal glory and external expansion. He led his armies on the successful campaign to capture Belgrade in August 1521. He invaded Hungary and won a resounding victory against Hungarian King Louis II at the Battle of Mohacs in August 1526. This battle lives on in the memories of Hungarians today, who view it as one of the lowest points of their history. Hungarian deaths included King Louis and around 25,000 of his army, survivors of whom were massacred following the battle. The defeat ushered in a period of 150 years of Ottoman domination in Hungary.

Less successful was the Ottoman siege of Vienna in 1529. Nevertheless, the victories and territorial expansion in eastern Europe, North Africa, and the Mediterranean islands meant that Europe was reminded of the extent of the threat posed by this new Islamic Empire, rivaling its Umayyad, Abbasid, and Saljuqid predecessors.

Ottoman Relations with the Christian World

Ottoman incursions into Europe would remain the focus of ongoing clashes between Islam and Christianity during succeeding centuries. The brutality of the Ottoman forces was legendary. Many massacres could be detailed, but we will focus upon that of the Armenians during the period when the Ottomans were struggling to hold on to an empire in decline.

The genocide of the Armenians occurred in two important phases. The first mass killings took place in 1894–96 during the reign of Sultan Abdul Hamid II (ruled 1876–1909). These events represented the Ottoman response to its Armenian subjects' pressure for reforms, supported by European governments. Estimates of Armenian victims murdered in this two-year period range up to 300,000, with associated destruction to livelihood and many thousands forcibly converted to Islam. However, an even worse campaign of genocide was to follow.

In 1912 the Armenian Partiarchate in Istanbul put the Armenian Christian minority population of the Ottoman state at 2.1 million.[7] The Ottoman state came under severe pressure due to military setbacks in the First World War, especially following a defeat by Russian forces in 1915. One group to feel the full brunt of Ottoman disfavor was the Christian minority. Following the Russian defeat, Armenians serving in the Ottoman forces were demobilized and subsequently massacred. Others throughout the Ottoman Empire were deported from their homes, compelled into forced labor schemes, abducted, and murdered by Ottoman authorities. There was an international outcry, but it had little effect. This sense of outrage combined with

---

7. A. E. Redgate, *The Armenians* (Oxford: Blackwell, 2000), 271.

guilt because of lack of international action is well expressed in the following 1918 letter from former American President Theodore Roosevelt to Cleveland Hoadley Dodge:

> The Armenian horror is an accomplished fact. Its occurrence was largely due to the policy of pacifism this nation has followed for the last four years. The presence of our missionaries, and our failure to go to war, did not prevent the Turks from massacring between half a million and a million Armenians, Syrians, Greeks and Jews—the overwhelmingly majority being Armenians. . . .
> . . . The Armenian massacre was the greatest crime of the war.[8]

In the First World War the Ottomans were defeated by the Allies. The revolution of Atatürk in the early postwar years led to the establishment of a secular republic and the abolition of the caliphate in 1924. This key decision has had a profound impact on the Muslim world, with many Muslims, especially Islamist activists, longing for the reestablishment of the caliphate as a mark of Islam's resurgence in the world.

Other Islamic Empires in the Modern Period

Ottoman power based in Turkey was complemented by a number of other great Muslim empires. These will receive less attention since our primary focus falls on the Muslim lands adjoining, and often in direct conflict with, Europe. But mention should be made of Persian, Indian, and Southeast Asian Islamic empires.

The Safavid Empire in Persia (1501–1722)

Persia had a history of imperial grandeur going back millennia. Following the conquest of Persia by the early caliphs, the region was absorbed within the Umayyad and Abbasid empires. However, as we have seen, Persians came to play an influential role in affairs of state under many Abbasid caliphs, and some of the greatest Islamic thinkers and writers in the classical period originated in Persia.

In due course Persia established its own great Muslim empire, that of the Safavids. With its capital at Isfahan, the Safavid dynasty of Iran made a significant move in establishing Shi'a Islam as the religion of state. Finally Shi'ism had moved from being a chronically persecuted minority to achieving majority status within a particular Islamic context.

8. Available on the World Wide Web: http://www.armenian-genocide.org/statements/roosevelt.htm. See also Redgate, *Armenians*, 272.

There were sporadic clashes between the Ottomans and the Safavid dynasty in Iran. A treaty in 1639 gave Baghdad and Iraq to the Ottomans, and the Caucasus to Iran, thus delineating relative spheres of influence. The rivalry between Turkey and Iran for influence in the Muslim world continues to this day.

The Mughal Empire

A succession of Muslim dynasties ruled a great empire based on Delhi in India for three hundred years. The Mughal Empire was established by Babur, of mixed Turkish and Mongol ancestry, who invaded India from Afghanistan. The Mughals reached their peak in the seventeenth century.

Babur's grandson Akbar the Great (ruled 1556–1605) was one of the greatest Mughal emperors. He was inclined toward pantheism and relatively tolerant of religious minorities. His grandson Shah Jahan was somewhat more orthodox in his religious doctrines. Shah Jahan's lasting legacy is the great Taj Mahal, which he built in memory of his wife, Muntaz Mahal.

Aurangzeb (ruled 1657–1707) succeeded Shah Jahan and was strictly orthodox. He destroyed Hindu temples and was strongly opposed to what he considered nonorthodox practice among Muslims. Under him the Mughal Empire reached its greatest extent.

By 1770 the Mughal Empire had declined considerably. It was finally destroyed by British imperial power, a fact held as a bitter memory by many Muslim revivalists in the Indian subcontinent.

Islam in Southeast Asia

Islam spread to Southeast Asia from the Middle East and India via trading contacts. In the late thirteenth century some coastal rulers in Sumatra embraced Islam, and this marked the establishment of the faith in the region, though individual Muslim travelers had been visiting the area long before this.

There are legendary accounts of nine Muslim missionaries or saints in local chronicles that testify to the arrival and spread of Islam on the island of Java. It established itself initially in coastal settlements, then spread inland, and thence eastward. Around the same time, Islamic expansion was taking place elsewhere in the Southeast Asian region: on the Malay peninsula and to the islands of the southern Philippines. Sufism played a particularly important role in defining the early identity of Islam in Southeast Asia.

Several Islamic empires came to prominence: Malacca, Aceh, Johor, Mataram, and Sulu. However, all had their power curtailed by European imperial expansion, whether Portuguese, Dutch, English, or

Spanish. This added poison to the pot of Christian-Muslim conflict and continues to corrupt the relationship between these faiths.

THE AGE OF EUROPEAN IMPERIALISM

A key theme to emerge from our study has been the clash of empires, representing Christian Europe and Muslim lands. One of the starkest ironies of the modern period lies in the recognition that as the Ottoman Empire squeezed Christian Europe from the east, Europe in turn squeezed communities allied with the Ottomans in other locations.

There were broadly three stages in the modern history of European imperialism. First came the phase of Mercantile Imperialism, lasting approximately 1500–1780 and taking place in the pre-Industrial era. This coincided with the peak of Ottoman power and its surge into eastern Europe and reflected European merchants' desire for an alternate route to Asia to avoid Muslim-controlled overland routes. During this period Portugal and Spain initially established colonies in the Americas, as well as trade links with India, China, and the East Indies. They were followed by Britain, France, and Holland, and by 1780 Britain had the most widely spread network of colonies. This phase is also characterized by commercial company control of the colonies, rather than direct control by governments. Examples were the British East India Company and the Dutch Verenigde Oostindische Compagnie (VOC).

The second phase of European imperialism took place in the early Industrial era (ca. 1780–1880). In this period the British expanded their empire after the loss of American colonies. France also expanded its holdings, while the Dutch government took control of the Dutch East Indies from the VOC. Spain held on to the Philippines, Cuba, and several other possessions after the loss of its South American colonies in the 1820s.

Finally came the phase of what is commonly called the New Imperialism (ca. 1880–1905). This was marked by intense rivalry between the great industrial powers. Britain was overtaken in industrial output by Germany and the United States. Historians speak of the "Grab for Africa" and the "Scramble for China," with vast areas carved up between the leading European powers. In fact, over half the world's population, including almost all of Africa and Asia, passed under varying degrees of control by Britain, France, Germany, Belgium, Holland, Italy, Russia, and new imperial powers such as Japan and the United States. The colonized peoples included many of the world's Muslims. Not included were those Arab Muslims under Ottoman control—yet many Arabs saw Ottoman rule as merely another form of foreign domination.

Thus Christian Europeans were threatened by Ottoman expansion and incursions from the east. Meanwhile Muslims throughout much of the world were threatened by Christian European colonialism in India, Indonesia, Africa, and other locations. The complex legacy of rivalry and enmity between Christianity and Islam was being fueled even further.

REFORMISM, NATIONALISM, AND ISLAM

By 1900 Ottoman Turkey was in advanced decline. This perception, combined with the fact that vast numbers of Muslims were under the colonial control of Europeans, caused many Muslim thinkers to engage in soul-searching. They were particularly preoccupied with one question: Why would God allow believers (i.e., Muslims) to be subjugated by non-Muslims?

A new school of reformist thinkers provided an answer to this dilemma. They proposed that God had allowed such a situation to develop because Muslims had not been good Muslims; they had been lax in their faith. There was a desperate need to reform Islam, this group argued. Such reform would include drawing on Western knowledge, especially in terms of scientific know-how. If such knowledge were then solidly grounded within an Islamic paradigm, Muslims would be able to recapture past Islamic greatness.

This development coincided with the rise of national consciousness throughout the colonized regions. In some locations secular nationalist movements came to the fore. In Muslim locations Islamic resurgence calling for reform emerged as the new challenge to the colonial powers.

Sayyid Jamal al-Din al-Afghani (1838–97) is considered the early pioneer of this reformist thinking. Al-Afghani emphasized the importance of religious faith and claimed that atheistic materialism led to decadence, debasement, and decay. He wrote *The Refutation of the Materialists* as a specific rebuttal of the Darwinian theory of evolution. But in addition to denouncing foreign powers and their control of Muslim countries, al-Afghani attacked Muslim rulers who opposed reforms, such as the Shah of Persia and those who did not actively resist European encroachments.

Another important name in this regard was Muhammad 'Abduh (1849–1905), who became the Grand Mufti of Egypt. 'Abduh's most influential written work is his *Theology of Unity*. He was ably assisted by his student Rashid Rida (1865–1935), who became the editor of the reformist journal *al-Manar*. These and other reformist leaders advocated various programs: first, a purification of Islam by eradicating non-Islamic influences, including secularism; second, a reformation of the education system to reestablish Islamic principles; third, a greater emphasis on reference to the primary Islamic sources to address modern problems, rather than uncritically accepting the religious dictates of traditional authorities.[9]

This surge in reformist thinking would have a profound influence on developments in the twentieth century. The emphasis upon getting back to Islamic scriptural basics would be carried through by later radical thinkers, as we shall see in subsequent discussion.

World War 2 and Decolonization

In the period following the end of the Second World War, a process of decolonization quickly swept away the great European empires. Many new states came into being, including a considerable number of nations that had Muslim-majority populations.

There was considerable competition among local forces vying to fill the power vacuum resulting from the departure of colonial authorities. This competition was typically played out between two different mind-sets appearing in Muslim communities: some groups favored the creation of states along the lines of Western parliamentary democracies; others more religiously conscious sought states that reflected an Islamic identity in varying degrees. This presented a set of crossroads of considerable significance, which the new Muslim nations had to traverse.

In most new countries that had Muslim majorities, such as Indonesia, Pakistan, and Tunisia, the Western democratic model asserted itself in the early years of independence, much to the chagrin of more self-consciously Islamic political and social groups. However, the initial sense of optimism was not to last. Many Muslim-majority countries found the adaptation to modern international economic and political systems extremely difficult. Governing authorities in many countries adopted political, social, and economic methods that were based on non-Muslim Western models; when these did not produce the desired degree of success or prosperity, dissatisfaction resulted. This led to political and social movements calling for a return to Islamic basics. Such reactions were breeding grounds for religious fundamentalism and political radicalism.

Typology

A host of labels have been widely used and misused in referring to different kinds of Muslims: fundamentalist, revivalist, radical, mod-

9. H. A. R. Gibb, *Modern Trends in Islam* (Chicago: University of Chicago Press, 1947), 33.

ernist, reformist, and other terms. To overcome resulting confusion, it is useful to identify a typology. The Canadian scholar Andrew Rippin offers a useful typology of different Muslim responses to the challenges of the modern world,[10] which will serve our purposes well in the remaining discussion. Rippin groups Muslims into three macrotypes:

- *Traditionalists* hold "to the full authority of the past and that change should not and does not affect the traditions of the past."
- *Islamists* use "the authoritative sources of the past to legitimize changes in the present day. . . . [Such use] opens up the possibilities of independent reasoning through the rejection of authority by that very process of the return to the text and the ignoring of traditional interpretation of those texts." This group harks back to a previous Golden Age and longs for an idealized perfect community in some imagined past time.
- *Modernists* consider that "greater advantage is to be found within the modern circumstance by embracing change and making religion itself subject to change. The Modernist position is frequently based upon a principle of differentiating basic moral precepts from specific legal prescriptions."

It is the Islamists who tend to capture the media headlines. They look back to a number of pioneers in radical thinking in the distant past, such as Ibn Hanbal (d. 855); in the fairly distant past, such as Ibn Taymiyya (d. 1328); and in the more recent past, such as Sayyid Qutb (d. 1966). All these men prioritized the Qur'an and Hadith as self-sufficient blueprints for the practice of the faith and for living in the world.

Sayyid Qutb is arguably the most important voice in the radical Islamism of the twentieth century. His vision for Islam was to recreate Muhammad's community in the modern world. He was virulently anti-Western, as the following quote from one of his works demonstrates:

Western civilization is unable to present any healthy values for the guidance of mankind. . . . It is essential for mankind to have new leadership!
. . . The period of the Western system has come to an end primarily because it is deprived of those life-giving values which enabled it to be the leader of mankind. It is necessary for the new leadership to preserve and develop the material fruits of the creative genius of Europe, and also to provide mankind with such high ideals and values as have so far remained undiscovered by mankind, and which will also acquaint hu-

10. Rippin, *Muslims: Their Religious Beliefs and Practices*, 182–85.

manity with a way of life which is harmonious with human nature, which is positive and constructive, and which is practicable. Islam is the only system which possesses these values and this way of life.[11]

He also considered that if Islam would be great again, it would need to purify itself from non-Islamic influences within. He was strongly opposed to traditionalist tendencies in Islam:

> If Islam is again to play the role of the leader of mankind, then it is necessary that the Muslim community be restored to its original form. It is necessary to revive that Muslim community which is buried under the debris of the man-made traditions of several generations, and which is crushed under the weight of those false laws and customs which are not even remotely related to the Islamic teachings, and which, in spite of all this, calls itself the "world of Islam."[12]

This typology will become much more prominent as, in the remaining chapters, we turn our attention to developments in the second half of the twentieth century.

11. Sayyid Qutb, *Milestones* (New Delhi: Naushaba Publications, 1995), 7–8.
12. Ibid., 9.

8

THE
MISSIONARIES

From its beginnings to the present a significant part of the history of Islam has been concerned with the interaction of successive Muslim and Christian empires.[1] But there has also been a subset of that history, the accounts of interaction between Muslims and Christians engaged in their respective missionary tasks.

According to United Nations statistics, in 1997 there were approximately 1.15 billion Muslims worldwide and 1.93 billion professing Christians, between them making up more than half of the world's population.[2] Christians engage in mission, in some sense responding to the so-called Great Commission given to the apostles by Jesus: "Go . . . and make disciples of all nations" (Matt. 28:19 NIV).[3] Muslims have the duty of *da'wa*, calling, summoning people to submit to Allah and to follow the sunna, the pathway trodden first by Muhammad.[4]

Although in the past Islam has developed few sustained initiatives

1. But that might be seen as overlooking the important element supplied by the history of the interaction of Muslims and Jews. For a detailed study of this history, see Ye'or, *Dhimmi: Jews and Christians under Islam*.

2. *World Population Prospects* (New York: United Nations, 1997). David Barrett, in his annual survey of the "Status of Global Mission," *International Bulletin of Missionary Research* (January 2000): 25, reports a total of 2.00 billion Christians ("of all kinds") and 1.19 billion Muslims.

3. Paul makes no reference to this Great Commission but in 1 Corinthians 9:15–23 does briefly explain his own motive for mission. See Peter Cotterell, "Matthew's Great Commission," in *Mission and Meaninglessness* (London: SPCK, 1990), 95ff.; and Donald Senior and Carol Stuhlmueller, *The Biblical Foundations for Mission* (London: SCM, 1983), 251f.

4. There is a question as to whether Sura 3:104 is addressed to the entire umma (Muslim community) or to only a select part of it. See the discussion of this question in David Kerr, "Islamic Da'wa and Christian Mission: Towards a Comparative Analysis," *International Review of Mission* 79, issue 353 (April 2000): 150–71. It is interesting that Colonel Gadhafi of Libya is said to lend his support to a Muslim mission that he refers to as "The Islamic Call Society." Cf. Norman Daniel, *Islam and the West*, 2d ed. (Oxford: One World, 1993), 143.

comparable to the Christian missionary movements, the situation has dramatically changed: "Today, Islamic 'Call' societies represent a rapidly growing and diversified socioreligious movement consisting of many organizations aimed not simply at non-Muslims but at calling Muslims themselves to return to Islam, to more fully and self-consciously reappropriate their Islamic identity."[5] These Islamic societies may well be showing the traditional Christian missionary agencies more effective patterns of calling people to faith than those currently practiced by the church. The da'wa organizations reach out to every element of Muslim society, with a strong emphasis on youth, and with it the call to Muslim youth to practice its own da'wa without waiting for the benefit of supporting structures. Schools, youth clubs, family centers, and health-care centers all contribute to the Islamic call.

However, it is by no means clear that Muslim mission has been more effective than Christian mission. Bishop Stephen Neill writes:

> In recent years we have been told a great many times, in a number of reputable Christian publications, that Muslim missions have been much more successful in Africa than Christian missions, and that five times as many people are becoming Muslims in a year as are becoming Christians. This has been endlessly repeated. On what evidence, if any, is this discouraging statement based?
>
> Personal investigation, as far as I have been able to carry it out, lends no support to it whatever.[6]

However, the statistics produced by David Barrett and Todd Johnson[7] certainly indicate a more rapid growth in total numbers of Muslims worldwide than in numbers of Christians. The figures are in millions:

		World Population	Muslims	Christians
1900	Total	1,620	200	558
1970	Total	3,696	554	1,236
	% increase 70 yrs	128	177	122
2000	Total	6,055	1,188	2,000
	% increase 30 yrs	64	114	62
2025	Projected total	7,824	1,785	2,617
	% increase 25 yrs	29	50	31

5. Esposito, *Islam: The Straight Path*, 249.
6. Stephen Neill, *Salvation Tomorrow* (Nashville: Abingdon, 1976), 126.
7. David Barrett and Todd Johnson, "Annual Statistical Table on Global Mission: 2002," *International Bulletin of Missionary Research* 26.1 (January 2002).

Though there is evidence of a massive strengthening of Islamic commitment in the twenty-first century, there is only a generally slow movement of Christians becoming Muslims (and of Muslims becoming Christians). Back in 1938 at the Tambaran Missionary Conference, Dr. Paul Harrison recounted the histories of the five converts to Christianity his mission could claim after fifty years of witness in Arabia.[8] But elsewhere the picture has sometimes been strikingly different. Indonesia is probably the clearest example of large numbers of Muslims becoming Christians. Stephen Neill comments, "It has to be noted that, from the point of view of numbers, no missions to Muslims have ever equaled the success of the Dutch missions in Indonesia."[9] One of the most significant missionary figures in nineteenth-century Indonesia was Ludwig Nommensen, a German who started his work in 1861. By 1917 the Batak church was nearly two hundred thousand strong.[10] It is striking, when compared to other settings, that large numbers of Muslims have become Christians in Indonesia. Writing in the *World Christian Encyclopedia* in 1982, David Barrett asserted: "Protestants and Catholics received well over 2.5 million converts from nominal Islam since 1965. The largest numbers came from . . . Central Java, East Java, North Sumatra, Alor, Timor, Lampung, Sulawesi and the interiors of Kalimantan and West Irian."[11]

Less striking is what Latourette describes as a "slow leakage" to Islam from the Coptic Church in Egypt in the mid-1930s. He comments:

This seems to have been chiefly from the pressure of Moslems upon Christians to accept Islam as a condition of employment and from a desire for divorce, a step easy in Islam but impossible in the Coptic Church. Yet some of the apostate Copts, having obtained their divorces, returned to the church of their fathers, a step which the Egyptian government allowed more readily than it did conversions from hereditary Moslems. Moreover, Copts did some preaching to Moslems and each year had a few baptisms from the latter.[12]

8. Stephen Neill, *A History of Christian Missions*, 2d ed. (London: Penguin, 1986), 311.

9. Ibid., 294.

10. At the beginning of the twenty-first century the Batak church numbered more than a million, while the total Indonesia church numbered more than eight million.

11. David Barrett, *World Christian Encyclopedia* (Nairobi, Oxford, and New York: Oxford University Press, 1982), 382. For details relating to the Greja Kristen Jawi Wetan (GKJW) Church, see S. Wismoady Wahono, "Christian Mission in Asia: The Colonial Past and Challenges for Today," *International Review of Mission* 87, issue 345 (April 1998): 197–212.

12. K. S. Latourette, *A History of the Expansion of Christianity*, vol. 7, *Advance through Storm* (Grand Rapids: Zondervan, 1970), 257.

In general it seems that the closer any religion is to Christianity, the less likely it is that members of that religion will convert. Followers of the Traditional Religions (which have little in common with Christianity) have often forsaken them in large numbers in favor of Christianity, while converts from Islam and Judaism (both of which have close ties to Christianity) have generally been few.

But though many may see this as a somewhat discouraging view of Christian mission to the Muslim world, it is a view primarily based on a preoccupation with numbers of converts. In a more profound way Islam has been deeply affected by the Christian witness. Once again this is to be traced to those occasions where the Christian emphasis has been on the person of Jesus, rather than specifically on Trinitarian theology. The picture of Muhammad that emerges from the Qur'an, from the Traditions, and from the early biographies raises some troubling issues for Christians; it is quite different from the pictures painted by Muslim apologists writing for the Christian world: "At point after point the figure was subtly Christianised until the desert ruler of Arabia became much more like the Carpenter of Nazareth than earlier students would have supposed to be possible."[13] This has had inevitable consequences: positively, Muslims who are influenced by such reformist views of Muhammad have no need to address what some see as failures in the character of the prophet of Islam. But negatively, it has made difficult, if not impossible, the pursuit of genuine open scholarship in Islam on certain topics, including the issue of the sources of the Qur'an and the search for a truly balanced biography of Muhammad.

Although the church has tried to approach Islam through academic debate and rational argument, this does not appear to have been particularly convincing to Muslims, who already have an abundance of academic theology. The doctrine of the Trinity, certainly a major stumbling block to Muslims, is not a doctrine easily understood by faithful Christians, still less by cautious Muslims. In a careful study of the Armenian Church and its relationship through the centuries with its mainly Muslim overlords, Hagop Chakmakjian suggests:

> All approach to Islam should be made first through the living example and spirit of Jesus Christ, rather than the dogmas of the Trinity, infallible Scriptures, divinity of Christ, and the formal doctrine of the Incarnation. Islam does not need more intellectual creeds, of which it has the simplest and holds to it firmly.[14]

13. Neill, *History of Christian Missions*, 446.
14. Hagop Chakmakjian, *Armenian Christology and Evangelization of Islam* (Leiden: Brill, 1965), 84.

DAR AL-ISLAM AND DAR AL-HARB

It is regrettably the case that both Christianity and Islam have resorted to violence and coercion in spreading their respective faiths whenever they have had the political clout to do so. Sayyid Qutb, the radical Muslim writer and political activist encountered previously, outlined Islam's progress toward violence in four stages:

> For thirteen years after the beginning of his messengership, [Muhammad] called people to Allah through preaching without fighting or *jizyah* and was commanded to restrain himself and to practice patience and forbearance. Then he was commanded to migrate, and later permission was given to fight. Then he was commanded to fight those who fought him, and to restrain himself from those who did not make war against him. Later he was commanded to fight the polytheists until Allah's din was fully established. After the command for jihad came, the nonbelievers were divided into three categories: those with whom the Muslims had peace treaties; the people with whom the Muslims were at war; and the *dhimmies*.[15]

There is little reason to doubt Qutb's analysis. It goes some way toward explaining the existence, over the centuries since Muhammad, of a pathway of violence determined in part by the classical Muslim division of the world into two components, the *dar al-Islam* and the *dar al-harb:*

> Jihad divides the people of the world into two irreconcilable groups: the Muslims—inhabitants of the dar al-Islam regions subject to Islamic law; and infidels—inhabitants of the dar al-harb (*harbis*), the territory of war, destined to come under Islamic jurisdiction, either by the conversion of its inhabitants [through da'wa] or by armed conflict [through jihad in its non-Sufi, militaristic sense].[16]

For Christianity there appears to be no parallel rationalization of the relationship between Christians and non-Christians, nor any *formal* justification proposed for violence under the aegis of the church, although it is interesting that the violence of the Crusades was *informally* excused by asserting that it was "to slay for God's love."[17] By the fourteenth century, to the shame of Christianity, "the position of Muslims in Christendom approximated temporarily to that of Christians in Islam, except that the ultimate goal was their conversion."[18]

15. Qutb, *Milestones* (1985), 43.
16. Ye'or, *Islam and Dhimmitude*, 43.
17. Daniel, *Islam and the West*, 136.
18. Ibid., 138.

THE CHURCH THROUGH TWO MILLENNIA

In his seven-volume *History of the Expansion of Christianity,* Kenneth Scott Latourette divided the Christian era into four periods. The first of these, which he labeled "The First Five Centuries," presented the extraordinary spectacle of the apparently insignificant and powerless church reaching out with its Good News into the Roman Empire and beyond.

By the end of the second century, Christianity had reached Britain to the west, and the third-century *Acts of Thomas* makes it clear that somehow the church had also reached India in the east. By the middle of the fourth century a Christian church was established in the Axumite kingdom of Ethiopia.

The church then moved into Latourette's second period, "The Thousand Years of Uncertainty." These were painful years (in some ways illustrating the situation of the church in Europe in the twenty-first century). The church exhausted itself in playing two disastrous games, politics and philosophy. Politically the church occupied itself with developing a hierarchical structure modeled on that of the empire. The philosophical game was baptized and relabeled "theology," but it was still philosophy. And out of these two concerns, politics and philosophy, new links were formed between church and state—links that had begun to be formed in the days of Constantine.

The Roman Empire was, of course, preoccupied with the problem of assuring the military security of the state, thus effectively leaving to the church the whole field of social action. So well did the church rise to its new responsibilities that early in the second millennium the previous dependence of the church on the state was reversed, and in good measure the church was able to impose its will on the state. In Pope Gregory VII and his *Dictatus Papae* (The Dictates [Assertions] of the Pope), 1075, we find not only the ultimate expression of papal authority over the church, but also the clearest possible claim to ultimate sovereignty over the state.[19] Among these assertions is one stipulating that only the Pope has the authority to use the *imperial* symbols, so drawing into one person both ecclesiastical and secular authorities.

The thousand years of preoccupation with politics and philosophy left the essential church neglected. Right at the beginning of the thousand years we have the rise of Islam and the shattering collapse of the

19. See Geoffrey Barraclough, *The Medieval Papacy* (London: Thames and Hudson, 1968), 85–89, for a facsimile of the original twenty-seven notes of the *Dictatus*. In more detail, see W. Ullmann, *The Growth of Papal Government in the Middle Ages* (London: Methuen, 1965). Chapter 9 is devoted to an examination of Gregory's contribution to papal government.

North African churches. This event should surely have attracted the full attention of church leaders everywhere. But politics and philosophy won out. By the end of the thousand years the situation was critical:

> The faith seemed threatened with internal disintegration. In Italy the Renaissance had brought a dry rot of scepticism. Even the Popes appeared in morals and aspirations more pagan than Christian. Criticism of the Church and of the clergy was rife. Most of the thirteenth and fourteenth century movements which had given such evidence of vitality had lost their first enthusiasm, had died out, or had been crushed by persecution.[20]

The third period, the "Three Centuries of Advance," takes Latourette forward to 1800. The period is neatly signposted at each end, at the beginning by Luther's tower experience, in which he rediscovered the principle of justification by faith,[21] and at the end by William Carey's *Enquiry into the Obligation of Christians to Use Means for the Conversion of the Heathen*, 1792. Luther recovered the doctrine of justification by faith, and Carey rescued it from the hyper-Calvinism that immobilized it. Indeed, Carey had to contend with the hyper-Calvinism then rampant in his Baptist denomination. When Carey presented mission as a matter for discussion at the Ministers' Fraternal in Northampton, no less a figure than Dr. John Ryland opposed him: "Young man, sit down, sit down. You're an enthusiast. When God pleases to convert the heathen, He'll do it without consulting you or me."[22]

So we arrive at Latourette's fourth period of mission history, "The Great Century" that marks out the era of classical Christian mission, studded with names such as Carey of India, Livingstone and C. T. Studd of Africa, Hudson Taylor and Jonathan Goforth of China, and the unsung officer of the British Royal Navy, Allen Francis Gardiner, founder of the South American Missionary Society, who died of starvation and exposure on the coast of Tierra del Fuego. The Great Century is marked by the creation of a sequence of missionary societies and an apparently inexhaustible stream of missionaries who were undeterred by the knowledge that the expectation of life for the newly arrived missionaries in some parts of Africa could be measured in weeks. It was a century of great contrasts in mission. Missionaries labored many hours daily learning new languages and reducing them to writing, translating the Bible, establishing schools, building clinics

20. Latourette, *History of the Expansion of Christianity*, 2:448.

21. James Atkinson (*The Great Light* [Exeter: Paternoster, 1968], 19) places the *Turmerlebnis* (tower) experience in the summer of 1513.

22. A. H. Oussoren, *William Carey* (Leiden: Suthoff, 1945), 29.

and hospitals, and fighting malaria and a dozen other diseases then scarcely known to Western medicine. On the other hand, missionaries were also waited on by their "boys," indulged their inherited sense of superiority, and practiced the consequent paternalism.

To these four periods Ralph Winter added "The 25 Unbelievable Years," 1945–69. On every continent the church was born and proved to be no sickly child. Between 1956 and 1968 the worldwide Protestant community almost doubled in size, from 162 million to 316 million. By the end of the second millennium there were more than a billion Roman Catholics, nearly a quarter of a billion in the Orthodox churches, and almost a billion Protestants, together constituting some 34 percent of the world's population.

THE MODERN MISSIONARY MOVEMENT

The earliest *Protestant* missionary society was the Danish-Halle Mission, which King Frederick IV of Denmark established to take Christianity to Tranquebar in India. He could find no Danish volunteers for the mission, so the first missionaries were Germans who arrived in India in 1706, more than eighty years ahead of William Carey's *Enquiry into the Obligation of Christians to Use Means for the Conversion of the Heathen,*[23] often taken as the starting point for the modern missionary movement. But long before either event stands the mission initiated by Francis of Assisi, who is often dismissed as the man who talked to the birds. In 1209 Francis persuaded Pope Innocent III to recognize what came to be known as the Franciscan Order. Ten years later Francis went to Egypt, where the "Christian" Fifth Crusaders faced a Muslim army. He was able to obtain an audience with the Muslim sultan. There is a widespread opinion that in going to Egypt and in going to his meeting with the sultan alone and unarmed, what Francis really hoped for was martyrdom.[24] Exactly what happened at the meeting we do not know; Christian writers have steadily embellished such facts as they had, even to the extent of asserting that the Sultan al-Malik al-Kamil became a secret convert to Christianity.[25]

Just as it was becoming apparent that the Crusades had failed to persuade Muslims to become Christians, a new figure appeared on the

23. Reissued by the Baptist Missionary Society (Didcot, Oxfordshire, U.K., 1991), to mark the two-hundredth anniversary of its first publication.

24. See Christine A. Mallouhi, *Waging Peace on Islam* (London: Monarch, 2000), 278: "There seems no doubt that he looked for martyrdom."

25. See ibid., 278–87, for a generally optimistic view of the outcome of the meeting between the missionary and Kamil.

scene, the mystic Ramon Lull (Llull).[26] He was born in 1232 on the island of Majorca, which had only recently been taken back from Muslim rule. Lull was raised in luxury and indulged in vices that wealth made possible. But when he became a Christian, he turned to mysticism and found himself fascinated by the Muslim Sufis. This in turn led him on to a desire to be a missionary to Muslims. He set up a training school for would-be missionaries to Islam, and gradually a series of principles of mission to Muslims began to emerge.

First, he saw language as a key to communication, so he learned Arabic and had Arabic taught in his training school. Second, although he did not entirely reject crusade as a tool of evangelism, he stressed rather the approach of philosophy and logic; his philosophical system included the "art of finding truth," a method of logic that was supposed to lead to the establishment of truth in any academic field. Third, he wanted the church to be reformed, replacing its luxury and ceremonies with a missionary vision, and especially a vision for the Muslim world. And fourth, he proposed that the church should set aside a tenth of its income to promote mission.[27]

Lull was more than a mystic and educator: he traveled widely, trying to persuade the church of the priority of mission to Muslims, and he made several journeys to North Africa to debate Christianity with Muslim academics. Even age failed to deter him; at eighty he was back in North Africa, where—possibly at Tunis—he was stoned with such severity that he died on board the ship taking him back to Majorca. Sixty years after his death his teaching was condemned by Pope Gregory XI, but with the passing years his work became better appreciated. Eventually he was beatified and his cultus approved by Pope Pius IX, though he was never canonized.

The modern missionary movement, not infrequently dated from William Carey's appeal, has attracted much criticism, often ill informed, arising from the fact that the movement ran parallel to the period of European imperialism. It was supposed that the missionaries were simply an arm of colonialism. It is probably still too early to give a genuinely balanced assessment of the period, but the Islamics scholar W. Montgomery Watt expressed his opinion in 1991:

> Most Muslims resented conversions to Christianity, and some accused the missionary movement of being an arm of colonialism. This charge is at most only partially true. It probably applies to the Portuguese missions in the centuries immediately after Vasco da Gama, and later to

26. See the biography of Ramon Lull by E. A. Peers, *Fool of Love* (London: SCM, 1946).

27. See Latourette, *History of the Expansion of Christianity*, 2:321–23.

Dutch missions in Indonesia, and German and Belgian missions in Africa. On the other hand, British administrators in India and Malaysia were mostly somewhat lukewarm toward Christian missionaries, and in Northern Nigeria they seem to have favoured Islam. In the Muslim native states of India under the British, missionary work was not permitted. In some British colonies, however, the administrators were pleased to hand over educational and medical work to the missions. Thus in the British colonies as a whole, although there was co-operation in varying degree between the colonial administrators and the missionaries, the latter were far from being mere agents of the former. Moreover, important missionary work was also done by American, Scandinavian and Swiss missions who had no colonies to go to.[28]

The modern missionary movement may be considered to have begun with William Carey in 1792, but arguably the greatest missionary to Islam was Bishop Thomas Valpy French,[29] who went to India with the Church Missionary Society in 1850. He saw the value of adapting to local Muslim life and culture, grew a beard, and dressed as did the Muslims. He worked hard at languages so that later he was able to establish schools where students could study in their own languages rather than in English. His emphasis on language is ingenuously revealed in a letter to a would-be missionary:

> You must, of course, commence with Urdu or Hindustani, so as to be able to talk to your servants, to help in the services of the church and in the schools. You had better give some six or eight hours a day to that, and also spend two or three hours at Punjabi, to be able to talk with the villagers. You should also try to give two or three hours to the study of Persian, which you will find invaluable in the schools, and all your spare time to the study of Arabic, so as to be able to read the Qur'an.[30]

Although India wore out French's body, it failed to quench his eager spirit. In 1890, at the age of sixty-five, he took on a task that younger men refused: evangelism in the Arabian peninsula. In addition to his Hindustani he had studied Pushtu for his time in Afghanistan, and Arabic for his discussions with Muslims. It is reported that in Jiddah, the Red Sea port for Mecca, he would sit in a coffeehouse and read the Scriptures aloud in Arabic. But the climate of Muscat proved to

28. W. Montgomery Watt, *Muslim-Christian Encounters* (London and New York: Routledge, 1991), 104.

29. See M. C. Griffiths, "Thomas Valpy French," in *Mission and Meaning*, ed. A. Billington and A. Lane (Exeter: Paternoster, 1995).

30. H. Birks, *Life and Correspondence of T. V. French* (London: John Murray, 1895), 1:47, quoted in Griffiths, "Thomas Valpy French," 185.

be too much for him, and he died after being there for less than six months.

The twentieth century was punctuated by two world wars. One incident between those wars perhaps most visibly illustrates the vast difference between that world and the world today. Winston Churchill was then at the British Colonial Office:

> In the spring of 1921 I was sent to the Colonial Office, to take over our business in the Middle East and bring matters into some kind of order. At that time we had recently suppressed a most dangerous and bloody rebellion in Iraq, and upward of forty thousand troops . . . were required to keep order. In Palestine the strife between the Arabs and the Jews threatened at any moment to take the form of actual violence. The Arab chieftains, driven out of Syria, . . . lurked furious in the deserts beyond the Jordan. . . . I therefore convened a conference at Cairo to which practically all the experts and authorities of the Middle East were summoned. Accompanied by Lawrence (of Arabia), Hubert Young and Trenchard from the Air Ministry, I set out for Cairo. . . . We submitted the following main proposals to the Cabinet. First we would repair the injury done to the Arabs and to the House of the Sherifs of Mecca by placing the Emir Feisal upon the throne of Iraq as King, and by entrusting the Emir Abdulla with the government of Trans-Jordania. Secondly we would remove practically all our troops from Iraq. . . . All our measures were implemented, one by one.[31]

It is difficult to realize that a handful of Western politicians could, so recently and in so sensitive an area, and without any particular reference to the peoples of the area, define territories and appoint their rulers.

Today we see a vastly different world. Quantitatively we may speak of a world of more independent nations, with more widespread education, a rising Gross International Product, and a steadily increasing average life expectation. But qualitatively it is a new world, with the old empires swept away and new empires emerging. The power of the new world lies less in individual nations than in conglomerates: the North Atlantic world of North America and the European Union, China and her satellites, and, of course, the Muslim world, where the pattern of mission has been influenced by the rise of missionary movements in the churches of the developing world. In 1977 the first Nigerian missionaries of the Evangelical Missionary Society, the missions arm of the Evangelical Churches of West Africa, arrived in the Sudan, and soon the mission reported that they had deployed 127 full-time missionary families there.

31. Winston Churchill, *Great Contemporaries* (London: Fontana, 1937), 131.

Christian mission to the Muslim world is always faced with the problem of Islam's concept of *ridda*, apostasy. Sura 3:77 places the apostate outside the Muslim community: "As for those who sell the faith they owe to Allah and their own plighted word for a small price, they shall have no portion in the hereafter: nor will Allah speak to them or look at them on the Day of Judgment, nor will he cleanse them: they shall have a grievous penalty." But while the penalty to be paid in the hereafter is made clear, the Qur'an does not stipulate the penalty to be imposed by the Muslim community. However, the Law Schools of Islam all agree that the punishment for apostasy is death.[32]

The Universal Declaration of Human Rights was unanimously adopted by the General Assembly of the United Nations in December 1948. The Declaration includes freedom of conscience and religion, a freedom not merely denied by the Muslim world (although not necessarily by Muslim states) but carrying a death threat if such freedom should be exercised. It is relevant that in the Islamic Universal Declaration, promulgated by the Islamic Council of Europe in 1980, there is no reference to freedom of religion, and section IV even states: "The Shari'a is the supreme law of the Muslim community and must be enforced in its entirety in all aspects of life. Each and every Muslim country must explicitly make Shari'a the criterion by which to judge the public and private conduct of all, rulers and ruled alike."[33]

Under the threat of death it is little wonder that, whatever they might think or wish, Muslims confronted with Christianity hesitate to take the step of a deeper and more profound commitment to Jesus, who is, after all, already an honored prophet of Islam. But there is another side to this denial of the right to freedom of religion. The history of Islam under the Umayyads, Abbasids, Fatimids, and Mamluks is replete with examples of forced conversions to Islam.[34] Not only are Muslims denied the right to a free choice of religion, but conversely, where the appropriate political conditions obtain, other religionists have been required to surrender their freedom to choose.

32. Doi, *Shari'ah*, 266–67.

33. See Salem Azzam, ed., *Islam and Contemporary Society* (London: Longmans, 1982). In 1981, the same council issued a further statement, now called the Universal Islamic Declaration of Human Rights. Section XIII, "Right to Freedom of Religion," states only that "every person has the right to freedom of conscience and worship in accordance with his religious beliefs." The Declaration does not address the issue of a person's right to *change* his or her religion. Available on the World Wide Web: http://www.alhewar.com/ISLAMDECL.html.

34. Ye'or, *Islam and Dhimmitude*, 87–88. In a footnote, Bat Ye'or provides an impressive list of authorities detailing forced conversions of both Christians and Jews to Islam.

9

CONFLICT
IN THE MIDDLE EAST

No assessment of the contemporary arena of Christian-Muslim interaction would be complete without discussing various conflicts that have taken place in the Middle East during the second half of the twentieth century. Most, though not all, of these surround the existence of the State of Israel. At the same time, no consideration of the State of Israel would be complete without taking into account significant factors from past history.

THE ESTABLISHMENT OF MODERN ISRAEL

The Jewish Diaspora was dispersed throughout Europe and the Middle East over the period surveyed in previous chapters. Jewish communities had experienced discrimination and persecution for almost two thousand years since being largely driven out of Palestine by the Romans after A.D. 70. The worst persecution had occurred in Christian Europe. Jewish communities had been expelled successively from European locations, with France (1182, 1306, and 1394) and England (1290) pioneering this practice, followed by Hungary (1349), Austria (1421), Spain (1492), Portugal (1496), Bohemia and Moravia (1744).[1]

The following contemporary account by the Christian monk Rigord describes the first expulsion from France:

> In the year of our Lord's Incarnation 1182, in the month of April, which is called by the Jews Nisan, an edict went forth from the most serene king, Philip Augustus, that all the Jews of his kingdom should be prepared to go forth by the coming feast of St. John the Baptist.[2] And then the King gave them leave to sell each his movable goods before the time

1. S. Apisdorf, "Anti-Semitism—Every Generation." Available on the World Wide Web: http://www.aish.com/holidays/passover/articles/antisemitism_every_generation.asp.
2. June 24.

fixed. . . . But their real estate, that is, houses, fields, vineyards, barns, winepresses, and such like, he reserved for himself and his successors, the kings of the French.[3]

The expulsion of Jews from England in 1290 under King Edward I followed a similar pattern:

On July 18, 1290, the king issued a decree to expel all the Jews from England. The emigrants were told to liquidate their affairs by November 1. . . . They were permitted to take along their belongings, or to sell them; their dwellings and synagogues became the property of the royal treasury; only a few were granted permission to sell their houses. Those who remained in England beyond the specified day were to be executed.[4]

The greatest calamity to befall European Jewry in the Middle Ages was the great expulsion of around 250,000 Jews from Spain as a result of King Ferdinand's edict of March 31, 1492:

We have decided to order all Jewish men and women to leave our kingdom, with the understanding that they will never return. . . . If they shall fail to comply with this order, and if they are to be found in our principalities, they shall be condemned to death, and their assets confiscated without any trial. We command that from the end of July, no citizen in our kingdom is to dare to keep openly or secretly a Jewish man or Jewish woman.[5]

As we saw in earlier discussion, there were also periods of persecution by various rulers of the Muslim empires though, on balance, Jews fared much better under Muslims than under Christianity. The portrayal of Jews in both Christian and Muslim sacred Scriptures created the potential for negative stereotyping, and discrimination and persecution typically resulted during periods of social upheaval or political chaos.

A Jewish community had always remained in Palestine after the Roman destruction of Jerusalem in A.D. 70. Its numbers ebbed and flowed, according to differing policies of the occupying powers and conditions of life.

3. This account was recorded in the *Gesta Philippi Augusti*, a contemporary Latin history by the monk Rigord, who first began this chronicle about 1186. Cf. Jacob Marcus, *The Jew in the Medieval World: A Sourcebook, 315–1791* (New York: JPS, 1938), 24–25.

4. Dubnov, *History of the Jews*, 3:69.

5. Ibid., 3:335.

The emergence of Zionism in the late nineteenth century coincided with the rise of nationalist sentiment in colonized countries. The term *Zionism* assumed negative connotations in the late twentieth century, yet it is historically no more than a sentiment of nationalism among Jews, and it parallels the same phenomenon among other communities that were seeking to take charge of their own destinies around 1900.

This Jewish desire for a national home was stimulated by massacres and pogroms in Eastern Europe during the same period and by ongoing widespread discrimination elsewhere. Theodor Herzl, a Jewish writer from Budapest and father of the Zionist movement, was witness to one of the most famous cases of anti-Jewish discrimination in the nineteenth century. He attended the infamous court-martial of the French Jewish soldier Alfred Dreyfus in 1894. This prompted him to develop his concept of a Jewish state, which he expressed in 1896:

> We have honestly endeavoured everywhere to merge ourselves in the social life of surrounding communities and to preserve the faith of our fathers. We are not permitted to do so. . . . In countries where we have lived for centuries we are still cried down as strangers. . . . It is useless, therefore, for us to be loyal patriots. . . . If only we could be left in peace. But I think we shall not be left in peace.[6]

After the declaration by Lord Balfour of the British government in 1917, the Zionist movement picked up momentum considerably. This declaration included the following crucial words:

> His Majesty's Government view with favour the establishment in Palestine of a national home for the Jewish people, . . . it being clearly understood that nothing shall be done which may prejudice the civil and religious rights of existing non-Jewish communities in Palestine, or the rights and political status enjoyed by Jews in any other country.[7]

In effect, this declaration made a series of promises that were difficult to reconcile with each other. It gave hope to the Jews for the creation of a Jewish national home in Palestine. It also tried to reassure both the resident Palestinian population as well as Jewish populations elsewhere that they would not suffer as a result. Subsequent history has shown the inherent tensions built into these promises.

6. Theodor Herzl, "The Jewish State," in *The Israel-Arab Reader,* ed. Walter Laqueur, 2d ed. (New York: Bantam, 1969), 6–7.
7. "The Balfour Declaration," in *Israel-Arab Reader,* ed. Laqueur, 17–18.

After the defeat of the Ottoman Empire in the First World War, the British were given responsibility for administering Palestine under a mandate from the newly formed League of Nations. The 1920s and 1930s brought large-scale Jewish migration from Europe to Palestine, both legal and clandestine. It increased after tight restrictions on immigration to the United States were imposed in 1924, following large-scale immigration of Jews in previous decades. It further surged after Adolf Hitler assumed power in Germany in 1933, and persecution of Jews increased. The growth in the Jewish community in Palestine is clearly reflected in population statistics: in 1921 Jews represented 11 percent of the population of Palestine, but by 1939 the Jewish proportion had risen to 29 percent.[8]

The Arab revolt of 1936–39 represented a response to Jewish immigration. A number of Jews were massacred by local Palestinian Arabs. The British army restored order, but by now British concern with deteriorating communal relations prompted them to make important policy decisions. In May 1939, the British government White Paper restricted Jewish immigration to 75,000 over the next five years, with the intention that it should cease after that.

However, international events took over. The Nazi Holocaust left an indelible mark upon European consciousness. When Allied armies came upon the death camps and found evidence of the Nazi murder of six million Jews, in one fell swoop the long European history of anti-Semitism became unrespectable and unacceptable.

The newly created United Nations looked for a permanent solution to the vulnerability of the Jews in Diaspora. In UN Resolution 181 of November 29, 1947, member nations voted to partition Palestine into two states, Jewish and Arab, with Jerusalem to be under international administration: "Independent Arab and Jewish States and the Special International Regime for the City of Jerusalem . . . shall come into existence in Palestine two months after the evacuation of the armed forces of the mandatory Power has been completed but in any case not later than 1 October 1948."[9]

History has also shown that this was arguably the best possible solution, given that the Israelis and Palestinians struggled unsuccessfully to reach an agreement somewhat resembling this early partition during the 1990s. It failed in 1947 because it was ahead of its time.

8. Randolph S. Churchill and Winston S. Churchill, *The Six Day War* (London: Heinemann, 1967), 12.

9. "United Nations General Assembly Resolution 181, November 29, 1947." Available on the World Wide Web: http://www.yale.edu/lawweb/avalon/un/res181.htm.

The Jewish community in Palestine accepted the UN decision, whereas the Arabs rejected it, arguing that they were being dispossessed of land to which they were entitled in full measure. Sporadic fighting between the two communities followed. The UN Security Council appealed for an end to the fighting:

> The Security Council . . . appeals to all Governments and peoples, particularly in and around Palestine, to take all possible action to prevent or reduce such disorders as are now occurring in Palestine.[10]

The State of Israel was declared on May 14, 1948, coinciding with the British relinquishing their mandate for Palestine. Several Arab armies immediately invaded the Jewish state but lost the war.

Muslims typically regard the resulting State of Israel as a European colonial implant along the lines of, first, the Crusader principalities that were established after 1099, and second, the European colonies of the nineteenth century in the Muslim world.

Another factor influencing Muslim attitudes was that during the long centuries of Muslim empires in the region, Jews had been regarded as dhimmis, second-class citizens acknowledging Islamic sovereignty. Although Muslim tolerance was relatively enlightened for its time, this relationship had set a pattern for the future. Furthermore, it accorded with Qur'anic injunctions on Muslim-Jewish relations. So the idea of a Jewish state being established in former Muslim lands, especially where sacred sites were located, was considered a blasphemy by vast numbers of Muslims. This attitude continues to plague attempts at reconciliation by Jews and Arabs today.

Thus bitterness and mutual suspicion have resulted in endemic hostility between Israel and its Arab neighbors since Israeli independence. This has led to a series of conflicts, roughly one each decade.

THE ARAB-ISRAELI CONFLICT

The 1948 War

At the outset of the war, Israel faced the armies of Egypt, Transjordan, Syria, Iraq, and Lebanon. The Jews were heavily outnumbered but, unlike their Arab adversaries, they were united. And also unlike the Arabs, Israel had to win to survive, which served as a significant motivating factor.

---

10. "United Nations Security Council Resolution 42, March 5, 1948." Available on the World Wide Web: http://www.yale.edu/lawweb/avalon/un/scres042.htm.

The only Arab army that was successful against Jewish forces was the British-trained Arab Legion. It captured the Jewish quarter of Jerusalem and defeated Jewish forces at Latrun. Elsewhere Jewish forces were victorious. By the time of the ceasefire in January 1949, the Jewish victory had extended the boundaries of the UN-defined Jewish state to three-quarters of Palestine. The remainder was taken over by Egypt and Transjordan.

The creation of Israel and the ensuing war resulted in massive population movements. Palestinian refugees fled, or were driven out, to refugee camps that were still operating in neighboring Arab countries fifty years later. These camps served as a festering sore, perpetuating the Palestinian refugees' hatred toward the new Jewish state.

The other significant population movement that receives less attention was that of the Jewish minorities in Arab domains. Hundreds of thousands migrated to Israel, often after being expelled from their ancestral homes in Cairo, Baghdad, and other locations, typically with only a few days' notice.

These population movements paralleled the case of the partition of India into independent India and Pakistan around the same time. Also parallel is the way the Muslim émigrés from India, the *mohajirs*, were left on the margins of Pakistani society, as occurred with the Palestinian refugees in neighboring Arab lands.

One cannot overestimate the instability resulting from the 1948 war. In the words of Patrick Seale: "For the Arabs, defeat in Palestine was a harsh lesson in power politics. . . . The brief, catastrophic war resulted in more bitterness than decades of semi-colonial occupation."[11] An intractable conflict was thus set on track, and the region has not yet emerged from its bitter legacy.

The 1956 and 1967 Wars

Within less than a decade, another war erupted between Israel and its Arab neighbors, triggered by the decision of President Nasser of Egypt to nationalize the Suez Canal. In partnership with Britain and France, Israel invaded and occupied the Sinai. The Israelis saw the Sinai as a buffer against the frequent attacks that Egyptian *fedayeen* fighters had made against Israeli communities across the border since 1949.

Israel was forced to withdraw from the Sinai under pressure from the United States and Russia. Thus Israel lost points in the public relations arena, but they made several significant gains. First, UN troops were sent to guard the Egyptian-Israeli border. This was important for

11. Patrick Seale, *The Struggle for Syria* (London: Oxford University Press, 1965), 3.

Israel because it hindered the free movement of fedayeen attacks. Furthermore, Egyptian President Nasser was forced to allow Israeli shipping to use the Gulf of Aqaba to access the Israeli port of Eilat.

These measures proved to be merely stopgap. In 1960 President Nasser clearly declared Egyptian intentions: "When we have brought our armed forces to full strength and made our own armaments, we will take another step forward towards the liberation of Palestine, and when we have manufactured jet aircraft and tanks, we will embark upon the final stage of this liberation."[12] Meanwhile, the Arab Summit Conference of 1963 agreed to form the Palestine Liberation Organization (PLO). This body consisted of diverse and multiple factions. A draft constitution was drawn up, with Palestinian exile Ahmed Shukairy designated to carry the planning forward.

Tensions on the Israeli-Syrian border were constant, without any UN forces to keep the sides apart, though observers from the United Nations Truce Supervision Organization (UNTSO) were present on the border. Frequent Syrian artillery shelling of Israeli communities in Galilee near the border attracted heavy Israeli air strikes in response. Between 1957 and 1962 Israelis reported to the UN on 422 fedayeen raids on Israeli territory and Syrian breaches of the truce.[13] Fedayeen attacks across the Israeli-Jordanian border also attracted heavy Israeli reprisals.

In November 1966, Egypt and Syria signed a Defense Alliance. In May 1967, in response to apparently contrived Russian reports (discounted by UNTSO observers)[14] that Israel had sent large numbers of troops to the Syrian border, Egypt massed a hundred thousand troops in the Sinai. At the same time they closed the entry to the Gulf of Aqaba to Israeli shipping and ordered UN forces to leave their bases on the Egyptian-Israeli border in the Sinai. At this time Nasser publicly declared:

> Recently, we felt we are strong enough, that if we were to enter a battle with Israel, with God's help, we could triumph. On this basis we decided to take actual steps.[15]

On May 30, King Hussein of Jordan traveled to Egypt to sign a defense agreement. Israeli politician Shimon Peres considered this a

12. "Speech by President Gamal Abdel Nasser at a Mass Rally of the Youth Organisations in Damascus (October 18, 1960)," in *Israel-Arab Reader*, ed. Laqueur, 139.

13. Churchill and Churchill, *Six Day War*, 21.

14. Ibid., 28.

15. "Nasser's Speech to Arab Trade Unionists (May 26, 1967)," in *Israel-Arab Reader*, ed. Laqueur, 175.

crucial development, saying, "Nasser and Hussein at Cairo airport. This was an historic and crucial kiss. . . . We were now surrounded by a sort of banana filled with Russian weapons."[16]

To avoid being caught unawares, Israel launched attacks on June 5, 1967. The primary targets were Egypt and Syria, but Jordan also entered the fray. Israeli military forces, with equipment from Western states, won sweeping victories over the Arab forces, equipped with Soviet hardware. The Arab forces were defeated within a week. Sinai, the West Bank, and the Golan Heights were captured from Egypt, Jordan, and Syria respectively. Israel had thus gained all the Palestinian land that had originally been divided between Jews and Palestinians by the UN in 1947.

The sense of Arab humiliation was profound. Nasser resigned, though under pressure he withdrew his resignation. But this defeat meant the end of his Arab nationalist ideology. The focus would move gradually toward more Islamist groups, who declared that God had allowed the Arabs to be defeated because they had drifted away from true Islam; only by returning to Islam could Arab pride be restored and Palestine recovered.

Thus the intractable conflict was made even more intractable, but it was assuming an increasingly Islamist hue. The Arab Islamic world was approaching another crucial set of crossroads.

Subsequent Tensions and Conflicts

Following the 1967 war, the UN Security Council issued Resolution 242, of November 22, 1967, which called for

> a just and lasting peace in the Middle East which should include the application of both the following principles: Withdrawal of Israeli armed forces from territories occupied in the recent conflict. Termination of all claims or states of belligerency and respect for and acknowledgement of the sovereignty, territorial integrity and political independence of every State in the area and their right to live in peace within secure and recognized boundaries free from threats or acts of force.[17]

This resolution has been reaffirmed by subsequent UN pronouncements. These calls were initially rebuffed by Arab leaders such as Yasir Arafat, who expressed the spirit of continuing rejectionism in 1969:

16. Churchill and Churchill, *Six Day War*, 60.
17. "United Nations Security Council Resolution 242, November 22, 1967." Available on the World Wide Web: http://www.yale.edu/lawweb/avalon/un/un242.htm.

The United Nations and the Big Powers have chosen to call their solutions "peaceful," whereas, in fact they are political solutions which are in no way related to peace as they all aim at safeguarding the state of Israel and ignoring the Palestinian Revolution. As such we declare that we will not under any circumstances accept any so-called peaceful solution which is being concocted by either the "Big" States or the "Small" States. We regard any such settlement as a document of self-humiliation which our people are forcibly asked to accept. I believe that if our generation is unable to liberate its homeland, it should not commit the crime of accepting a fait accompli, which will prevent the future generations from carrying on the struggle for liberation.[18]

In a key development, the Palestinian National Covenant was finalized in 1968.[19] It set in cement Palestinian policy vis-à-vis the Jewish state for the next two decades. The ninth article of this covenant called for armed struggle, and the nineteenth article denounced the original UN partition plan:

The partition of Palestine in 1947 and the establishment of the state of Israel are entirely illegal, regardless of the passage of time, because they were contrary to the will of the Palestinian people and to their natural right in their homeland, and inconsistent with the principles embodied in the Charter of the United Nations; particularly the right to self-determination.

The 1970s and 1980s would be characterized by conflict. Various PLO factions implemented the policy of the Palestinian National Covenant, using civilian airline hijackings as one of their favorite tactics. In 1972, ten Israeli athletes were kidnapped and murdered by Palestinian fedayeen at the Munich Olympics. Israeli forces launched reprisal raids across borders in response to infiltration from neighboring Arab lands. King Hussein of Jordan, increasingly concerned at Palestinian attacks on Israel from Jordan and Israeli reprisals, drove the PLO from his country in a bloody campaign in September 1970.

In October 1973 Egypt and Syria launched massive and synchronized attacks on Israeli fortifications in the occupied Sinai and Golan Heights. The new President of Egypt, Anwar Sadat, hoped to gain a crucial bargaining ploy for future diplomatic attempts to regain the Sinai from Israel. The initial military successes were in favor of the Arab states, but the situation was reversed as Israel mobilized. The Is-

18. Yasir Arafat in an interview, "Free Palestine," August 1969, cited in *Israel-Arab Reader*, ed. Laqueur, 381.

19. "The Palestinian National Charter: Resolutions of the Palestine National Council July 1–17, 1968." Available on the World Wide Web: http://www.yale.edu/lawweb/avalon/mideast/plocov.htm.

raelis received a massive airlift of military supplies from the United States, while the Arabs received airlifts from the Soviet Union. The final battle lines at the time of the ceasefire did not favor the Arab states. However, they had gained considerable pride and kudos from their initial military successes.

Another key development at this time was the oil crisis. In the mid-1970s ten Arab oil-producing nations between them held 60 percent of the known oil reserves.[20] They used this to extract retribution on the West for its support of Israel. At the height of the 1973 war, these states increased the price of oil by 60 percent in one day and banned oil supplies to the United States. This introduced an important new factor in future relations between Middle Eastern nations and the West.

The 1980s were not long in progress before a new war in the region broke out. Israel launched an invasion of Lebanon in 1982. The PLO had based itself there after being expelled from Jordan in 1970. Regular PLO raids across the border into northern Israel followed. The 1982 invasion was designed to destroy the PLO once and for all. However, the PLO Chairman Yasir Arafat and his leadership escaped to Tunisia. Israel then occupied a buffer zone in Southern Lebanon, only eventually withdrawing in 2000.

SETTLEMENTS AND THE FIRST INTIFADA

Following the 1967 war, Israeli settlements were increasingly constructed in strategic locations in the occupied West Bank and Gaza. There was particularly heavy construction during the 1980s and 1990s, especially under governments led by the right-wing Likud party. From 1984 to 2002 the settler population in the occupied West Bank and Gaza increased from 30,000 to approximately 200,000.[21] Religious settler movements such as Gush Emunim, arguing for a biblical mandate for settlement throughout the biblical land of Israel, have strived to spur on the settlement process, seeing it as a bulwark against any future Israeli government relinquishing land to the Palestinian population. The presence and continuing growth of these communities has seriously complicated the situation and made almost impossible a complete Israeli withdrawal from the occupied areas as part of a peace settlement.

20. Robert W. Stokey, *America and the Arab States: An Uneasy Encounter* (New York: John Wiley and Sons, 1975), 259.

21. David Newman, "How the Settler Suburbs Grew," *New York Times*, May 21, 2002.

Until the late 1980s, wars between Israel and its Arab neighbors had been fought in a conventional mode between professional armies. However, the First Intifada (uprising; 1987–93) added a new dimension to Israeli-Palestinian conflict. It broke out in late 1987 and represented a crucial development by involving a shift of the heart of Palestinian opposition from Palestinian diaspora communities and Arab allies to the Palestinian populations under Israeli occupation in the West Bank and Gaza. The Palestinians engaged in civil disobedience and popular uprising, and Israel was unable to exert the same degree of dominance over this type of opposition as it had enjoyed in conventional warfare. This was an important factor in triggering the peace process of the 1990s.

The Israeli-Palestinian Peace Process (1991–2000)

The 1990s brought a new spirit of hope to this most intractable of conflicts, with the holding of a series of meetings and the signing of several Israeli-Arab Accords. First came the Madrid Conference (1991), followed by the Oslo Accords (1993), the Peace Treaty between Jordan and Israel (1994), and the Wye River Agreement (1998). The 1993 joint statement signed by Israelis and Palestinians included the following agreement:

> The Government of the State of Israel and the Palestinian team representing the Palestinian people agree that it is time to put an end to decades of confrontation and conflict, recognize their mutual legitimate and political rights, and strive to live in peaceful coexistence and mutual dignity and security to achieve a just, lasting and comprehensive peace settlement and historic reconciliation through the agreed political process.[22]

This led to the handover of major urban centers in the occupied West Bank and Gaza to the newly established Palestinian Authority. The handover was carried out in return for a Palestinian recognition of Israel's right to exist. However, this development left pending a final status agreement that would include a decision about Jerusalem.

The peace process lurched along but was beset by a range of problems. Not least was the fact that radical Islamist groups among the Palestinians—Hamas and Islamic Jihad—sought to undermine the peace process by terrorist actions against Israeli military and civilian targets, with particular focus on devastating suicide bombings. The Hamas Covenant embodies this spirit of rejectionism: "There is no so-

---

22. "Israel-Palestine Liberation Organization Agreement: 1993." Available on the World Wide Web: http://www.yale.edu/lawweb/avalon/mideast/isrplo.htm.

lution for the Palestinian question except through Jihad. Initiatives, proposals and international conferences are all a waste of time and vain endeavors. The Palestinian people know better than to consent to having their future, rights and fate toyed with."[23]

A spate of suicide bombings in the mid-1990s by Palestinian Islamist radicals produced heavy military and bureaucratic retaliation from the Israelis, and a resultant slowdown in the peace process. This further exacerbated tensions and mutual suspicion. Nevertheless, final status discussions between teams led by Israeli Prime Minister Ehud Barak of the Labor Party and Yasir Arafat were held at Camp David in the United States in July 2000 under President Clinton's patronage. Joel Beinin, professor of Middle East history at Stanford University, has summarized key elements of the failed negotiations:

[Barak] agreed to recognize a Palestinian state on as much as 94 percent of the West Bank and to transfer some desert areas near the Gaza Strip to Palestinian control in exchange for annexing territory, including three large Jewish settlement blocs in the West Bank, to Israel. He broke the Israeli taboo on negotiating over Jerusalem and talked about Palestinian administrative autonomy over Arab neighborhoods in East Jerusalem and Muslim control and a Palestinian flag flying over the Noble Sanctuary/Temple Mount, though Israeli sovereignty over the entire city would remain. He agreed to the resettlement of some 100,000 Palestinian refugees inside Israel proper in the framework of a family unification program, and to Israeli participation in an international fund to compensate the 4–5 million other refugees. Certainly, no other Israeli leader has gone this far. . . . Both Barak and Palestinian negotiator Saeb Erekat agreed that the main sticking points were Jerusalem and the refugee question. Barak refused to accept any form of Palestinian sovereignty in Jerusalem.[24]

Kalil Osman, writing in the Muslim activist periodical *Crescent International*, gives voice to Palestinian reservations on the Jerusalem question:

On Jerusalem, the American proposal for shared sovereignty offered the Palestinians only access to the Aqsa mosque and broad civilian and administrative autonomy in scattered parts of East Jerusalem; i.e., the

23. "The Covenant of the Islamic Resistance Movement, 18 August 1988." Available on the World Wide Web: http://www.yale.edu/lawweb/avalon/mideast/hamas.htm. For a detailed study of the Hamas Covenant and ideology, see Peter G. Riddell, "From Qur'an to Contemporary Politics: Hamas and the Role of Sacred Scripture," in *Fundamentalisms*, ed. C. H. Partridge (Carlisle: Paternoster, 2001).

24. Joel Beinin, "Camp David II," *MERIP Press Information Note 26*, July 26, 2000.

right to collect their own garbage, change their street lamps and the like. . . . Although Arafat agrees in principle to the idea of sharing sovereignty of Jerusalem, the formula presented at Camp David amounted to abandoning the long-held Palestinian dream of the city as the capital of an independent Palestinian state. As such, it gave Arafat no room to save his defeated face.

After tortuous discussions, the negotiations fell apart. In prophetic tones, Kalil Osman suggested that this failure in negotiations might lead Palestinians to consider armed struggle as a more effective means of achieving their goal of statehood. He offered as a model the Israeli military withdrawal from south Lebanon in early 2000 after eighteen years of occupation, widely seen in the Arab world as an Israeli military defeat at the hands of the Lebanese Shi'a militia Hizbullah (or Hezbollah, Party of God):

> The Palestinian "president" could ill afford to concede points on the questions of Jerusalem and the refugees' right of return. He has been coming under increasing pressure since the liberation of south Lebanon, which had the effect of a match thrown into the tinderbox of accumulated Palestinian fury. Hizbullah's example has given Palestinians a powerful and attractive contrast, an example worthy of being emulated. In Lebanon, the Islamic resistance's unwavering determination succeeded in bringing about total liberation with no strings attached. In contrast, Arafat's string of compromises has brought the Palestinian people nothing but an unjust peace based on an acute asymmetry of power: economic misery, dependency and poverty; corruption, nepotism and cronyism; repression, tyranny and one-upmanship; and the replacement of zionist occupation soldiers with Arafat's equally-brutal security men.[25]

Palestinian-Israeli relations deteriorated dramatically within weeks of the failed discussions. A visit by right-wing Israeli politician Ariel Sharon to the Temple Mount in October 2000 triggered widespread Palestinian protests. After Yasir Arafat's return to the Palestinian areas from the Camp David meeting, Hamas and Islamic Jihad activists who had been detained in Palestinian Authority prisons were released. Between October 2000 and October 2002 dozens of suicide bombings against Israeli military and civilian targets by Palestinian Islamist militants took place, triggering heavy Israeli military reprisals against Palestinian security and civilian locations. The second Intifada thus erupted and is ongoing; some 1,600 Palestinians and 600 Israelis had

25. "Palestinians Want New Intifada as Camp David II Ends without Deal after 15 Days," *Crescent International*, August 1–15, 2000.

been killed since the outbreak of the Intifada by the end of October 2002. In Israeli national elections in February 2001, the hardline Ariel Sharon of the Likud Party was elected as Prime Minister, and this also had a negative effect on the whole peace process. The unsuccessful outcome of this venture is undoubtedly a significant factor in worsening relations between the Islamic world and the West in the early twenty-first century.

INTRA-MUSLIM TENSION AND CONFLICT

Alongside the Israeli-Arab conflicts, the Middle Eastern region has been plagued by tensions and conflicts between Arab or Muslim states. Most are linked in some way with the Israeli-Arab conflict, but they nevertheless deserve comment in their own right.

The Egyptian-Israeli Peace Treaty

Continuous calls by the UN and the U.S. government for peace negotiations between Israel and the Arab states were initially unsuccessful, for the reasons given in previous discussion. However, things changed when President Sadat of Egypt broke ranks with other Arab states. He visited Israel in November 1977 and addressed the Knesset, the Israeli Parliament. American President Jimmy Carter then hosted Egyptian-Israeli peace discussions at Camp David in the United States in September 1978, which led to an agreement including the following statements:

> The parties are determined to reach a just, comprehensive, and durable settlement of the Middle East conflict through the conclusion of peace treaties based on Security Council resolutions 242 and 338 in all their parts. Their purpose is to achieve peace and good neighborly relations. They recognize that for peace to endure, it must involve all those who have been most deeply affected by the conflict. They therefore agree that this framework, as appropriate, is intended by them to constitute a basis for peace not only between Egypt and Israel, but also between Israel and each of its other neighbors which is prepared to negotiate peace with Israel on this basis.[26]

One year after the signing of this peace treaty, Israel handed over the Sinai to the Egyptian authorities. However, Egypt would pay a high price for this agreement with the Israelis. Other Arab states rejected the Egyptian efforts to represent them in the peace discussions. Egypt was shunned by the rest of the Arab world for over a de-

26. "Camp David Accords; September 17, 1978." Available on the World Wide Web: http://www.yale.edu/lawweb/avalon/mideast/campdav.htm.

cade and was expelled from the Arab League. Furthermore, President Sadat, the architect of this peace treaty, was assassinated by a radical Islamist group in October 1981. These radicals, driven by their reading of Islamic scripture, considered Sadat to have betrayed his faith by negotiating with a group portrayed as deceitful and untrustworthy by these scriptures. The march of Islamism was well under way.

The Iran-Iraq War (1980–88)

Islamism was rampant in other areas as well. After the Iranian revolution of 1979, the new Islamist government of Iran moved quickly to introduce Islamic legal codes in place of the more secular codes of the previous regime. However, sweeping changes were carried out in other parts of government and administration. Crucially, purges in the military forces left the new Iranian state dangerously exposed.

The Iraqi governing regime under President Saddam Hussein took advantage of the chaos in Iran to launch a military offensive in order to gain control of the disputed Shatt al Arab waterway on the Iran-Iraq border. The Iraqis ignored UN Security Council Resolution 479 of September 1980 calling for a halt to hostilities. The resulting war lasted eight years and caused over one million casualties.

Both sides at different times declared it to be a jihad (holy war) against the other.

The Gulf War (1990–91)

The unsuccessful military adventure against Iran did not quench the appetite of Iraqi President Saddam Hussein for territorial expansion. On August 2, 1990, Iraqi forces invaded neighboring Kuwait, claiming that it was historically part of Iraq and had been hived off by British cartographers during the colonial period. The UN Security Council issued Resolution 660 on the day of the attack, condemning it and demanding "that Iraq withdraw immediately and unconditionally all its forces to the positions in which they were located on 1 August 1990."[27]

In response to the Iraqi refusal to cooperate, the UN Security Council issued Resolution 678 on November 29, 1990, authorizing

> member States co-operating with the Government of Kuwait, unless Iraq on or before 15 January 1991 fully implements . . . the foregoing resolutions, to use all necessary means to uphold and implement resolution 660 (1990) and all subsequent relevant resolutions and to restore international peace and security in the area.[28]

27. Available on the World Wide Web: http://www.un.org/Docs/scres/1990/660e.pdf.
28. Available on the World Wide Web: http://www.un.org/Docs/scres/1990/678e.pdf.

This resolution sanctioned the use of force against the Iraqis to expel them from Kuwait. An international coalition of forces under American leadership thereupon launched a campaign to liberate Kuwait. The coalition included military forces from over twenty nations, including a number of Muslim nations such as Egypt, Syria, Saudi Arabia, and the other states of the Gulf Cooperation Council, Bangladesh, Morocco, and others.

Iraqi forces were driven from Kuwait in February 1991, though the coalition forces stopped short of entering Baghdad and driving Saddam Hussein and his regime from power, not being authorized to do so by the UN mandate. Zones in the north and the south of Iraq were declared by the UN as no-go zones for Iraqi military forces after the war, in recognition of local opposition among Kurdish and Shi'ite minorities to Saddam Hussein's regime and of the continuing threat posed by this regime to neighboring states. These measures did not eliminate this threat, as recognized by Muslim journalist Amir Taheri, who wrote: "Saddam Hussein has dragged the people of Iraq, and to some extent the rest of the Arabs, into several tragic adventures in the past three decades. Soon, he may drag them into yet another, one that may be his last."[29]

CONCLUSIONS

Parts 1 and 2 of this book have focused on history. We have seen that the history of Islam is one of greatness and decline, of empires and occupation. There have been recurring flashpoints between Islam and Christianity through the centuries:

636	Fall of Jerusalem to Muslims
7th–8th centuries	Loss of Byzantine lands to Muslims
Early 8th century	Loss of Spain to Muslims
12th–13th centuries	Christian response—the Crusades
11th–15th centuries	Christian response—reconquest of Spain
1453	Loss of Constantinople to Ottomans
15th–17th centuries	Ottoman incursions into Europe
15th–20th centuries	European colonization of Muslim lands
20th century	Conflicts in the Middle East

29. Amir Taheri, "Saddam Hussein's Delusion," *New York Times*, November 14, 2002.

Each of the above developments is like a link in a chain or a piece in a mosaic. One piece cannot be extracted and examined in isolation from others if one is to understand how history informs specific events.

Likewise, there have been recurring flashpoints between Islam and Judaism through the centuries:

- Rejection by Medinan Jews of Muhammad's claims as a prophet.
- Embedding of anti-Jewish comments in the Qur'an and Hadith have served to poison the relationship between Muslims and Jews in succeeding periods.
- Ambiguous conditions of the Jews under Islam; it was better than being in Europe, but there were periods of great difficulty under Islamic rule too.
- The establishment of modern Israel was entirely out of keeping with the Muslim view of Jews based on (a) Islamic scriptural portrayals and (b) the history of Jews as dhimmis.

Similarly, each of the above developments is like a link in a chain or a piece in a mosaic. One piece cannot be extracted and examined in isolation from others. For example, the Israeli-Palestinian conflict cannot be fully evaluated without reference to Qur'anic and Hadith statements on Jews, the history of Jews under Islam, and other key historical moments.

In addition to the tension and rivalry between Islam and its fellow monotheistic faiths, the internal history of Islam itself has suffered from periods of great fragmentation and rivalry between competing groups. For the first 1,350 years of its existence, Islam has had to negotiate its way through a series of internal crossroads, where different ideologies and theologies competed to define the identity of the faith. Such rivalries were periodically resolved, only to resurface in other forms at later points in Islamic history.

We will now turn our attention to the modern day, keeping in mind aspects of history that have left a clear imprint on events unfurling around us at the beginning of the twenty-first century, and considering how internal tensions are playing themselves out as different Islamic groups vie to define the identity of the faith in the new millennium.

PART 3

LOOKING AROUND

10

THE MUSLIM MASSES AND WESTOPHOBIA

THE TERRORIST ATTACKS OF SEPTEMBER 11, 2001

On September 11, 2001, nineteen terrorists hijacked four civilian airliners in the United States. Three were deliberately flown into the twin towers of the World Trade Center in New York and the Pentagon in Washington. The fourth crashed in a field in Pennsylvania, seemingly en route to another unidentified destination. These attacks led to the deaths of approximately three thousand people, mostly civilians, in the hijacked aircraft and within the targeted buildings.

Evidence pointed overwhelmingly to the responsible group being the al-Qa'ida organization led by the Saudi radical Osama bin Laden.[1] Al-Qa'ida has thus come to the fore in public discourse following these terrorist attacks, but they were far from dormant before September 11, 2001.

During the 1990s a series of terrorist actions were linked with the radical network. A massive explosion at the World Trade Center in 1993, attacks on American military personnel in various parts of the Arabian peninsula in 1996 and 2000, the destruction of the American embassies in Kenya and Tanzania in 1998, and an abortive attempt to bomb Los Angeles airport in 2000—all carried the imprint of the al-Qa'ida radical network. Furthermore, in 1996 and again in 1998 Osama Bin Laden issued *fatwa*s (edicts) declaring jihad against the United States.[2]

1. For evidence compiled and published by the British government, see *Responsibility for the Terrorist Atrocities in the United States, 11 September 2001—An Updated Account*. Available on the World Wide Web: http://www.number–10.gov.uk/default.asp?PageID=5322. In late June 2002, bin Laden's spokesman, Suleiman Abu Ghaith, admitted on Al Jazeera television that al-Qa'ida was responsible for the attacks. See Kahled Abou El Fadl, "Moderate Muslims under Siege," *New York Times*, July 1, 2002.

2. For the text of these declarations, see Y. Alexander and M. Swetnam, *Usama bin Laden's al-Qaida: Profile of a Terrorist Network* (Ardsley, N.Y.: Transnational Publishers, 2001), appendix 1A and 1B.

Three days after the September 11, 2001, attacks, British Prime Minister Tony Blair made the first of his several pronouncements regarding the nature of Islam. "I say to our Arab and Muslim friends, neither you nor Islam is responsible for this," declared the prime minister as he addressed the House of Commons on the crisis.[3]

In similar vein, George W. Bush staked a claim to credentials as a specialist in Islam in his public statements. Ten days after the September 11 attacks, the U.S. President informed a joint session of Congress that the nineteen terrorists involved represented "a fringe movement that perverts the peaceful teachings of Islam."[4] President Bush reiterated this theme in his Ramadan message to Muslims in November 2002, which included the statement that "Islam is a peace-loving faith."[5]

Of course, both men took their cues from advisers within, or connected with, their respective administrations. But the effect of such a stream of pronouncements triggered questions in the minds of the public regarding the nature of Islam. Is it inherently peaceful, or do those nineteen men who killed themselves and thousands of others in the name of their faith represent the true face of Islam?

Answers should be sought not from presidents and prime ministers, but rather from the faith's insiders, those who live Islam in all its fullness. Before answering the question regarding "the true face" of Islam, we will initially examine the concerns of the Muslim masses around the world, and then see how different groups try to win the support of the masses.

VIEWS OF THE MUSLIM MASSES

The terrorist attacks of September 11 triggered mixed responses from Muslims around the globe. Many were shocked and appalled at the loss of innocent life. Spontaneous candlelit vigils in sympathy with Americans were held in Iran.[6] Expressions of condolence for the families of the victims flooded into the United States from Muslim locations. Yasir Arafat, chairman of the Palestinian Authority, gave blood as a symbolic statement of support for the victims. Friday prayers at many mosques in the week of the attacks were devoted to praying for the victims and their families. Muslims throughout Brit-

3. From the 10 Downing Street Newsroom, September 14, 2001. Available on the World Wide Web: http://www.pm.gov.uk/output/page3428.asp.
4. "Text of George Bush's Speech," *The Guardian*, September 21, 2001.
5. "President Bush Sends Ramadan Greetings," Office of the Press Secretary, The White House, November 5, 2002.
6. Thomas L. Friedman, "The Best of Enemies?" *New York Times*, June 12, 2002.

ain also observed the two-minute silence called by the British government to remember the dead.

However, such a sympathetic response did not represent the whole picture. One of the most ugly scenes on the day of the attacks was captured on film when journalists broadcast images of Palestinians rejoicing in East Jerusalem. The *Church Times* reported that "tens of thousands of Palestinians in refugee camps across the Middle East joined in, as did smaller groups in Egypt, Jordan, Pakistan, and elsewhere in the world."[7]

Such rejoicing was not restricted to Palestinian communities. The Egyptian newspaper *Al-Arabi* devoted several pages of its issue of September 16, 2001, to focusing on Egyptians celebrating at the September 11 attacks. In one article, Ahmed Murad wrote: "I am rejoicing over America's misfortunes. And I will be more frank and say that I am happy for this great number of victims." In another article Ahmed Abu Al-Ma'ati warned:

> The American government would be mistaken if it believed the consolation telegrams sent to it by the poor and forgotten developing countries on the occasion of last Tuesday's attacks. The overflowing happiness [of the people] of these countries tells things completely differently from what its presidents and kings say. . . . What happened was nothing but America being given a sip of hatred from the grail it made the people of many countries drink.[8]

In Britain, too, some members of the Muslim minority found cause for celebration at the tragic events of September 11. *The Telegraph* reported that a school librarian in a British Home Counties school with mainly Muslim pupils related that her "15-year-old pupils cheered and chanted anti-American slogans when one of their classmates walked into the room during registration, punching the air and shouting about the attacks."[9]

Why the Antipathy?

Because of such scenes of Muslim rejoicing at America's suffering, many Western and Christian commentators chose to place a primary focus not upon calls for retaliation, but rather upon a process of self-examination. Scott McConnell commented: "Before Americans set

7. Gerald Butt, "Why America Is Hated So Much," *The Church Times*, September 14, 2001.

8. Religious News Service from the Arab World, September 12–18, 2001.

9. Stewart Payne, "Extremists 'Are Targeting Children,'" *The Telegraph*, London, September 15, 2001.

their sights on revenge, . . . they should at least understand why this attack delighted many, why United States foreign policy makes it hated in much of the world."[10] Philip Lawler, writing in the *Catholic World Report*, asked, "Why do so many people hate America? Why are young men ready even to die in order to harm us? If we cannot answer those questions, we cannot hope to conquer terrorism."[11] Dudley Woodberry, emeritus professor of Islamic studies at Fuller Theological Seminary in California, took a similar approach with his article in the *International Bulletin of Missionary Research*, suggesting a "direction of fit": American policy caused grievances, which caused hatred, which caused terrorism: "Terrorism is a response to built-up grievances, real or imagined. Therefore, one cannot drive out terrorism without dealing with the grievances that lead to it."[12]

The prominent Sri Lankan Christian scholar Vinoth Ramachandra endorsed such a direction of fit, providing a long list of U.S. actions that he saw as triggering the kind of response seen on September 11:

> Have Americans forgotten that they are the only nation in the history of the world to have unleashed nuclear weapons on civilian populations? . . . Question: What do Pol Pot, Saddam Hussein and Osama bin Laden have in common, apart from being mass murderers? Answer: They were all equipped and supported by the CIA until American interests changed. . . . Where were the CNN cameras focused when apartment blocks, factories and offices in Baghdad (1991) and Belgrade (1999) were bombed, night after night, by decent, law-abiding American youth as if it were a computer war-game? . . . The American public has watched idly by while the Israeli occupation of Arab lands, backed up by a vicious system of apartheid, state-sponsored executions, and indiscriminate bombings of Palestinian villages, [has] continued unabated.[13]

Such statements further imply that since the United States, and indeed the West in general, has taken actions and adopted policies that have alienated the Muslim masses, by changing these actions and pol-

10. Scott McConnell, "Why Many Arabs Hate America." Available on the World Wide Web (cited November 26, 2001): http://www.mediamonitors.net/scottmcconnell 1.html.

11. Philip Lawler, "The Looming Showdown," *Catholic World Report*, 11.9 (October 2001).

12. J. Dudley Woodberry, "Terrorism, Islam, and Mission: Reflections of a Guest in Muslim Lands," *International Bulletin of Missionary Research* 26.1 (January 2002): 3.

13. Vinoth Ramachandra, "Response to Terrorist Attacks: An Open Letter to American Students and the American Church." Available on the World Wide Web: http://www.urbana.org/feat.wtc.vinoth.cfm.

icies the Muslim masses will cease to support radicals and be more favorably disposed to Western countries.

We should not assume that the direction of fit proposed by the above commentators is correct. Furthermore, while some causes of Muslim antipathy toward the West might be reasoned and defensible, we should not necessarily assume that all are. We should closely scrutinize all views, whether by such commentators or by Muslims.

In the following paragraphs, we will look first at those causes most frequently advanced for antipathy toward the West among the Muslim masses. We will then consider a range of other factors that must be taken into account if our analysis is to avoid superficiality.

The Most Frequently Stated Causes

There are undoubtedly policies and actions pursued in the recent past by the United States and other Western countries that have caused much resentment in the Muslim world. An indication can be gleaned from statements by Muslim radicals, who claim to articulate the concerns of the masses. Suleiman Abu Ghaith, an al-Qa'ida spokesman and aide to Osama bin Laden, spoke as follows in a recorded message: "The storm will not calm as long as you [the United States and Britain] do not end your support for the Jews in Palestine, lift your embargo from around the Iraqi people, and have left the Arabian peninsula."[14]

The Israeli-Palestinian Conflict

The establishment of the State of Israel in 1948 is seen by most Muslims as an attempt to reassert European colonial control via a latter-day crusader state. European and American economic and military links with Israel since its creation are taken as evidence of the West's expansionist goals. The humiliating defeat of Arab armies by Israel in several wars since 1948 is considered to have been facilitated by the West.

Many non-Muslims challenge such views as simplistic monochrome representations of a complex conflict. First, Western, and indeed American, support for Israel is not monolithic. Second, such views tend to ignore how Palestinian and other Arab actions and policies have contributed to the intractable nature of the conflict over the years. Furthermore, they also ignore the vigorous debate within Israeli society concerning policies vis-à-vis its Arab neighbors. Israeli Defense Minister Benjamin Ben-Eliezer spoke as follows in June 2002:

14. Available on the World Wide Web: http://au.dailynews.yahoo.com/headlines/20011014/aapworld/1003011993–873209894.html.

Whoever ignores the need for the existence of a Palestinian state, or for the existence of two entities, simply doesn't know what he's talking about. . . . There's no way around it; two nations are going to have to live side by side. It would be well if they would do it very quickly, to find the basis for co-existence.[15]

Nevertheless, among Palestinians in the West Bank and Gaza, support for the Israeli-Palestinian peace process plummeted during 2001. A Bir Zeit University poll taken in October of that year showed that support for rejectionist radical Islamist groups had risen by 12 to 31 percent over a twelve-month period. Over the same period support for the mainstream Fatah organization, which had been guiding the Palestinian participation in peace discussions with Israel, fell from 33 to 20 percent.[16] This reflects a widespread feeling among Palestinians, one echoed by Muslim masses in other countries, that a two-state solution would be a sellout of Palestinian rights. Their preference would be for Israel to disappear as a state, since they consider it to be an alien Western implant in the Muslim heartlands. Rightly or wrongly, such views are widely held throughout the Muslim world. They represent a significant ingredient in a feeling of antipathy toward America and the West in general that is held by the Muslim masses.

United Nations Sanctions against Iraq

Another key festering sore that is poisoning the relationship between the West and the Islamic world is the issue of United Nations sanctions against Iraq, imposed following Iraq's 1990 invasion of Kuwait to dissuade Iraq from pursuing its production of weapons of mass destruction.

The sanctions resulted in great hardship for the Iraqi people, and details have been widely reported in both Muslim and non-Muslim media. For example, the Egyptian broadsheet *Al-Ahram* frequently has provided its readers with depressing statistics, such as the increase of deaths of Iraqi children due to malnutrition from 35 per 1,000 (1989) to 131 per 1,000 (2000).[17] Such details inevitably and understandably cause much anti-Western feeling in countries that have strong historical ties with Iraq, such as Arab countries.

In response, Western leaders have called attention to what they see as the continuing threat posed by President Saddam Hussein's Iraq

15. "Ben-Eliezer: The Solution Is Palestinian State, Not Fence," *Ha'aretz*, June 17, 2002.

16. J. Bennet, "A New Mideast Battle: Arafat vs. Hamas," *New York Times*, December 6, 2001.

17. Rasha Saad, "It's Called Genocide," *Al-Ahram Weekly Online*, July 6–12, 2000.

and its continuing production of weapons of mass destruction,[18] and his past willingness to use such weapons against the Iraqi Kurdish minority in 1988 and during the Iran-Iraq War. Furthermore, Western supporters of continuing sanctions have pointed out that medical supplies were not subject to sanctions, and they therefore have claimed that the Iraqi government was itself increasing the suffering of its own people in order to generate social dissension in the West.

However, few Muslims are persuaded by such comments from Western supporters of ongoing sanctions. Muslims see the sanctions as further evidence of Western colonial ambitions, and Western denials of this fall on deaf ears.

American Military Presence in Saudi Arabia

A substantial American military presence remained in Saudi Arabia after the 1990–91 Gulf War. The U.S. troops were originally sent to expel Iraq from Kuwait after its August 1990 invasion, and a number of American military bases with personnel remained in Arabia at the request of the Saudi regime, to dissuade Iraq from further military adventures.

However, the presence of non-Muslim troops near the principal Muslim holy sites is considered an affront by large numbers of Muslims throughout the world, not least in Saudi Arabia itself, where intelligence surveys suggested that 95 percent of educated Saudis between twenty-five and forty-one years of age supported Osama bin Laden in his conflict with the West.[19] The Lebanese American Christian academic Professor Fawaz Gerges stresses the importance of this issue in the formation of radical thinking:

> I have spent the last ten years or so studying the various videotapes and [bin Laden's] speeches and everything he has said, and the most critical, important issue is neither Palestine nor Iraq. It's basically the American military presence in the bilad al-haramayn, the land of the two holy places, and the authorities in Saudi Arabia's willingness, not only to allow the Americans to have . . . a military presence in Saudi Arabia but also their implicit and indirect alliance with what he calls the crusaders and the Jews.[20]

The American military presence is taken as further evidence of Western intentions to resurrect its colonial past, and this strikes pow-

18. For a chilling analysis of Iraqi weapons production, see "Iraq's Weapons of Mass Destruction: The Assessment of the British Government." Available on the World Wide Web: http://www.ukonline.gov.uk/featurenews/iraqdossier.pdf.

19. Saad al-Fagih, "The Coming Saudi Eruption," *The Guardian*, January 29, 2002.

20. *Osama bin Laden*, prod. Simon Berthon, dir. Jon Blair (3BM Television for Channel 4: Channel Four Television Corporation, 2001).

erful negative chords among the Muslim masses. Assurances by American leaders to the contrary also fall on deaf ears.

Other Less Frequently Mentioned Causes

The three issues mentioned above are modern, and while they certainly deserve closer examination, commentators need also to acknowledge that the underlying causes of tension between Islam and the West go far beyond any one of these modern conflicts considered alone. Indeed, Fawaz Gerges's reference in the preceding quote to "crusaders and Jews" points to sentiments of antipathy among the masses that the radicals are able to play upon.

We will now address various other factors contributing to Westophobic sentiments among the Muslim masses.

Negative Stereotyping of Non-Muslims in Islamic Sacred Scripture

Islamic sacred scriptures, the Qur'an and Prophetic Traditions (Hadith), include a vast array of verses that serve to mold Muslims' views toward non-Muslims. Throughout the Muslim world, an important part of the educational formation of young children includes study of the scriptures. In this way, from an early age Muslim children's views toward non-Muslims, both conscious and unconscious, are fashioned by their encounter with the Muslim sacred texts.

It should be noted that the Qur'an and Prophetic Traditions send out mixed messages on this issue. Verses can be identified that portray Christians and Jews in a positive light. But equally apparent are verses that cast non-Muslims in a bad light.

An example of Qur'anic verses that portray non-Muslims negatively is Sura 5:51: "O ye who believe! Take not the Jews and the Christians for your friends and protectors: They are but friends and protectors to each other. And he amongst you that turns to them (for friendship) is of them. Verily Allah guideth not a people unjust." Similarly, the canonical collection of Prophetic Traditions by Abu Dawud includes the following account:

> Narrated Abu Hurayrah: Suhayl ibn Abu Salih said: "I went out with my father to Syria. The people passed by the cloisters in which there were Christians and began to salute them. My father said: 'Do not give them salutation first, for Abu Hurayrah reported the Apostle of Allah (peace be upon him) as saying: "Do not salute them (Jews and Christians) first, and when you meet them on the road, force them to go to the narrowest part of it."'"[21]

21. Abu Dawud, *Sunan*, bk. 41, no. 5186. Available on the World Wide Web: http://www.usc.edu/dept/MSA/reference/searchhadith.html.

Another authoritative collection of Traditions, that by the eminent theologian Muslim, includes the following account: "Abu Hurayrah reported Allah's Messenger (may peace be upon him) as saying: 'The Jews and the Christians do not dye (their hair), so oppose them.'"[22] The result of regularly encountering such statements within texts considered to carry the word of God is that, at the very least, Muslim children are taught to regard non-Muslims with feelings of ambivalence. When other factors come into play, this ambivalence can easily turn into antipathy and overt hostility.

The Legacy of History

Another key ingredient contributing to a sense of anti-Western feeling among the Muslim masses is connected with the 1,400-year relationship between the Islamic world and the Christian West that we surveyed in previous chapters. Much of this history is marked by warfare, respective gains and losses through imperial expansion, and resulting endemic mutual mistrust.

Most of the Eastern Christian Empire centered on Constantinople was lost to Islamic armies between 632–1453. The Crusades represented a Christian counterattack, and its brutality has never been forgotten by Muslims in the Arab world. The Ottoman Turkish incursions into Europe from the sixteenth century created an abiding fear among the European populations living on the front line. Then Western colonization of Islamic lands around the world around 1800–1945 left Muslims with bitter memories of being exploited and subservient to non-Muslim rule.

So when modern-day conflicts, such as the Israeli-Palestinian conflict and the issues surrounding Iraq, are examined, it needs to be clearly understood that many Muslims (and Westerners) view these modern conflicts against the backdrop of past history and its living legacy.

Globalization

Prince Hassan of Jordan identified an important ingredient of antipathy toward the West in the Muslim world when he said, "Globalisation ('awlamah) in our part of the world is held in deep suspicion."[23] Concerns with the effects of globalization have been evident to Western audiences observing violent demonstrations in Seattle, Gothenburg, and Genoa between 1991 and 2001. However, similar concerns felt in the Muslim world have not been so visible to Western audiences.

22. Muslim, *Sahih*, III, chap. 831, no. 5245, 1156.
23. Hassan bin Talal, "Towards a World with 10,000 Cultures," *Discourse* 1 (August 2000): 9.

Muslim writers articulate the concerns of many Muslims when they criticize economic globalization. A. S. Gammal sees globalization as essentially trade driven and attributes responsibility ultimately to the United States:

> Globalization is essentially an economic process that begins in America and eventually involves its trilateral partners in Europe and Japan. Taking the ideology of neo-liberalism as its rhetorical fuel, globalization seeks to create a world economy that benefits American corporations, first and foremost, and other transnational companies that operate by American-defined rules.[24]

However, it is not only journalists who express such concerns. President Husni Mubarak of Egypt articulated a similar viewpoint at the meeting of the eight most populous Muslim nations (D8) in February 2001, saying: "Open markets in today's world are basically accessible for the products of advanced countries, while our exports . . . are faced every day with new protectionist procedures, overt or covert, that impede their access to the advanced countries' markets."[25]

The effects of globalization extend beyond the realm of economics and impact wide-ranging social and cultural issues. Thus Zafar Bangash similarly writes with concern about cultural globalization, which he sees primarily in terms of Americanization:

> Globalization means not merely uniformity but also conformity to the dominant, primarily American culture. This applies as much to food as it does to music and clothes. People around the world are expected to eat greasy McDonald hamburgers, drink pepsi or coke, wear Levi jeans and gyrate to Michael Jackson music. If they have any spare time left, then the ubiquitous CNN is there to occupy it.[26]

Globalization as a political phenomenon causes concern to many Muslims as well. The advantages of democracy, so often articulated by Western leaders, is seen by many Muslims as undermining the rightful place of God. Pakistan's Jamaat-e-Islami organization captures this well:

---

24. A. S. Gammal, "The Global Protests against Anti-globalization and the Media's Coverage of Them," *Crescent International*, June 1–15, 2001.

25. "Leaders of the Most Populous Muslim Nations Debate Response to Globalization," February 27, 2001. Available on the World Wide Web: http://www.khilafah.com/1421/category.php?DocumentID=1100&TagID=1#.

26. Zafar Bangash, "McDonaldization of Culture: America's Pervasive Influence Globally," *Crescent International*, February 1–15, 1998.

Democracy at the philosophic level, which affirms the principle of sovereignty of man and denies existence of eternal and absolute religious and moral values, is at variance with the Islamic concept of world and society. Islam affirms the sovereignty of God and believes that man needs divine guidance. By definition the Muslim is one who accepts the divine law as the source of guidance for his individual and collective behaviour.[27]

Though statements such as those listed above by Muslim spokesmen are highly critical of globalization as a phenomenon, searching questions need to be asked of such critiques. A Muslim concern with worldwide umma, leading many to argue that Muslim identity should be focused on faith rather than national loyalty, is a form of globalization in its own right. Islamic economics operates on a global dimension. Muslim concerns with moral issues, leading to a surge in Muslim women wearing head-covering, is a worldwide trend. It could thus be argued that Muslim opposition to globalization is driven by a dissatisfaction with the particular forms it takes, rather than opposition to globalization per se. Islamic globalization is desirable; Western globalization is not.[28]

Westophobia in the Muslim Media

The perception among Muslims of Western culture being decadent and debased is fueled by regular statements in the Muslim media, both in the Middle East and among Muslim minorities in the West, that reflect and often exaggerate moral decay in Western societies. The following quote from *Invitation to Islam* encapsulates this view: "Men in the West feel no obligation to protect women from the harms of society. This is why a man will allow his wife to be a stripper, call-girl and even a prostitute. Honour knows no place in the West."[29] Likewise, the prominent British Islamist, the late Kalim Siddiqui, made a powerful contribution to the negative stereotyping of all Westerners with regard to moral attitudes: "Women throughout Europe have been brought up to regard men in uniform as qualifying for instant favours. . . . Offering free and frequent sex to soldiers is a well established part of European women's war effort."[30] Such comments have tarred all Westerners with

27. "Islam and the New World Order," *Worldview* (Jamaat-e-Islami, Pakistan). Available on the World Wide Web: http://www.jamaat.org/world/worldorder.html.

28. For a fuller discussion of this topic, see Peter G. Riddell, "Islamic Perspectives on Globalisation," *St. Mark's Review* (2003).

29. *Invitation to Islam*, 8, cited in *The Westophobia Report: Anti-Western and Anti-Christian Stereotyping in British Muslim Publications*, Occasional Paper, no. 1 (London: London Bible College Centre for Islamic Studies, 1999), 6.

30. Kalim Siddiqui, *Islam and the West after Bosnia* (London: Muslim Parliament of Great Britain, 1993), 9, cited in *Westophobia Report*, 6.

the same brush. No doubt Hollywood has played a significant role in this process of stereotyping through its worldwide distribution of films including sexually explicit material. However, such a factor explains, but does not justify, the broad extent of negative stereotyping of the West by the Muslim media around the world.

This negative stereotyping of the West has been termed *Westophobia* by recent studies.[31] Westophobia refers to entrenched and endemically hostile attitudes to the West and to perceived cultural traits of the West. The term parallels that of *Islamophobia*, fear or hatred of Muslims and Islam, a phenomenon that was studied in detail in a British context in a 1997 report produced by the Runnymede Trust.[32]

The phenomenon of Westophobia is encapsulated in a comment printed in *Common Sense*, the newsletter of the Islamic Party of Britain: "There is nothing in Western societies . . . that remotely resembles good behaviour. They all walk in haughtiness, vanity and pomp; insolent, arrogant and boastful."[33] The regular appearance of such views in the Muslim media around the world also contributes to the perpetuation of a sense of antipathy on the part of Muslims toward the West.

Conspiracy Theorizing

Another more intangible yet powerful factor in causing Muslim antipathy to the West is the prevalence of conspiracy theorizing in much of the Muslim world. This is closely linked with issues of power and disempowerment. Up to 70 percent of the world's refugees are Muslims, and some of the poorest countries in the world are predominantly Muslim. Hence, the Muslim world has developed a tendency to attribute responsibility for economic, social, and political problems to the world's rich and powerful nations and societies. In today's world, wealth and power lie predominantly in the West.

Thus international organizations, such as the United Nations and its multiple agencies, and even Western and Christian nongovernmental organizations (NGOs), are often portrayed in the Muslim media as agents of Western, and especially U.S., government policy. The Muslim magazine *Impact International* lambastes the NGO Save the Children, saying it "is one of the largest U.S. government contractors patrolling the so-called 'third world'—running programmes in scores of places where political sensitivities would hinder the overt presence of

31. *Westophobia Report*.
32. *Islamophobia: A Challenge for Us All* (London: Runnymede Trust, 1997).
33. *Common Sense* (summer 1997): 7; cited in *Westophobia Report*, 8.

U.S. government personnel."[34] In a similar but even more accusing vein, the periodical *Crescent International* declares:

> Foreign non-governmental organisations (NGOs) operating in the Muslim world have become the primary vehicle for spreading western culture and pornography. Operating under the guise of providing "help" and support, their principal target are [sic] the most vulnerable peoples in these societies. Where pornography and western culture—the two are virtually synonymous these days—cannot be pushed down the throats of people directly, Christian missionaries soften up the target population first.[35]

The issue of conspiracy theorizing is closely linked with Westophobic comment in the Muslim media. This phenomenon is deeply embedded within the Arab mind-set and surfaces in times of trouble or crisis. For example, during the Six-Day War in June 1967, as Israel quickly gained the upper hand, the prominent Egyptian broadsheet *Al-Ahram* reported the involvement of American and British military forces on the side of the Israelis, to account for the Israeli success.[36] These reports were also repeated in a speech by Egyptian President Nasser at Cairo University on July 23, 1967.[37] Though sheer fabrications, these reports were carried by a prominent organ of the media and repeated by a head of state, thus ensuring their wide distribution.

In relation to the terrorist attacks of September 11, 2001, this phenomenon of conspiracy theorizing manifested itself in a particularly disturbing way.

Soon after the attacks, most Muslim commentators quickly showed their reluctance to believe that Osama bin Laden's al-Qa'ida network, or indeed any Muslim group, could have been responsible for the attacks. For example, an article in the prominent Egyptian newspaper *Al-Hayat* a few days after the attacks concluded that Osama bin Laden could not have been responsible since only a professional with specialist engineering knowledge could have brought down the World Trade Center towers.[38]

In seeking a scapegoat, speculation about Israeli complicity spread like wildfire. The Egyptian Sheikh Muhammad Al-Gamei'a, the Al-Azhar University representative in the United States and Imam of the

34. "Save the Children? Save Your Money!" *Impact International*. Available on the World Wide Web: http://www.africa2000.com/IMPACT/savechildren.html.
35. Mohammad Abul-Hayat Jalal-Abadi, "NGOs Spread Pornography in Muslim Bangladesh," *Crescent International*, 27.10, August 1–15, 1998, 8.
36. Churchill and Churchill, *Six Day War*, 160–61.
37. "Nasser's Revolution Anniversary Speech at Cairo University, July 23, 1967," in Laqueur, *Israel-Arab Reader*, 198–207.
38. Religious News Service from the Arab World, September 12–18, 2001.

Islamic Cultural Center and Mosque of New York City, was interviewed on October 4, 2001. He carried the previous comment a step
further: "Only the Jews are capable of planning such an incident, because it was planned with great precision of which Osama bin Laden
or any other Islamic organization or intelligence apparatus is incapa-
ble." In more anti-Semitic terms, he continued:

> On the news in the U.S. it was said that four thousand Jews did not come
> to work at the World Trade Center on the day of the incident, and that
> the police arrested a group of Jews rejoicing in the streets at the time of
> the incident. . . . This news item was hushed up immediately after it was
> broadcast. . . . The Jews who control the media acted to hush it up so
> that the American people would not know. If it became known to the
> American people, they would have done to the Jews what Hitler did![39]

Although there is absolutely no basis for such reports, they served
the desired purpose. Because they were issued by prominent spokes-
persons, they were picked up by individual journalists and news agencies in the Muslim world, and with each repetition these reports
seemed to gather a measure of undeserved credibility. This provides a
clear example of the impact of deliberate disinformation.

Leading Muslim world broadsheets repeated this theme of Jewish
responsibility for the September 11 attacks. Mustafa Mahmoud, writing in Egypt's *Al-Ahram*, speculated: "What if it proved that the ones
behind all this were not the Afghans but more likely the Israelis. . . .
The attacks against America could be from within America itself and
Israel could be playing a role in creating the West's hatred of Arabs
and Muslims."[40] Similarly Nabil Luka Babawi said in *Al-Akhbar* on
September 30, 2001:

> By promoting the idea that Arabs and Muslims were the ones behind
> the [September 11] attacks, the Zionist lobby mobilized American pub-
> lic opinion against Arabs and Muslims and destroyed the untroubled
> state between Muslims and Christians. The only beneficiaries of all this
> are the Jews.[41]

This form of conspiracy theorizing, when transmitted by the mass
media, has a powerful effect on attitudes toward other societies and
countries. The effect of such conspiracy theorizing in this instance

39. Available on the World Wide Web: http://www.lailatalqadr.com/stories/p5041001
.shtml.
40. Mustafa Mahmoud, "Illusion or Truth?" *Al-Ahram*, October 20, 2001, 13, cited
by Religious News Service from the Arab World.
41. Religious News Service from the Arab World, September 26–October 2, 2001.

was first to reinforce a view that Jews were devious and scheming, second to create the impression of America being controlled by its Jewish minority, and third to discourage Arab communities from asking why the actual perpetrators of the September 11 attacks had come from their midst.[42]

CONCLUSIONS

While Muslim antipathy for the United States and the West in general is undoubtedly linked to certain aspects of recent American and Western foreign policy, it is far too simplistic to suggest that the antipathy exclusively results from these foreign policy issues. Rather, it derives from a potent cocktail of ingredients that go far back in time, to the beginnings of Muslim-Christian historical contact and to the very Islamic texts themselves. This long-term antipathy and hatred is fed by modern issues: matters of foreign policy, the effects of globalization in its various forms, Westophobia in the Muslim media, and rampant conspiracy theorizing.

It is not correct to suggest that America's foreign policy preceded and caused anti-Western and anti-American sentiment in the Muslim world. Rather, the preexisting antipathy has been fueled by the foreign policy issues that have been discussed.

As stated at the beginning of this chapter, anti-Western antipathy is not the whole picture as far as the Muslim masses are concerned. The Muslim masses hold many positive attitudes toward the West and at times admire the West. The movement of populations through immigration is largely one way, from the Muslim world to the West. This reflects a view held by many Muslims that the West has much to offer that they find attractive.

However, the widespread sense of antipathy toward much that is of the West represents a potential for exploitation by the more radical members of Islamic communities. We will now turn our attention to the radicals, to see how they attempt to galvanize the Muslim masses into action against the West. Then we will see how more moderate voices strive to guide the masses in a quite different direction.

---

42. The Jews were not the only ones blamed by conspiracy-minded Muslims for destroying the World Trade Center. Sheikh Abu Hamza al-Masri of London's Finsbury Park Mosque asserted in an interview that the FBI was responsible for the destruction of the Twin Towers ("Today Programme," *BBC Radio 4*, July 26, 2002). Available on the World Wide Web (cited July 26, 2002): http://www.bbc.co.uk/radio4/today/listen/listen .shtml.

11

THE RADICAL
ISLAMIST
WORLDVIEW

Although a feeling of antipathy toward the West is prevalent among the Muslim masses, relatively few would be willing to participate in the type of anti-Western violence and terrorism seen in the attacks on U.S. sites on September 11, 2001. In order to understand the thinking of those Muslims who would be ready to take part in such action, we need to move beyond the masses to focus on small groups of radical Islamists. We will consider them from three angles: mind-set, membership, and modus operandi.

MIND-SET AND MOTIVES

Radical Islamists are driven by a range of factors. Central is their particular literalist reading of Islamic scripture, reflecting a belief that they can re-create a "golden age" from the past—the community of Muslims led by the prophet Muhammad in Madina in the early seventh century. In the words of the Egyptian contemporary writer Diaa Rashwan, "For those groups advocating violence the contemporary world resembles the one confronted by the Muslims in Medina."[1] In order to re-create this past utopian society, radical Islamists believe that they must use Islamic scripture as a blueprint for their society. Hence, their statements and declarations are typically heavily interspersed with quotations from Islamic scripture to sanction the particular policy being articulated.

Our discussion of radical Islamist mind-set and motives will be grounded in living history by focusing upon responses by radical groups to the terrorist attacks of September 11, 2001.

1. Diaa Rashwan, "God and the Cause," *Al-Ahram Weekly Online*, May 30–June 5, 2002.

Scriptural Dictates

In the days following the attacks, radical Muslim voices were heard loudly. Friday prayers at London's Finsbury Park mosque on September 14 were marked by statements of support for Osama bin Laden, the chief suspect in the terrorist attacks.[2] The Imam of Finsbury Park Mosque, Sheikh Abu Hamza Al-Masri, had previously achieved notoriety in 1999, when he was accused of sending young British Muslims as jihad (holy war) fighters to Yemen.

Al-Masri's group, Supporters of Shariah (SOS), always drew on the Islamic scriptures to justify their policies and statements. The SOS Web site quoted the *Islamic Traditions* in praising death in jihad, promising that this will lead to great rewards, including forgiveness of sins, guaranteed salvation on the day of resurrection, and entry into Paradise.[3]

The jihad theme was quite prominent in the statements of radical Islamist groups following the events of September 11. After allied air strikes in Afghanistan commenced on October 7, 2001, al-Qa'ida spokesman Suleiman Abu Ghaith on an Al-Jazeera television broadcast exhorted: "The Jihad is a duty of every Muslim. God says fight for the sake of God and to uphold the name of God."[4]

A representative of the radical Muslim Youth Association picked up on this theme, saying in an interview on British television that the Qur'an and the Islamic Traditions called for Muslims to respond jointly to any retaliatory attack by Western military forces on al-Qa'ida bases in Afghanistan. He warned that an assault on Osama bin Laden would trigger a response from Muslims throughout the world, and stressed that Muslims in Britain, who primarily identified themselves by their faith rather than their nationality, would willingly join in the defense of Islam.[5]

The militant group al-Muhajiroun organized a gathering on September 15 in Birmingham, England, entitled "USA, the Enemy of Islam," and issued a press statement the following day: "O Muslims, stand together and unite our Ummah [community] to fight against the enemies of Allah . . . and his Messenger Muhammad in this time of need. The Book of Allah calls you, the Ummah cries for your help and Paradise awaits you."[6] It cited Sura 9:41 in support of this call for

2. *The Times* (London), September 15, 2001.
3. Available on the World Wide Web: http://www.supportersofshariah.org/Eng/aj/ajindex.html.
4. *Daily Telegraph* (London), October 10, 2001.
5. *Channel 4 News Special,* September 13, 2001.
6. Al-Muhajiroun press statement, September 16, 2001.

Muslims to stand together and fight against the enemies of Allah, with Paradise being the promised reward.

Likewise, Hizb al-Tahrir (HuT), an international group that embraces a similarly radical ideology,[7] released a communiqué to coincide with the commencement of American bombing of Afghanistan on October 7. It also turned to the pages of the Qur'an in support of its call to arms: "Fight them, and Allah will punish them by your hands, cover them with shame, help you (to victory) over them, heal the breasts of believers."[8] Anticipating indifference among Muslims to this call to arms, HuT quoted Qur'an Sura 9:38 in order to urge Muslims to join in jihad: "O ye who believe! What is the matter with you, that when ye are asked to go forth in the cause of Allah (Jihad) ye cling heavily to the earth? Do ye prefer the life of this world to the Hereafter? But little is the comfort of this life, as compared with the Hereafter." Throughout such statements, the theme of death in holy war as a ticket to Paradise was prominent in the rhetoric of Muslim radicals.

What of the terrorists themselves, those nineteen men who deliberately hijacked four airliners carrying civilian passengers for the express purpose of flying them into buildings and killing as many people as possible? There is no doubt that they, too, were driven by scriptural motivations. A document left by one of the hijackers is replete with references to Islamic scripture, the prophet Muhammad, and the early history of Islam. These references served to undergird the actions of the hijackers on September 11. The writer of this document urged his colleagues to consider Muhammad as their model: "Remember the battle of the prophet . . . against the infidels, as he went on building the Islamic state." They are exhorted to keep God uppermost in their minds as they carry out their task, and to refer to scripture: "You should pray, you should fast. You should ask God for guidance, you should ask God for help. . . . Continue to recite the Koran." The writer then urges his fellow hijackers to overcome their natural human fear by remembering that Paradise awaits them at their moment of death:

> You have to be convinced that those few hours that are left you in your life are very few. From there you will begin to live the happy life, the infinite paradise. Be optimistic. The prophet was always optimistic. . . . Always remember the verses that you would wish for death before you meet it if you only know what the reward after death will be. . . . You

7. Founded in Jordan in 1953 by Taqi al-Din al-Nabhani, HuT aims to restore the caliphate.
8. Sura 9:14.

will be entering paradise. You will be entering the happiest life, everlasting life. . . . We are of God, and to God we return.[9]

When allied air strikes on Afghanistan began on October 7, Osama bin Laden issued a statement overtly expressing his support for the September 11 terrorist attacks. Above all, he emphasized the supposed divine sanction for the attacks:

Here is America struck by God Almighty in one of its vital organs, so that its greatest buildings are destroyed. Grace and gratitude to God. . . . God has blessed a group of vanguard Muslims, the forefront of Islam, to destroy America. May God bless them and allot them a supreme place in heaven. For He is the only one capable and entitled to do so.[10]

Capitalizing on Westophobia among the Masses

In order to galvanize the Muslim masses to action against the West, radical Islamists typically appeal to causes that they know will resonate with the masses. They make frequent references to the Israeli-Palestinian conflict, UN sanctions against Iraq, and the presence of American troops in Saudi Arabia. However, they also stress the historical dimension to tension between Muslims and the West (discussed earlier), including frequent allusions to the Crusades and other past conflicts.

The Crusade theme appeared regularly in statements by Osama bin Laden. On November 3, 2001, he issued a call to Muslim audiences: "Let us investigate whether this war against Afghanistan that broke out a few days ago is a single and unique one or if it is a link to a long series of crusader wars against the Islamic world."

In the same speech bin Laden emphasized the historical dimension to the struggle between Islam and the West: "This war is fundamentally religious. The people of the East are Muslims. They sympathized with Muslims against the people of the West, who are the crusaders." He goes on to stress that conflicts between Islam and the West, both in the past and in the present, are merely realizations of what was foretold in the Islamic scriptures:

This fact is proven in the book of God Almighty and in the teachings of our messenger (may God's peace and blessings be upon him). Under no circumstances should we forget this enmity between us and the infidels. For, the enmity is based on creed. God says: "Never will the Jews or the

9. "Oh God, Open All Doors for Me," *The Washington Post*, September 28, 2001.
10. Fred Halliday, *Two Hours That Shook the World: September 11, 2001: Causes and Consequences* (London: Saqi Books, 2002), 233.

Christians be satisfied with thee unless thou follow their form of religion" [Sura 2:120]. It is a question of faith, not a war against terrorism, as Bush and Blair try to depict it.[11]

Thus bin Laden is clearly attempting to capitalize on the reasons for anti-Western feeling among the Muslim masses: scriptural references, historical factors, and late-twentieth-century conflicts.

It is important to remind ourselves that radical Islamists would not immediately embrace the West if the modern issues were quickly resolved: that is, if suddenly Israel were dismantled, Iraqi sanctions were dropped, and U.S. troops withdrew from Arabia. If these three steps were taken, Muslim radicals would find other causes for complaint because in essence—and this is the key point—their particular literalist reading of Islamic scripture leads them to conclude that nonbelievers (non-Muslims) are infidels and should be fought. The issues of Israel, Iraq, and U.S. military bases—plus other struggles such as those in Chechnya and Kashmir—are merely manifestations of the radicals' conflict with the West, rather than its causes.

Rejecting Criticism by Other Muslim Leaders

Another significant characteristic of Islamic radicals is their readiness to dismiss the religious credentials of Muslims who do not share their views. In response to the September 11 attacks, many Muslim leaders around the world issued strong condemnations of Muslim radical approaches, as we shall see in subsequent discussion.

In a significant example of this, the head of Egypt's Al-Azhar University issued a fatwa (edict) declaring that the views and beliefs of Osama bin Laden did not reflect true Islam. In response, bin Laden said in interview:

> The *fatwa* of any official *aalim* (religious figure) has no value for me. History is full of such ulema (clerics) who justify Riba (interest), who justify the occupation of Palestine by the Jews, who justify the presence of American troops around Harmain Sharifain (holy places in Saudi Arabia). These people support the infidels for their personal gain. The true ulema support the jihad against America.[12]

This dogged insistence on military jihad and rejection of more moderate approaches to adversarial situations on the part of radicals

11. Osama bin Laden, speaking on November 3, 2001. Available on the World Wide Web: http://news.bbc.co.uk/low/english/world/monitoring/media_reports/newsid_16360 00/1636782.stm.

12. "Muslims Have the Right to Attack America," *The Observer* (London), November 11, 2001.

strongly resembles the Kharijite ideology, the extremist rejectionist approach that first emerged during the caliphate of Ali in the mid–seventh century. Kharijite thinking is expressed succinctly by Joseph Kenny: "Khârijism, in its true revolutionary spirit, never was a permanent movement, but it is an ever-recurring ideology, taking on different names, which appeals to Muslims who are marginalized and desperate in a Muslim society."[13]

Educational Formation

In early November 2001, Malaysian Prime Minister Mahatir Mohamed warned that a group of radical Islamists had undergone instruction at an unnamed religious school in Pakistan, followed by military training in Afghanistan under the Taliban, in preparation for overthrowing the governments of Malaysia, Indonesia, and the Philippines. Their aim, according to Dr. Mahatir, was to set up an Islamic state in the region.[14]

While such warnings by non-Muslim authorities attract considerable attention, the effect of a prominent Muslim leader issuing such a statement is even more profound. Dr. Mahatir had in fact identified a key element in the program of radical Islamists: using Islamic religious schools to prepare young Muslim activists for engaging in jihad campaigns to establish Islamist regimes in majority Muslim locations.

Western audiences and even political leaders had been largely unaware of the key role of such religious schools in manufacturing extremism. But all became clear following the events of September 11, 2001. This strategy is clearly articulated by Mohamed Charfi, former president of the Tunisian Human Rights League and Tunisian minister of education from 1989 to 1994:

> Since Sept. 11, the world has come to know more about the educational systems prevalent today in Muslim countries and their role in promoting hostility toward the West. . . . Many Muslim children still learn at school the ancient ideology of a triumphant Muslim empire, an ideology that held all non-Muslims to be in error and saw its mission as bringing Islam's light to the world. And yet young people see their governments working to live in peace with non-Muslim powers. Such discordant teachings do not prepare children to live in a changing world. Osama bin Laden, like the 15 Saudis who participated in the criminal

13. Joseph Kenny, "The Sources of Radical Movements in Islam," *Skepticos* 1 (1990): 19.

14. "Mahatir Tuduh Kelompok Militan Berniat Menjatuhkannya," *Kompas*, November 10, 2001.

operations of Sept. 11, seems to have been the pure product of his schooling.[15]

Pakistani Islamic religious schools, or *madrasas*, had played a key role in preparing those young activists who later came to form the leadership of the Taliban movement in Afghanistan. The network of Pakistani madrasas runs parallel to the state educational system. Official Pakistan government reports record around 6,500 such madrasas in Pakistan with around 600,000 students enrolled. Yet such figures appear to understate the extent of the phenomenon since they do not take into account the number of mosques offering the same religious education. During the 1980s and 1990s they were instrumental in fostering a climate of religious extremism, both in Pakistan and across the border in Afghanistan.

Peshawar is the heartland of such radical madrasas. The number of religious schools in the Peshawar area of Pakistan jumped from 13 in 1980 to 87 by the end of 1998, with an estimated student population of around 18,000. Syed Inayetullah, an eighteen-year-old Pakistani in his third year at the Rahatabad madrasa in Peshawar, gave voice to the radical ideology produced by such institutions: "Everything you [Americans] do is wrong. America's wealth, its resources, are in the hands of Jews, and they are not using it for a noble cause."[16]

Jeffrey Goldberg closely examined the Haqqania madrasa in the Northwest Frontier Province of Pakistan. Goldberg describes the Haqqani madrasa as a "jihad factory." At the time of his visit in 2000, this madrasa offered an eight-year course of study for high-school-age and university-age students focused on interpretation of the Qur'an and of the Hadith, Islamic jurisprudence, and Islamic history. Goldberg pointed out that "very few of the students . . . study anything but Islamic subjects. There are no world history courses, or math courses, or computer rooms or science labs at the madrasa."[17] The ages of the 3,000 students at the Haqqania madrasa, most of them poor Afghani boys who live and study without charge, range from 9 to 35. There are no girls at the school.[18]

15. Mohamed Charfi, "Reaching the Next Muslim Generation," *New York Times,* March 12, 2002.

16. Tyler Marshall and John Daniszewski, "Spreading Hate: Pakistan's Muslim Schools Preach Dark View of U.S.," *Los Angeles Times,* September 19, 2001.

17. Jeffrey Goldberg, "Inside Jihad U.: The Education of a Holy Warrior," *New York Times Magazine,* June 25, 2000.

18. Mark McDonald, "Radicals Wield Political Force," *Miami Herald,* September 24, 2001.

An Agence France-Presse report noted that "more than 100 religious schools in Pakistan are engaged in brainwashing girls as young as five to women as old as 65 preparing them to 'attain martyrdom' by fighting in Kashmir and elsewhere."[19]

Much of Pakistan's domestic support for the Taliban and opposition to the U.S.-led air strikes on Afghanistan in late 2001 came from militant students studying at madrasas in Peshawar, Quetta, and other Pakistan border towns.

In recognition of the significance of these schools in fostering conflict, and under pressure from the U.S. government, the Pakistan authorities sought to bring the madrasas under a closer level of scrutiny. In late October 2001, Pakistan Federal Education Minister Zubeda Jalal said at a press conference at the Quetta Press Club that the network of madrasas had agreed to be registered with the Pakistan government and to receive official assistance. Under this arrangement, the government would provide the madrasas with textbooks on three subjects—Urdu, mathematics, and science—and would also provide computers. Training would be given to teachers in selected subjects.

In June 2002, Pakistan Information Minister Nisar Memon announced a government ordinance giving all madrasas six months to register formally with the government or face closure.[20]

However, this was not the first time the Pakistan government had tried to bring the madrasas under its umbrella. After earlier attempts to bring about government influence on the madrasa curriculum, many madrasa teachers refused to cooperate. "We do not accept the government syllabus," said Allah Ditta, a teacher at the Jamia Qurania Arabia Madrasa in the village of Macchikay in Pakistan's central Punjab province. "Their syllabus does not make a man religious. The aim of our religion is to reach God."[21] The issue of potential noncooperation with Pakistan government directives was no doubt a key element in the Pakistan government decision in early 2002 to expel thousands of Arabs, Afghans, and other foreigners studying at Islamic religious schools in Pakistan, a move that some international observers described as "a bold step in the right direction."[22]

The role of the Pakistan madrasas in preparing young Muslim radicals for participation in jihad campaigns is reflected in many other countries as well. In Indonesia, the terrorist bombing on the island of

19. Agence France-Presse, October 24, 2001.
20. Susannah Price, "Pakistan Religious Schools Deadline," *BBC News Online,* June 19, 2002.
21. "Myth and Reality of a Pakistani Madrasa." Available on the World Wide Web: http://www.rediff.com/news/2001/aug/21pak1.htm.
22. "Terrorists' Aim in Pakistan," *Christian Science Monitor,* March 20, 2002.

Bali on October 12, 2002, was shown to be linked with radical Islamic instruction provided at several Islamic schools in neighboring East Java.[23] This phenomenon also applies among Muslim minorities in Western countries, where after-hours madrasa equivalents attached to radical mosques have prepared many young men to take part in overseas jihad campaigns.

MEMBERSHIP

There is a risk in seeking to identify which organizations and groups could be considered members of an international Islamist movement. Such an analysis could be taken to imply that all member groups share a degree of commitment and the same views on necessary action. This is not the case. While some radical Islamist groups willingly participate in terrorist attacks against civilian targets, such as those seen on September 11, others avoid direct participation in such actions. However, the latter group might express support for the ideals of the terrorists and go so far as to send members to fight alongside terrorist groups subjected to retaliatory attacks by non-Muslim powers.

Al-Qa'ida

Of those groups committed to violent action against perceived enemies, the al-Qa'ida network is the most prominent. It was established by Osama bin Laden in the late 1980s to bring together Arabs who fought in Afghanistan against the Soviet invasion.

Following its founding, al-Qa'ida forged alliances with like-minded fundamentalist groups around the world. In late 2001, al-Qa'ida cells had been identified or were suspected in wide-ranging locations, including Afghanistan, Pakistan, Bangladesh, Saudi Arabia, Qatar, Yemen, Jordan, Egypt, Libya, Lebanon, Algeria, Tunisia, Mauritania, Sudan, Azerbaijan, Uzbekistan, Tajikistan, Chechnya, Somalia, Eritrea, Kenya, Tanzania, Uganda, Ethiopia, other parts of Africa, Malaysia, the Philippines, Uruguay, Ecuador, Bosnia, Kosovo, Albania, the United Kingdom, Canada, and allegedly the United States itself.

With such diversity, al-Qa'ida clearly operates as a loose network of affiliates. The groups coordinate through al-Qa'ida's Shura Council, a kind of board of directors that includes representatives from the many groups. Prior to the war in late 2001, the council met on a regular basis in Afghanistan to plan operations.[24]

23. John Aglionby, "Police Swoop on Home Village of Bali Bomb Suspect," *The Guardian*, November 11, 2002.

24. Alexander and Swetnam, *Usama bin Laden's al-Qaida*, 3.

Other Radical Groups in the Muslim World

While direct cooperation between al-Qa'ida and other groups can be difficult to define precisely, a shared ideology can more easily be identified. The glue that binds such groups together tends to be associated with the theme of jihad, and this often reflects itself in the names of like-minded radical groups.

It was widely reported that bin Laden's al-Qa'ida network had formed an alliance with the Egyptian jihad groups. The jihad movement in Egypt has been active since the late 1970s, and has split into two factions. The first, led by Ayman al-Zawahiri, was closely involved in al-Qa'ida operations in Afghanistan, where al-Zawahiri spent long periods of time. The second was the Vanguards of Conquest (Tala'a al-Fateh), led by Ahmad Husayn Agiza. For their spiritual leader, both factions looked to Sheikh Umar Abd-al Rahman, imprisoned in the United States for involvement in the abortive 1993 attempt to bomb the World Trade Center.

In terms of ideology the Palestinian radical group Hamas shares much with al-Qa'ida. The group organized public rallies in the Gaza Strip in early October 2001 in support of Osama bin Laden after U.S.-led air strikes against Afghanistan. A Hamas spokesman in Gaza, Abdel Aziz Rantisi, endorsed statements by bin Laden, commenting in a special interview with Al Jazeera television station that "bin Laden does not practice terrorism. The terrorist is the Zionist enemy (Israel), and the Palestinian people are those who are burned by the fire of this terror."[25] Some researchers suggest that Hamas and al-Qa'ida are formally affiliated[26] and report that a network of Palestinians within al-Qa'ida was active in recruiting Hamas members to undergo training in al-Qa'ida camps in Afghanistan before these camps were destroyed by Western forces in late 2001.[27]

Radical Islamist activity is not confined to the Arab world. In Indonesia, the period 1998–2002 witnessed the flourishing of Islamist radicalism, due in no small part to inputs from the al-Qa'ida network. The chief local agent of radicalism is the Jemaah Islamiyah (JI), formed in the 1970s by Abdullah Achmad Sungkar, who met Osama bin Laden in Afghanistan in the early 1990s. After this meeting, JI quickly became an associate group of al-Qa'ida.[28] Confirming the warning of

25. "Palestinian Officials Reject bin Laden Statement," *Ha'aretz*, October 8, 2001.

26. Alexander and Swetnam, *Usama Bin Laden's al-Qaida*, 30.

27. Y. Barsky, "Hamas—The Islamic Resistance Movement of Palestine," American Jewish Committee Briefings, February 7, 2002.

28. Rohan Gunaratna, *Inside Al Qaeda: Global Network of Terror* (London: Hurst, 2002), 187.

Malaysian Prime Minister Mahatir, cited previously, Rohan Gunaratna observes:

> Al Qaeda's Asian arm—Jemaah Islamiyyah (JI: Islamic Group)—aims to
> establish an Islamic republic unifying Malaysia, Indonesia, Brunei,
> southern Thailand and Mindanao in the Philippines. Originally an In-
> donesian group, under Al Qaeda's influence JI established cells through-
> out the region, its plan being to carve out smaller Islamic states from
> within the existing state borders and later unify them in an Islamic
> republic.[29]

Dozens of foreign Islamist jihad fighters, mostly from the Middle
East, were reported as openly operating with local Islamist groups in
various parts of the country. The majority were in the eastern Maluku
islands, helping the militant Java-based Laskar Jihad (Holy War
Force) organization in the war it has conducted against local Christians since 1999. So many had arrived that Laskar Jihad even opened
a special welcome desk for them at the local airport.[30]

The movement of radical activists with connections to Indonesia
was not one way. Laskar Jihad leader Ja'far Umar Thalib trained at
an al-Qa'ida camp in Afghanistan, while some of his subordinates
studied in Libya. Other radical Indonesian groups, such as the Islamic Defenders Front, the Laskar Hizbullah, and the Islamic Youth
Movement (GPI), openly acknowledge having close ties to al-Qa'ida.[31]
As the war in Afghanistan unfolded in October 2001, some 300 Indonesians traveled to that country to fight alongside the Taliban regime against the United States. The Islamic Youth Movement
claimed to have arranged their departure, and as the war turned
against the Taliban, spokesmen for the Islamic Youth Movement
said that 50 of the 300 Indonesians had managed to flee Afghanistan into Pakistan.[32]

In the neighboring Philippines, the Moro Islamic Liberation Front
and the Abu Sayyaf group have known links with al-Qa'ida and other
radical groups based in Pakistan and Afghanistan. Philippine intelligence agencies were tracking transmissions of financial support
from al-Qa'ida to several small Islamic fundamentalist groups in the

29. Ibid., 192–93.
30. For a detailed study of intra-Muslim debates in Indonesia and the surge in radicalism, see Peter G. Riddell, "The Diverse Voices of Political Islam in Post-Suharto Indonesia," *Islam and Christian-Muslim Relations* 13.1 (January 2002): 65–84.
31. John Aglionby, "Islamists in SE Asia Linked to bin Laden," *The Guardian*, October 11, 2001.
32. Abu Hanifah, "Gov't in Dark about Indonesian Fighters in Afghanistan," *Jakarta
Post*, November 19, 2001.

southern Philippines, sent through the International Islamic Relief Organization.[33]

Radical Cells in Western Countries

Two organizations based in Britain readily fall into the category of radical Islamist ideologues. They are al-Muhajiroun and Supporters of Shariah (SOS). Both openly admit to recruiting and sending jihad fighters to foreign conflicts. But there is no evidence that either has any links with the terrorist acts of the al-Qa'ida network in recent years.

Nevertheless, ideological support for Osama bin Laden's struggle against non-Muslim powers is clear in the statements of both groups about the September 11 attacks. The leader of al-Muhajiroun, Sheikh Omar Bakri Muhammad, said when interviewed on BBC Radio 4's *Today* program on September 12: "What happened was a direct consequence of the evil foreign policy of the USA. This is the compensation and payback for its own atrocities against Muslims."[34]

An al-Muhajiroun press release of November 7, 2001, included repeated calls for jihad:

> Muslims will proclaim that the only solution to the atrocities being committed against them in Palestine, Kashmir, Chechnya or Afghanistan is Jihad; an obligation to engage in physically upon those nearest and an obligation upon the Muslims around the world to support verbally, financially and physically![35]

Furthermore, the organization called upon British Muslim jihad fighters "to give up their Citizenship before they go to Afghanistan, as Islam forbids us to commit treason. Calling Muslims that hold citizenship to go to Afghanistan."[36] Moreover, al-Muhajiroun had clear advice for British and American Muslims contemplating service in the countries' armies, issuing a clear warning to them not to engage in the allied military operations in Afghanistan, and declaring that participation in these operations would be seen as "an act of apostasy."[37]

33. For a detailed discussion of al-Qa'ida penetration of the Philippines, see Gunaratna, *Inside Al Qaeda*, 174ff.

34. Yotam Feldner, "Radical Islamist Profiles: Sheikh Omar Bakri Muhammad—London," *Inquiry and Analysis*, Middle East Media Research Institute, October 24, 2001. Available on the World Wide Web: http://www.memri.de/uebersetzungen_analysen/themen/islamistische_ideologie/isl_bakri_24_10_01.html.

35. Press release, November 7, 2001. Available on the World Wide Web: http://www.almuhajiroun.com.

36. Ibid.

37. Ibid.

Unlike the case of al-Muhajiroun, the SOS Web site was disabled within one week of the September 11 attacks. Nevertheless, the organization's statements and actions around the time of the attacks clearly showed its ideological position. Abu Hamza Al-Masri, leader of SOS, described the terrorist attacks as "self-defense."[38] Demonstrators at the Finsbury Park Mosque in North London, where SOS bases itself, were reported as publicly joking about "yuppies" falling from the World Trade Center and urging worshipers to make similar attacks. The name of Osama bin Laden was proclaimed repeatedly in laudatory terms during the service of Friday prayers on September 14.[39]

Following the September 11 terrorist attacks, individuals and groups belonging to radical Islamist organizations were arrested in several European locations. In particular, police in France and Spain moved quickly to detain a number of people suspected of involvement in radical Islamist activities. This reflected a worldwide response: by the end of March 2002 more than 1,300 extremists believed to be linked to al-Qa'ida had been arrested in more than 70 countries.[40]

In a particularly chilling development, President Hosni Mubarak of Egypt reported that a communiqué from Osama bin Laden had been received in June 2001, revealing a plan to assassinate American President George W. Bush and other heads of state attending the G8 summit in Italy in July.[41]

Unanswered Questions

The nature of shadowy radical groups is such that many questions are left unanswered. In an attempt to find answers, researchers must of necessity deal with much material that is unconfirmed, at times relying on rumor and speculation drawn from sketchy and inconclusive evidence.

One such issue surrounds possible links between radical Islamist groups and communities of refugees and asylum seekers. Australian media reports suggested that refugee newcomers to Australia from Egypt, Jordan, and Tunisia were identified as being members of, or having connections with, the radical Al-Gama'a Al-Islamiyya, Al-Maqdisi, Al-Da'wa, and Al-Nahda groups.[42] Such suggestions were given greater

38. *Channel 4 News Special*, September 14, 2001.
39. *The Times* (London), September 15, 2001.
40. Available on the World Wide Web: http://story.news.yahoo.com/news?tmpl=story &u=/nm/20020319/ts_nm/attack_cia_dc_1&cid=578.
41. Interview on French television on September 25, 2001, reported in *New York Times*, September 26, 2001.
42. Available on the World Wide Web: http://news.com.au/common/story_page/ 0,4057,3034364%5E2%5E%5Enbv,00.html.

substance in the wake of the October 2002 terrorist bombings in Bali, when it was found that asylum seekers in previous years had included several people interviewed by the Australian Refugee Tribunal in 1999 who admitted to being

> members of the Australian branch of Jemaah Islamiyah. One person seeking a visa claimed to be fourth in the international line of command of Abu Bakar Bashir's now banned organization. A former member of the Refugee Tribunal in the 1990s, Bruce Haigh, says members of fundamentalist groups gained residence in Australia on the grounds of religious persecution under the Indonesian government of the time.[43]

Furthermore, Germany's governmental Agency for the Protection of the Constitution reported that Iraqi radicals, posing as refugees, had been smuggled into Western Europe via the German-Czech border for the purpose of promoting radical activities.[44] Moreover, such claims find support in al-Qa'ida documentation. For example, a police search in Manchester, England, found a training manual in an al-Qa'ida member's home. Lesson 12 of the manual is entitled "Espionage: Information-Gathering Using Covert Methods" and includes the following instructions:

> Recruiting agents is the most dangerous task that an enlisted brother can perform. . . . Candidates for Recruitment Are: 1. Smugglers 2. Those seeking political asylum.[45]

Another unconfirmed issue surrounds the possible involvement of particular governments in promoting international radical and terrorist activities. Chief suspect in this regard is the Iraqi government of Saddam Hussein. There was strong evidence of an Iraqi intelligence officer meeting with Mohammed Atta, one of the ringleaders of the September 11 terrorist attacks on the United States, just five months before the series of attacks. In reporting this meeting, the *New York Times* added that this evidence did not amount to proof of Iraqi involvement in the attacks.[46] Furthermore, two defectors from Iraqi intelligence admitted in November 2001 that they had worked for several years at a

43. "Video Interviews Confirm Refugees Linked to JI," *ABC News*, November 20, 2002.

44. Available on the World Wide Web: http://dailynews.yahoo.com/h/nm/20011031/wl/attack_germany_iraq_dc_1.html.

45. *Al Qaeda Training Manual.* Available on the World Wide Web: http://www.usdoj.gov/ag/trainingmanual.htm.

46. Patrick E. Tyler with John Tagliabue, "Czechs Confirm Iraqi Agent Met with Terror Ringleader," *New York Times*, October 27, 2001.

secret Iraqi government camp training Islamic terrorists in rotations of five or six months since 1995. The defectors said they knew of a highly guarded compound within the camp where Iraqi scientists, led by a German, produced biological warfare materials.[47]

Modus Operandi

What methods do radical Islamist groups use to achieve their desired ends? Groups that seem not to be directly involved in violence carry out a range of activities. First is the establishment of their ideological approach as dominant in particular mosques. A clear example of this is the Finsbury Park Mosque in London, where the radical group SOS has presented its radical ideology for some years, and from where young jihad fighters have been recruited and sent to foreign conflicts.

Skillful use of the Internet is also a feature of radical Islamist groups. The Al-Maddad group maintained a professionally produced Web site focusing on international Islamic struggles in Chechnya, Palestine, Philippines, Sudan, and Kashmir, and claimed to have sent dozens of Islamic fighters to these areas. The Khilafah.com Web site preaches a radical anti-Western ideology that exhorts young Muslims to join the Islamic struggle against "American-led oppression."

Following the September 11 attacks, increased pressure from security agencies on such sites resulted in some closures. Azzam Publications ran one of the larger jihad-related Internet sites, Azzam.com, offering primers such as "How Can I Train Myself for Jihad?" Founded in late 1996, Azzam Publications was named after Dr. Sheikh Abdullah Azzam, a mentor to Osama bin Laden. The Azzam.com Web site was closed down after complaints. Azzam Publications then opened the www.qoqaz.co.za Web site, which continued to report on jihad from the front line, eulogizing those who have been "blessed with martyrdom."

Other radical Islamist groups involved themselves more directly in campaigns of violence, and in this domain the al-Qa'ida network is without peer. A fundamental pillar of such groups revolves around finances. A French intelligence report commented that "the dominant trait of bin Laden's operations is that of a terrorist network backed by a vast financial structure."[48]

47. Chris Hedges, "Defectors Cite Iraqi Training for Terrorism," *New York Times*, November 8, 2001. Addressing the UN on February 5, 2003, U.S. Secretary of State Colin Powell presented additional compelling evidence of links between the Iraqi government and al-Qa'ida. Available on the World Wide Web: http://www.un.int/usa/03print_clp0205.htm.
48. "Al-Qaida and the Gold Trail That Leads through Dubai to September 11," *The Guardian*, February 19, 2002.

In terms of financial operations, bin Laden brought to the al-Qa'ida network a massive personal fortune estimated at up to $300 million. This has been supplemented by millions of dollars collected by radical clergy and mosques in the form of alms donations, and then distributed through certain Islamic charitable organizations.[49] Dubai has served as an established financial hub for radical Islamist groups. There are reports that the $500,000 used to fund the attacks of September 11, 2001, was funneled through Dubai. When allied attacks on Afghanistan began in early October 2001, couriers transported al-Qa'ida financial resources out of Afghanistan by using it to buy gold, and Dubai was an essential staging point on the journey.[50]

Financial operations in Britain were also key to the policies of the radicals, with details sometimes articulated in parliamentary debates. For example, Baroness Cox, speaking in the House of Lords on October 18, 2001, provided information on the methods of businessmen with radical Islamist leanings penetrating into the financial systems of key strategic organizations.[51] Even before the World Trade Center attack in September 2001, Britain had frozen at least £47 million of assets in U.K. bank accounts of suspected Afghan terrorists and members of the Taliban regime.[52] Thus the problem identified by Baroness Cox was real, though it would seem that government action in response to such reports was inadequate.

Military training serves as a key plank in the operations of the radical Islamist groups. Documents captured by allied forces at al-Qa'ida training camps in Afghanistan included student notebooks, instructor lesson plans, course curricula, training manuals, reference books, and memorandums. These pointed to a two-tier military training program. The first, which occupied most recruits, prepared them to be irregular ground combatants. The other tier provided volunteers with advanced units that prepared them for terrorist assignments abroad.[53] The *New York Times* estimated that approximately twenty thousand recruits passed through the al-Qa'ida training camps since they were established in 1996 with bin Laden's arrival in Afghanistan from the Sudan.[54]

49. Alexander and Swetnam, *Usama Bin Laden's al-Qaida*, 29.

50. "Al-Qaida and the Gold Trail."

51. "International Terrorism—Motion to Take Note," *Parliamentary Debates (Hansard), House of Lords Official Report* 627/29 (October 18, 2001).

52. Available on the World Wide Web: http://www.guardian.co.uk/waronterror/story/0,1361,558813,00.html.

53. C. J. Chivers and David Rohde, "Afghan Camps Turn Out Holy War Guerrillas and Terrorists," *New York Times*, March 18, 2002.

54. David Rohde and C. J. Chivers, "Al Qaeda's Grocery Lists and Manuals of Killing," *New York Times*, March 17, 2002.

Once training was completed, the jihad fighters engaged in field operations that drew on a mixture of methods: murder, suicide attacks, and hijackings, such as were seen on September 11, 2001. Since that day, radicals allied with al-Qa'ida have been prevented from carrying out a number of acts of violence.[55] On September 13, 2001, a plot to blow up the American Embassy in Paris was foiled. In December 2001, a team of al-Qa'ida members was arrested in Singapore as they prepared plans to blow up embassies of the United States, Israel, Britain, and Australia. On December 22, 2001, Richard Reid, a British citizen, was overpowered on a Miami-bound flight as he attempted to detonate explosives.

Along with these failed operations, al-Qa'ida sympathizers have accomplished a number of successful terrorist activities since September 11, 2001. On April 16, 2002, a suicide bomber drove a vehicle packed with explosives into the El Ghriba synagogue on the resort island of Djerba in Tunisia, killing 21 people, including 14 Germans.[56] On May 8, 2002, a car bomb was detonated in Karachi, killing 11 French nationals and 3 Pakistanis. On June 14, 2002, another car bomb was detonated by a suicide bomber outside the American Consulate in Karachi, killing 8 people. On October 12, 2002, bombs were detonated outside tourist nightclubs in Bali, Indonesia, killing almost 200 people.

However, much more sinister plans have also been attributed to the al-Qa'ida network, showing that its leaders are committed to using ever more destructive methods.

Before the American air strikes on Afghanistan that commenced in October 2001, it was widely reported that Osama bin Laden and his al-Qa'ida network had acquired nuclear materials for possible use in their terrorism war against the West. With the rapid fall of the various Taliban strongholds in November 2001, these fears were confirmed by various findings. *The Times* of London discovered partly burnt documents in a safe house in the Karta Parwan quarter of Kabul, hastily abandoned by the Taliban. Written in Arabic, German, Urdu, and English, the notes included detailed designs for missiles, bombs, and nuclear weapons, including descriptions of how the detonation of TNT compresses plutonium into a critical mass, sparking a chain reaction and ultimately a thermonuclear reaction.[57]

55. "Qaeda's New Links Increase Threats from Global Sites," *New York Times*, June 16, 2002.

56. Available on the World Wide Web: http://story.news.yahoo.com/news?tmpl=story &ncid=578&e=1&cid=578&u=/nm/20020623/ts_nm/attack_qaeda_synagogue_dc_3.

57. *The Times* (London), November 15, 2001.

The greater the territory abandoned by the Taliban, the greater the body of evidence unearthed pointing to al-Qa'ida's planning to produce and use nuclear devices. American intelligence agencies concluded in early December 2001 that the al-Qa'ida network had made greater strides than previously suspected toward fashioning crude radiological weapons that would spread radioactivity over a wide area. This conclusion was reached after interrogation of captured al-Qa'ida members and examination of evidence gathered at al-Qa'ida facilities in Afghanistan by American forces.[58]

The fears of American authorities were realized in June 2002 when an American citizen, Jose Padilla, alias Abdullah al-Muhajir, a suspected al-Qa'ida operative returning to America from Pakistan, was arrested for planning to detonate a radiological dispersion device, or "dirty bomb," in the United States.[59]

Clearly, much more water will pass under the bridge before al-Qa'ida's conflict with the West reaches resolution.

58. Available on the World Wide Web: http://dailynews.yahoo.com/htx/nm/20011204/ts/attack_osama_nuclear_dc_2.html.

59. "U.S. Says It Halted Qaeda Plot to Use Radioactive Bomb," *New York Times*, June 11, 2002.

12

THE MODERATE
WORLDVIEW

As we surveyed the history of Islam in parts 1 and 2 of this book, we became aware of internal tensions that erupted into open rivalry and conflict among Muslims at different points of that history. Some of these rivalries derived from power struggles, such as the Umayyad-Abbasid split in the mid–eighth century. Other tensions derived from a different approach to interpreting the primary texts of Islam. An example of this latter opposition was the literalist approach of conservative ulama (clerics) versus the more reason-based approach of the Mu'tazila (philosopher-theologians) in the ninth century.

The literalist versus rationalist tension was never permanently resolved, though at different times each gained the ascendancy. It is fair to say that the former established itself as normative for much of Islam's history. However, the modernist movements of the twentieth century saw a reassertion of rationalist approaches to interpreting the Qur'an and Hadith among many scholars.

This tension has resurfaced in no small measure in the present day and has become especially acute since the events of September 11, 2001. It would be most misleading to assume that the literalist approach of radical Islamists speaks for all Muslims. Indeed, a moderate voice within Islam is regularly articulated and seeks to firmly ground any interpretation of the Qur'an and Hadith within modern-day realities. This approach offers a sense of hope and optimism to non-Muslim observers of the Islamic world.

We will now turn our attention to listening to these moderate voices, in order to fill in another piece of the mosaic that is Islam. Again, we will focus on the events of September 11, 2001, and its aftermath. We will pay particular attention to the British context since this provides one of the most dynamic arenas for the struggle that is taking place between literalist and moderate rationalist Islamic theologians.

Moderate Muslims were quick to speak out, denouncing the terrorist attacks on the American sites. Their denunciations drew on both
theological and humanitarian perspectives.

SCRIPTURAL AND HUMANITARIAN CONSIDERATIONS

Dr. Zaki Badawi was one of the first moderates to speak out. In addition to serving as director of the Muslim College (London), Dr.
Badawi was also the head of the Council of Imams and Mosques in
Britain at the time of his writing. He is thus not only a prominent and
respected academic, but he also exerts profound influence within the
religious hierarchy of Islamic Britain.

Dr. Badawi was quick to point to the teachings of the Qur'an in condemning the September 11 attacks. Speaking on BBC Radio 4 two days
after the attacks, Badawi quoted the Islamic scripture as saying: "We
ordained that if anyone killed a person . . . not in retaliation of murder
or in punishment, . . . it would be as if he killed all Mankind. And if anyone saved a life it would be as if he saved the life of all Mankind."[1] He
offered his own interpretation of the significance of this verse: "Those
who plan and carry out such acts are condemned by Islam, and the
massacres of thousands, whoever perpetrated it [sic], is a crime against
God as well as against humanity."[2] Other prominent Muslims within
Britain and without made similar recourse to scripture in condemning
the violent attacks on American sites. Dr. M. Sa'id Ramadan Al-Bouti,
an academic from the University of Damascus, while writing for Q
News, the leading British Muslim magazine, quoted certain Qur'anic
verses as calling for piety, justice, fairness, and moderation. Hamza
Yusuf, an outspoken American Muslim activist who writes for the same
periodical, cited the Islamic prophet Muhammad as warning against
extremism: "For it is that which destroyed the peoples before you."[3]

Taking a slightly different angle, yet still rejecting the interpretation
of the radicals' scriptural injunctions, American Muslim academic
Zayn Kassam said: "I'm not sure I worship the God the pilots of the
[September 11 hijacked] plane did . . . since mine is a God of compassion, mercy, and looks down on people who take innocent lives."[4] In a

1. Sura 5:32.
2. *Thought for the Day*, BBC Radio 4, September 13, 2001.
3. "A Time for Introspection," *Q News*, October 14, 2001. This Hadith account is reported by the traditionists al-Nasa'i and Ibn Maja. Cf. Yusuf al-Qaradawi, "Extremism,"
in *Liberal Islam: A Sourcebook*, ed. Charles Kurzman (New York: Oxford University
Press, 1998), 197.
4. Zayn Kassam, "September 11, 2001, and Islam," *Council of Societies for the Study
of Religion* 31.1 (February 2002): 8.

remarkable article, British Muslim academic Ziauddin Sardar called for urgent recognition of a problem that the Islamic community should address: "Muslims are in the best position to take the lead in the common cause against terrorism. The terrorists are among us, the Muslim communities of the world." This theme was picked up by *Q News:* "Terrorism has no place in the vocabulary of Islamic law. . . . The Muslim world now needs to become more stern with extremists."[5] Sardar further sought to invoke Islamic law himself in condemning the terrorists:

> To Muslims everywhere I issue this fatwa: any Muslim involved in the planning, financing, training, recruiting, support or harbouring of those who commit acts of indiscriminate violence against persons or the apparatus or infrastructure of states is guilty of terror and no part of the Ummah [Muslim community]. It is the duty of every Muslim to spare no effort in hunting down, apprehending and bringing such criminals to justice.[6]

Likewise, *Q News* declared the terrorists to be beyond the pale: "We need to tell the world that Islam is guiltless, and that terrorism is carried out by members of an aberrant cult, called Kharijism, which borrows some Islamic forms but is in fact a separate religion."[7] Hamza Yusuf, the California-based activist, placed a similar focus on aberrant Kharijite views in identifying Islamic radicalism with the ancient breakaway sect: "Unfortunately, the West does not know what every Muslim scholar knows; that the worst enemies of Islam are from within. The worst of these are the khawaarij who delude others by the deeply dyed religious exterior that they project."[8]

The Egyptian scholar Yusuf al-Qaradawi, writing before September 2001, is particularly critical of extremist views, seeing them as having distant roots:

> Extremism reaches its utmost limit when a single group deprives all people of the right to safety and protection, and instead sanctions their killing and the confiscation of their lives and property. This, of course, occurs when an extremist holds all people—except those in his group—to be unbelievers. . . . This is the trap into which the Khawarij fell during the dawn of Islam.[9]

5. "There Are No Muslim Terrorists," *Q News,* October 2001, 9.
6. Ziauddin Sardar, "My Fatwa on the Fanatics," *Sunday Observer* (London), September 23, 2001.
7. "There Are No Muslim Terrorists," 9.
8. Hamza Yusuf, "A Time for Introspection," *Q News,* October 2001, 14.
9. Qaradawi, "Extremism," 202.

The American-based Iraqi writer Kanan Makiya prefers to draw a parallel between bin Ladenism and a notorious radical offshoot of Christianity: "[Bin Ladenism] is not Islam any more than the Ku Klux Klan is Christianity. No concessions can be made to either mind-set which have more in common with one another than they do with the religions they claim to represent."[10]

Condemnation also came from organizations and representative groups. The mainstream Muslim Council of Britain (MCB) quickly issued a press statement on September 14, 2001, affirming that "the values, principles and precepts of Islam stand absolutely against wanton acts of terror."[11] In a news release reporting a meeting of British Islamic scholars on September 29, 2001, the MCB issued a warning about the possible impact of British Muslim radicals:

> Islamic values are being misrepresented or corrupted by individuals and vocal groups within the Muslim community. . . . The Muslim community is thus threatened from within and one of its primary duties is to protect the community—in particular the youth—from the activities of such groups. . . . In interaction with and dealing with such groups, there is no substitute for logic and clear argument and a forthright disavowal of the obnoxious positions they often adopt and the tactics that they use.

A gathering of Muslim scholars in Europe meeting on October 16, 2001, denounced the al-Qa'ida network:

> The so-called Qa'ida Organization . . . is not in any way an Islamic organization and its activities should not be linked to Muslims. The statements of the spokesmen of this organization are not in keeping with the teachings of Islam and have nothing to do with the Sunna. Not one of the leaders of this group enjoy the attributes that give him the right to issue fatwas.[12]

International gatherings of leading Muslim politicians echoed these views. In an emergency one-day meeting, the fifty-six members of the Organization of the Islamic Conference, held in Doha, Qatar, rejected bin Laden's claim that the emerging conflict was between Islam and

10. Kanan Makiya, "Fighting Islam's Ku Klux Klan," *The Observer* (London), October 7, 2001.

11. "Justice with Responsibility," a statement by the Muslim Council of Britain on the occasion of the special House of Commons Debate, September 14, 2001. Available on the World Wide Web: http://www.mcb.org.uk.

12. *Al-Hayat*, October 23, 2001, cited by Religious News Service from the Arab World, October 24–30, 2001.

the West. The conference's final communiqué said: "[The September 11] terror acts run counter to teachings of the divine religions as well as ethical and human values."[13]

Muslim condemnation of the September 11 attacks also appealed to humanitarian perspectives. The Muslim Council of Britain stated, "The perpetrators of these atrocities, regardless of their religious, ideological or political beliefs, stand outside the pale of civilised values."[14] The Director of the Islamic Foundation in Leicester, Dr. Manazir Ahsan, decried the events as "an attack on civilisation,"[15] while Baroness Uddin, a member of the British House of Lords from the Labour Party, called for the perpetrators to be brought to justice, stating that the terrorist assaults were "a most horrendous attack on all human beings."[16]

Further afield, the Palestinian Authority strongly criticized Osama bin Laden. Palestinian Cabinet Minister Nabil Shaath denounced bin Laden for broadcast remarks in which bin Laden linked his campaign to the cause of the Palestinians. Shaath insisted that Palestinians did not support bin Laden: "If [bin Laden] thinks that he serves the Palestinian cause this way, then let him be responsible for his remarks. We will not be." Bin Laden had said in a videotaped interview that neither "America nor the people who live in it will dream of security before we live it in Palestine."[17]

Palestinian Chairman Yasir Arafat also criticized bin Laden, declaring that the Saudi-born militant had turned the suffering of the Palestinian people into a tool to advance his own interests, and in the process was harming the interests of the Palestinians.

Support for Military Action against Radicals

Some moderate Muslims chose to express support for direct action against the radical groups responsible for the September 11 terrorist attacks.

Hesham El-Essawy, president of the Islamic Society for the Promotion of Religious Tolerance in Britain, said he believed the allied attacks on the Taliban were "fully justified." He added: "These people

---

13. Ewen MacAskill, "Muslim Nations Reject al-Qaida Dogma," *The Guardian,* October 11, 2001.

14. MCB press statement, September 13, 2001.

15. Available on the World Wide Web (dated September 12, 2001): http://www.islamic-foundation.org.uk/pressrelease.html.

16. House of Lords Hansard text for September 14, 2001 (210914–05). Available on the World Wide Web: http://www.parliament.the-stationery-office.co.uk/pa/ld199900/ldhansrd/pdvn/lds01/text/10914–05.htm.

17. "Arafat Blasts bin Laden for Exploiting Palestinian Cause," *Ha'aretz,* October 10, 2001.

[the Taliban] are doing everything that is un-Islamic. . . . They're harming Muslims more than they're harming non-Muslims. In some ways you could see this [war on terrorism] as an action for Islam, not against it."[18] In a similar vein, Masood Akhdal, the Imam of Luton's Central Mosque, said: "I do not agree that this is a war against Islam. This is a war against terrorism."[19]

King Abdullah of Jordan backed the war on terrorism and praised Tony Blair's efforts to reinvigorate the Middle East peace talks. In an address to members of the House of Commons in London, King Abdullah said that Jordan stood "shoulder to shoulder" with Britain in the coalition against terror. King Abdullah said military action against prime terrorist suspect Osama Bin Laden and his network should be pursued "with caution but also with unflinching resolve."[20]

Similar statements of support for British and American actions came from Kuwait's acting Prime Minister, Sabah al-Hamad al-Sabah, and President Pervez Musharraf of Pakistan.

Opposition to Military Action against Radicals

Nevertheless, many moderate Muslim individuals and organizations came out strongly against American military attacks on Afghanistan.

Tariq Ali, a prominent British Muslim writer, criticized the American choice of a military response to the September 11 terrorist attacks, suggesting instead that "a lesson could have been learnt from Israel's patient stalking, capture and trial of Adolf Eichmann, who was accused of a far more serious crime."[21]

The MCB leveled thinly veiled accusations of Western double standards: "The first acts of the 'coalition against terrorism' show that power is being wielded without ethics and the result is tyranny and terror. They can in no way be described as being 'in defence of democracy and civilised values.'"[22] In support of its argument, the MCB referred to various Qur'anic verses that preached a message of justice, fairness, and moderation.

Other British Muslim bodies, such as the Islamic Society of Britain and the Union of Muslim Organizations (UMO) of the United Kingdom and Ireland, reacted in a fashion similar to the MCB. Dr. Syed

18. "UK Muslim Leaders Divided over Afghan War," *BBC News*, November 14, 2001.
19. Available on the World Wide Web: http://www.thetimes.co.uk/article/0,,200137 0002–2001373874,00.html.
20. Available on the World Wide Web: http://www.thisisbradford.co.uk.
21. Tariq Ali, "Yes, There Is an Effective Alternative to the Bombing of Afghanistan," *The Independent* (London), October 17, 2001.
22. MCB news release (September 29, 2001) reporting a meeting of Imams and Ulama.

Aziz Pasha, general secretary of the UMO, argued somewhat optimistically: "We should have negotiated with the Taliban. They would have handed bin Laden over to an international court."[23]

Elsewhere, criticism of American actions by Muslim moderates was widespread. The Indonesian president and vice president were vocal in their criticism of America's decision to respond militarily. These views were widely echoed by leaders of many Muslim countries around the world. No doubt they were driven in large part by the divided nature of their respective constituencies, pulled in opposite directions by radical Islamist and moderate voices.

WHAT IT COULD BE

Although there was much comment by moderate Muslims distancing themselves from radical Islamists, as we have seen, the thrust of such statements was figuratively to "excommunicate" the radicals from the Islamic fold, rather than to engage with some of the most challenging issues touching upon Islamic scripture and doctrine itself.

Some who know the Muslim community firsthand have had cause to accuse it of closing ranks in times of difficulty, rather than engaging in necessary self-criticism. Ziauddin Sardar, writing in the *Sunday Observer* on September 23, 2001, observed that "Muslims are quick to note the double standards of America. . . . But we seldom question our own double standards." In unpacking this remarkable statement, Sardar was courageous enough to address a topic virtually taboo among Muslim commentators:

> For example, Muslims are proud that Islam is the fastest growing religion in the West. Evangelical Muslims, from Saudi Arabia to Pakistan, happily spread their constricted interpretations of Islam. But Christian missionaries in Muslim countries are another matter. They have to be banned or imprisoned.

In making this comment, he was not merely referring to the Taliban's imprisonment and trial of twenty-four Western and Afghani Christian aid workers in mid-2001; he was also referring to the numerous Muslim countries (such as Malaysia and Egypt) where legislation forbids Christians from engaging in mission among Muslims.

23. "UK Muslim Leaders Divided over Afghan War," *BBC News*, November 14, 2001. Dr. Pasha was perhaps unaware that the UN had long demanded that the Taliban hand over bin Laden for trial; the UN calls were ignored by the Taliban leadership. Cf. UN Security Council Resolution 1267 (1999). Available on the World Wide Web: http://www.un.org/Docs/scres/1999/99sc1267.htm.

Yasmin Alibhai-Brown, a prominent British Muslim writer, also spoke out on this same issue:

> One of the things Muslims have to learn to do is treat people the way they expect to be treated themselves, and also to make demands of themselves that they make on others. I feel very, very strongly that we must have respect, yes, but it has to go both ways. For example, I don't see many Muslims at the moment worrying at all about the fact that Christians living in Muslim countries have a very hard time, and there are, frankly, not as many churches in Pakistan as there are mosques in [Britain].[24]

Alibhai-Brown also candidly acknowledged the Muslim penchant for conspiracy theorizing: "When you are confronted by certain unpalatable truths, you just run the other way and produce all sorts of stupid evidence to the contrary. I fear that some of my Muslim brethren are locked in that at the moment."[25] Although her comments preceded the September 11 attacks, they are of direct relevance to the widely circulating accusations that Israeli agents carried out the attacks, rather than a group of radical Islamists.

An even more powerful Muslim critique was articulated by the Pakistani scholar and author Izzat Majeed in his "Open Letter to Osama bin Laden":

> Look at what you have done, Osama bin Laden. . . . The vast majority of the Muslims of the world do not care about your proclamations and your antiquated notion of Islam. You helped create the Taliban (some say you actually rule over them). If the sheer barbarism of the Taliban regime is your version of an Islamic society, then you must be a true dreamer to think that any Muslim with half a brain will listen to you. The long-lost tribal simplicity and austerity that once characterised the practice of Islam interest no one today. The self-inflicted death of intellect in Islam a thousand years ago is the main cause of the retrogressive and unenlightened mullah culture in Muslim societies today. . . . The majority of the Afghans want you and your "foreigners" to leave them alone. By helping create and then lording over the Taliban you have lost any chance of winning the hearts and minds of the long-suffering people of Afghanistan. I am sure every single Afghan woman would love to put you in a burqa and flog you for your medieval and tyrannical version of Islam.

24. Yasmin Alibhai-Brown, "All Due Respect," *Third Way* 24.8 (November 2001): 18.
25. Ibid.

This document also contains statements echoing views of Sardar
and Alibhai-Brown that the world's ills are not all the fault of the
West. Majeed goes on:

> We Muslims cannot keep blaming the West for all our ills. We have to
> first get our own house in order before we can even make any credible
> struggle possible to rid us of ignorance, living-in-the-past chest
> thumping and intolerance of the modern world. Holy Prophet Mu-
> hammad (peace be upon him) on returning from a battle, said: "We re-
> turn from little jihad (jihad al-asghar) to greater jihad (jihad al-
> akbar)." True jihad today is not in the hijacking of planes but in the
> manufacturing of them. . . . Without a reformation in the practice of
> Islam that makes it move forward and not backward, there is no hope
> for us Muslims anywhere.[26]

In similar vein the Iraqi Muslim writer Kanan Makiya of Harvard
University challenges Muslims to think hard about the nature of anti-
American (and by extension anti-Western) sentiment in Muslim societies. In an article in the English broadsheet *The Observer,* Makiya
writes:

> Arabs and Muslims need today to face up to the fact that their resent-
> ment at America has long since become unmoored from any rational
> underpinnings it might once have had; like the anti-Semitism of the in-
> terwar years, it is today steeped in deeply embedded conspiratorial pat-
> terns of thought rooted in profound ignorance of how a society and a
> polity like the United States, much less Israel, functions.

Makiya continues, pointing to a curious convergence between radical Muslim and certain Western liberal viewpoints trying to attribute
ultimate blame for Western-Muslim tensions simply to matters of
Western foreign policy:

> To argue, as many Arabs and Muslims are doing today (and not a few
> liberal Western voices), that "Americans should ask themselves why
> they are so hated in the world" is to make such a concession; it is to pro-
> vide a justification, however unwittingly, for this kind of warped mind-
> set. . . .

> Worse than being wrong, however, it is morally bankrupt, to say nothing
> of being counterproductive. For every attempt to "rationalise" or "ex-

26. Izzat Majeed, "Open Letter to Osama bin Laden," *The Nation,* November 9,
2001. Cf. also Thomas Friedman, "Breaking the Circle," *New York Times,* November 16,
2001.

plain" the new anti-Americanism rampant in so much of the Muslim and Arab worlds bolsters the project of the perpetrators of the heinous act of 11 September, which is to blur the lines that separate their sect of a few hundred people from hundreds of millions of peace-loving Muslims and Arabs.[27]

Such voices provide cause for optimism. However, they are few and far between, and they are the voices of individuals. At the organizational level, Muslims tended to close ranks when challenged, with the clearest example in the British context being the Muslim Council of Britain. Instead of providing the kind of honest critique expressed by people such as Sardar, Alibhai-Brown, Majeed, and Makiya, the MCB engaged in carping criticism of British government policy once the military campaign in Afghanistan had begun. This was justified in the name of community solidarity. In a news release at the end of September 2001, the MCB showed that for it, a semblance of unity is considered to be paramount: "It [is] crucial to do everything to enhance and not undermine the unity of the Muslim community. The use of such terms as 'moderates' and 'extremists' should be avoided as this would create division and polarization."[28] With such a commitment to unity, one must ask how groups such as the MCB, as the most prominent umbrella body for the British Muslim community, could commit itself to the kind of forthright action that is sometimes necessary to hold radicals to account. Such action is thus left to non-Muslims, as was seen in the case of Afghanistan. The Muslim writer Zayn Islam similarly speaks out against those Muslims who maintain silence in the face of radical Islamist actions:

Muslims everywhere [are] complicit in not speaking out against Islamist discourses that narrow a profound and noble religious tradition into a tool of aggression against women, against minorities, against plural societies, that indoctrinate children, re-establish laws that are so archaic as to be laughable and no longer within the ethics or spirit of Islam, and who turn the Compassionate One into a fuel-loaded jet. . . . The problem is that if the educated and the wise in the Muslim world and elsewhere continue to be silenced by fear of retaliation, then there is no hope for many Muslim societies.[29]

27. Makiya, "Fighting Islam's Ku Klux Klan."
28. MCB news release (September 29, 2001) reporting a meeting of Imams and Ulama.
29. Paul C. Johnson, "Death and Memory at Ground Zero: A Historian of Religion's Report," *Council of Societies for the Study of Religion* 31.1 (February 2002): 6.

CONCLUSIONS: THE ESSENTIAL CHARACTER OF ISLAM?

The non-Muslim public is left in a state of confusion by these contradictory Muslim voices, and especially by the significantly different readings of Islamic scripture. Is Islam a religion of peace, as the Muslim moderates (and Tony Blair and George W. Bush) say, or is it a religion prone to violence and holy war, as statements by radical groups suggest?

The passionate commitment of insiders to one or other of these opposing viewpoints suggests that non-Muslim outsiders have a role to play in seeking an answer to this burning question.

In fact, the answer lies not in an either/or response, but rather in a "both . . . and" response. The Islamic sacred texts offer the potential for being interpreted in both ways. It depends on how individual Muslims wish to read them.

Muslim moderates would wish to affirm Dr. Badawi's use of Qur'an 5:32 (cited previously) to condemn violence and killing. It seems unambiguous. But if one continues to the next verse, the message is significantly different:

> The punishment of those who wage war against Allah and His Messenger, and strive with might and main for mischief through the land is: execution, or crucifixion, or the cutting off of hands and feet from opposite sides, or exile from the land: that is their disgrace in this world, and a heavy punishment is theirs in the Hereafter. (Sura 5:33)

Thus, while Dr. Badawi has sincerely chosen to emphasize a more compassionate interpretation of these verses, someone inclined to a more literalist reading of the Islamic scriptures could easily emphasize verse 33, which talks of execution, crucifixion, and cutting off hands and feet.

In this way, one mind-set, that of the Muslim moderates, takes a subtle and reason-based approach to the Islamic sacred texts, reading them in the light of the modern world and adapting them accordingly. Radicals, on the other hand, read the texts in a literalist way, focusing on the surface meaning. For them, the specific struggles such as Palestine, Iraq, and Chechnya are not even what is at issue; rather, it is that they read their Islamic texts to call for non-Muslim infidels to be fought, regardless of the cause.

In effect, there is a titanic struggle taking place between moderates and radicals for the hearts and minds of the Muslim masses in the middle. Who is winning? It is too early to say, but there are certain pointers that provide an indication of what is happening among the Muslim masses.

Salman Rushdie, in a letter to the *New York Times,* sounds a note of warning: "Paranoid Islam, which blames outsiders, 'infidels,' for all the ills of Muslim societies, and whose proposed remedy is the closing of those societies to the rival project of modernity, is presently the fastest growing version of Islam in the world."[30]

When the American air strikes on Afghanistan began on October 7, 2001, several organizations in Britain surveyed British Muslims to assess their response to developments. These surveys took place after detailed evidence of Osama bin Laden's involvement in the September 11 attacks had been published. We will draw upon two such surveys for the British context: the BBC canvassed five hundred British Muslims, and the reputable Muslim publication *Q News* consulted over a thousand of its readers. The results were consistent across the two polls.

A sizeable majority of 79 percent of *Q News* readers were not convinced that bin Laden and al-Qa'ida were responsible for the September 11 attacks, while the BBC showed a majority of 67 percent sharing this view. About a quarter of respondents to both polls indicated willingness to fight alongside bin Laden and the Taliban as jihad fighters against American and allied military intervention. Around 54 percent of *Q News* readers said they did not feel that the moderate MCB represented them; 44 percent of the same group said they would trust Osama bin Laden; but only 8 percent would trust British Prime Minister Tony Blair. Of those surveyed for the BBC poll, 15 percent said the terrorist attacks of September 11 were justified or somewhat justified.

What of other Muslim communities around the world? In December 2001 and January 2002, researchers conducted hour-long, in-person interviews in Saudi Arabia, Iran, Pakistan, Indonesia, Turkey, Lebanon, Kuwait, Jordan, and Morocco in order to determine popular views regarding world events and the Afghanistan crisis. These interviews, conducted by the prominent survey organization Gallup Poll, were held with a total of 9,924 Muslims.[31] Of this number, 61 percent said they believed Arabs were not involved in the September 11 attacks; only 18 percent said they believed Arabs carried out the attacks on the sites in New York and Washington. The most common attribution of blame was to Israel, reflecting the anti-Jewish conspiracy theorizing discussed earlier. Furthermore, 77 percent of those polled said

30. Cited in *Christianity Today* 46.1 (January 7, 2002): 34.
31. Frank Newport, "Gallup Poll of the Islamic World," Gallup Poll, Government and Public Affairs (February 26, 2002); cf. "Poll: Muslims Doubt Arabs Mounted Sept. 11 Attacks," Reuters, February 27, 2002.

American military action in Afghanistan was morally unjustified; only 9 percent said it was justified.

Elsewhere, other surveys suggested that vast numbers of Muslims around the world held perspectives on the world crisis that were diametrically opposed to those held by the majority in Western countries. For example, joint public surveys carried out by the Palestinian Center for Policy and Survey Research and the Hebrew University of Jerusalem's Truman Research Institute revealed that only 16 percent of Palestinians accepted that Osama bin Laden was involved in the September 11 attacks.[32]

So it would seem that when faced with two competing voices, those of the moderates and those of the radical Islamists, Muslims around the world are clearly divided. In terms of the world crisis of late 2001, evidence suggests that a majority of Muslims were strongly influenced by the arguments of the radicals, though many were not. The following comment by the leading French Muslim scholar Mohamed Arkoun seems to have been borne out by recent events: "[Muslim] thinkers and intellectuals . . . are having great difficulties inserting their critical approach into a social and cultural space that is, at present, totally dominated by militant ideologies."[33]

---

32. Available on the World Wide Web: http://truman.huji.ac.il/poll-dec-1-2001.htm.

33. Mohamed Arkoun, "Rethinking Islam Today," in *Liberal Islam: A Sourcebook*, ed. Charles Kurzman (New York: Oxford University Press, 1998), 206.

13

RESPONSES TO TERRORISM

RADICAL ISLAMISM AND TERRORISM

In the modern world Islamist radicalism has been responsible for terrorist acts in Israel, the United States of America, Indonesia, India, and a range of other locations. Of course, Islamist radicals are not behind all the terrorism in the world, but a detailed study of terrorist activities by non-Islamic groups is not of direct relevance to this present book.

The al-Qa'ida attack on New York and Washington stirred the Western world to a realization that it was now faced with a new kind of war, not against identifiable nations, nor with identifiable battlefields, but the new war of the terrorists. President George W. Bush did not start the war with the terrorists; the terrorists first declared war on the democratic world.

But what exactly *is* terrorism? According to a common saying, "It is like an elephant on your doorstep: you'll know it when you see it."[1] There seem to be three elements to terrorism:

- It is violence directed against noncombatants.
- It is violence delivered without warning.
- It is a group violence.

An individual acting alone may be violent, but he is not a terrorist until he belongs to an organized group. Irish Republican Army activists were terrorists, and the fact that they were fighting against British rule made no difference to their status. Hamas suicide bombers were terrorists when they blew themselves to pieces in a Jerusalem bus station, even though they were fighting against Israel. Pakistani fighters

1. Timothy Garton Ash, "First, the Biography . . . ," *The Guardian*, November 10, 2001.

for the liberation of Kashmir were terrorists when they attacked the Indian parliament.

Al-Qa'ida was and is a terrorist organization, and it has claimed validity on the authority of the Qur'an. As we have already seen, the Qur'an *does* have passages that encourage such violence. So what is the proper response to radical Islamist terrorism?

A Preliminary Caveat

In responding to terrorism, we can too easily produce wrong responses. The "right" responses will inevitably depend on our own beliefs. One may certainly argue that Christian beliefs must ultimately find their source in Jesus and that Muslim beliefs must ultimately find their source in Muhammad the messenger. Immediately we are presented with a striking contrast: there is little in common between these two persons.

Muhammad was born into an influential family, his uncle the Hashimite clan leader, his grandfather guardian of the Ka'ba, born in Mecca, the principal city of Arabia. Jesus was born into the family of an artisan, a carpenter, born in the little town of Bethlehem and raised in the insignificant village of Nazareth in Galilee. Arabia was free; Palestine was under Roman rule. Muhammad claimed to have received his first visions when he was forty years old, and was sixty-two when he died; Jesus died before he was thirty-five. Muhammad claimed no more than to be a prophet of God; Jesus claimed to be no less than Son of God, God incarnate. Muhammad performed no miracles other than those created for him by later pious believers;[2] according to the New Testament, Jesus performed numerous miracles of healing. Muhammad died in old age, among his family, having gained the allegiance of the nation; Jesus died like a criminal, on a cross, with only a handful of followers to show for his brief years of ministry. Muhammad was married many times; Jesus never married. Of greatest importance for our purposes is the last contrast: Muhammad, according to his biographer Ibn Ishaq, was personally engaged in twenty-seven military raids;[3] Jesus was a man of nonviolence throughout his earthly life.

Christianity has no excuse at all for those many occasions when it has resorted to violence. The Crusades are an obvious example, but even some missionaries were willing to use force when persuasion failed. Geoffrey Moorhouse has graphically illustrated this unfamiliar and fortunately rare aspect of nineteenth-century missionary en-

2. See, for example, Bukhari, *Sahih*, IV, LVI, chap. 26, nos. 831, 832, 533–34.
3. Guillaume, *Life of Muhammad*, 659.

deavor, detailing the use of British Royal Navy gunboats in West Africa in support of their work.[4] But there can be no New Testament justification for violence: certainly Jesus was uniformly pacific,[5] refusing even divine aid to escape from the cross.

That last sentence points to our caveat: it is too easy for Christians to produce a wrong response to violence by making reference to the wrong covenant. The Bible is divided into two parts: the first part, shared with the Jews, is called the Old Testament;[6] the second part, peculiarly Christian, is called the New Testament. The unfamiliar term *testament* tends to lead to confusion, suggesting a mere book. It would be better to use the term *covenant*. The Bible contains two covenants, and Christianity stands firmly under the second of the two, the *New* Covenant.[7]

The Old Covenant was made with a particular ethnic group, the Jews, eventually living in a particular country, Palestine. Although theoretically Israel was a theocracy, it had a capital city, Jerusalem, and a king. It had a community, requiring a civil law, and it had criminals, requiring a criminal law code. It was surrounded by potentially invasive nations and needed an army. Provision was made for all of these in the Old Covenant. The first part of the Bible contains a frank and often shocking account of the wars in which Israel engaged.

Either of two mistakes may be made in any Christian treatment of the Old Covenant Scriptures: on the one hand setting them aside as entirely irrelevant, and on the other hand quoting them uncritically as though they were New Covenant Scriptures. A response to violence, for example, might be to point to Exodus 21:23–25, which advocates "life for life, eye for eye, tooth for tooth, hand for hand, foot for foot, burn for burn, wound for wound, stripe for stripe." But Christianity asserts that the Old Covenant Scriptures are fulfilled under the New Covenant. Some, including the criminal law, are simply made irrelevant to the church. Others, including the Scriptures relating to sacrifices, are transformed and explained by the sacrifice of the cross. The promises of material prosperity in re-

4. Geoffrey Moorhouse, *The Missionaries* (London: Eyre Methuen, 1973), 88–95.

5. Some have pointed to the cleansing of the temple, in John 2:13–22, and the whip Jesus used. But the text makes it clear that the whip was used to drive out the animals, not the traders: "He drove all of them out of the temple, both the sheep and the cattle."

6. Jews refer to this as the Bible or as Tanakh, an acronym for its three major components (Torah = Law, Nevi'im = Prophets, Kethuvim = Writings).

7. The two covenants are clearly set out in Jeremiah 31:31. Paul takes up the issue in 1 Corinthians 11:25, and Hebrews has an extended discussion of the character of the new and "better" covenant in chapter 8. Cf. Mark 14:24.

turn for obedience to the Law are replaced by promises only of spiritual prosperity.[8]

The New Covenant is different. Its people are found among virtually all nations. They have no capital city beyond the heavenly Jerusalem, no king but Jesus, and look to their respective earthly governments for civil and criminal law. They do not expect governments to be Christian, nor do they expect the activities of their governments to be determined by Christian principles. And yet they sense a duty to advise, commend, and explain Christian principles to those who do not necessarily hold to them. Perhaps most important, Christians have no wars to fight except those directed against spiritual powers.

So we look first at the response to terrorism appropriate to governments and second at the response appropriate to Christians living under the New Covenant.

THE RESPONSE OF GOVERNMENTS

The New Covenant Scriptures indicate that specific responsibilities rest on the state. Writing somewhere between A.D. 57 and 59,[9] Paul says:

> Rulers are not a terror to good conduct, but to bad. Do you wish to have no fear of the authority? Then do what is good, and you will receive its approval; for it is God's servant for your good. But if you do what is wrong, you should be afraid, for the authority does not bear the sword in vain! It is the servant of God to execute wrath on the wrongdoer. (Rom. 13:3–4)

Peter, writing a little later than Paul,[10] echoes the same message: "Accept the authority of every human institution, whether of the emperor

8. Most of the Bible texts appealed to by teachers of prosperity theology come from the Old Covenant, and those taken from the New Testament are invariably misinterpreted. In the matter of prosperity a favorite New Testament verse is 2 Corinthians 8:9 NIV: "You know the grace of our Lord Jesus Christ, that though he was rich, yet for your sakes he became poor, so that you through his poverty might be made rich." But in both places "rich" refers to spiritual riches, not material wealth (as though Jesus had a large bank balance in heaven). See Peter Cotterell, *Mission and Meaninglessness* (London: SPCK, 1990), 269ff.

9. See Donald Guthrie, *New Testament Introduction*, 4th ed. (Leicester: Apollos; Downers Grove, Ill.: InterVarsity, 1990).

10. Assuming, with Guthrie (*New Testament Introduction*, 786ff.), that the epistle refers to the Neronic persecution, A.D. 62–64. But see P. J. Achtemeier, *1 Peter*, Hermeneia (Minneapolis: Fortress, 1996), 43ff. Achtemeier prefers "a date sometime between 80 and 100 C.E., most likely in the earlier years of that range." That would place Peter's writing in the context of Domitian's reign.

as supreme, or of governors, as sent by him to punish those who do wrong and to praise those who do right" (1 Pet. 2:13–14). When Paul and Peter mention governments and rulers, both are referring to the Roman government and the Roman emperor or governor. The reference to bearing "the sword" is almost certainly a reminder that Roman law was enforced by Roman soldiers,[11] and it indicates that their task of enforcing the law was still biblically appropriate even when they were operating in Rome's extended empire. Paul and Peter both had in mind the type of government that in a general way rewarded good and punished evil. There is room left here for the supposition that in the case of a corrupt government that does the reverse, rewarding evil and punishing good, and particularly if it moves to persecuting Christians, the principle may no longer apply.

Biblically we do not find any suggestion that Christian charity should result in the wrongdoer being spared punishment. What we do find is the principle that the state punishes, not the church.[12]

Orthodox Islam sees the non-Islamic world as promoting an economic and sociological system that is contrary to that laid down by the Qur'an, Tradition, and Shari'a law. Radical Islamism goes further and insists that the two systems cannot coexist: the democratic and capitalist system must be replaced by Muslim Shari'a.

Among other things, Shari'a law conflicts with what is almost fundamental to Western economics, the practice of paying interest on deposits and loans to banks or companies. Even in the church nearly a thousand years ago the Third Lateran Council condemned "usury" because it provided profit that did not correspond to any labor by the lender. Any transaction should carry a just price that reflects the labor involved in it.[13]

However, there is among scholars today a strong minimalist understanding of biblical texts that relate to economic matters since the worlds of the Bible, whether Old Testament or New Testament, are so

11. See C. E. B. Cranfield, *A Critical and Exegetical Commentary on the Epistle to the Romans*, International Critical Commentary (Edinburgh: Clark, 1975–79), 2:667.

12. Here is a good argument for the disestablished church. Since the dubious blessing of Constantine's patronage of the church, we have always suffered the paradox of state churches. Inevitably this brings confusion: the actions and decisions of the state are identified as the actions of the church or at least actions approved by the church. On the whole issue of establishment, see Donald Reeves, ed., *The Church and the State* (London: Hodder and Stoughton, 1984), and especially the contribution from Tony Benn. See also Cotterell, *Mission and Meaninglessness*, chap. 13. The United States has always tried to maintain a careful separation between church and state for the benefit of both.

13. J. F. Sleeman, "Usury and Interest," in *A Dictionary of Christian Ethics*, ed. John Macquarrie (London: SCM, 1967).

far removed from our world. Consequently it is argued that we can
only marginally take its dictates for today's economics.[14] But Islamic
Law is quite clear on this matter: taking "usury," *riba*, is forbidden. The
attack on New York in 2001 was undoubtedly an attack on Western
economics. The success of this attack can be seen in a succession of
failed businesses (including Swissair and the Belgian national airline
Sabena)[15] and the drop in stock markets around the world. In London
the FTSE Index stood at 6,200 in January 2001, at 5,800 in April, at
5,400 in August, and hit its lowest point (4,400) in mid-September, a
fall of some 20 percent in that month. By December it was back at
5,200, indicating the relative resilience of Western economies.

The violence of radical Islamism ought not to cause great surprise;
it conforms to the generally rugged and sometimes violent character
of Muhammad. Characteristic of both radical Islamism and of liberal
Islam is hagiography, the idealization of the life of Muhammad. Stephen
Neill comments:

> Many lives of the Prophet Muhammad have been written by Muslims
> for western and Christian consumption. In all of these the less agreeable
> features in the character of Muhammad have been softened down and
> subtly christianised, so that the rugged Prophet of Arabia has been
> transformed into a kindly and beneficent reformer.[16]

Compare, for example, the picture painted by Ameer Ali, a liberal
and Westernized Muslim, in his book *The Spirit of Islam*. He wrote of
Muhammad's

> purity of heart, austerity of conduct, refinement and delicacy of feeling.
> . . . A nature so pure, so tender, and yet so heroic inspires not only rever-
> ence but love. . . . His singular elevation of mind, his extreme delicacy
> and refinement of feeling, his purity and truth, form the constant theme
> of traditions.[17]

But that stands in stark contrast to the Hadith (Tradition) of Anas
ibn Malik. Bukhari records the Tradition passed on by Anas that eight
starving men of the tribe of 'Ukil came to Muhammad and asked for
milk. He advised them to go to the herds of camels and drink their

14. Ian Smith, "God and Economics," in *God and Culture*, ed. D. A. Carson and J. D.
Woodbridge (Carlisle: Paternoster; Grand Rapids: Eerdmans, 1993).
15. Swissair was eventually rescued, at least in some measure, by the Swiss government, and the Belgian government replaced Sabena with a truncated version employing some 50 percent of the original workforce.
16. Stephen Neill, *Crises of Belief* (London: Hodder and Stoughton, 1984), 90.
17. Syed Ameer Ali, *The Spirit of Islam* (London: Chatto and Windus, 1964), 117f.

milk. They did so and gradually regained their strength. They then attacked and killed the shepherds guarding the camels and fled with the camels. Muhammad learned of what they had done and ordered them to be pursued. They were captured and brought back to him. He ordered that their hands and feet be cut off, their eyes put out with heated nails, and that they then be exposed out in the desert to die.[18]

Throughout Islam's history violence has thus received a measure of official sanction from its primary scripture. And from its radical wing violence has appeared in the twenty-first century. It is the responsibility of governments to punish violence. But we may go further and say that since this form of violence and terrorism knows no frontiers, it is right for governments to work together to defeat it.

There is a need to go beyond punishment and to try to address modern-day issues fueling Islamic terrorism. Only then can the sickness be healed. Many Muslims have suggested that a major issue is the need for a Palestinian homeland. The West in general and the United States specifically have tended to support Israel against the Palestinians. The United Nations allocated half of Palestine to Israel in 1947, and in subsequent fighting, admittedly usually provoked by the Arab world, Israel has taken control of the rest. There seems to be in intractable problem of providing a Palestinian homeland, with the parallel need to gain unequivocal Arab recognition of the State of Israel and acceptance of its right to exist and flourish. And yet perhaps a twenty-first-century Middle East Marshall Plan would resolve the problem as it solved the equally desperate problem posed after World War 2 by a prostrate Europe.

But it is doubtful whether the question of a Palestinian homeland, of the status of Jerusalem, and/or of American military bases in Saudi Arabia are the real issues underlying Islamic militancy. These are far more complex, as we have seen in earlier discussion, and include the equivocal teaching of the Qur'an. Until the Islamic community as a whole deals with the problem of the interpretation of Qur'anic passages that appear to promote violence against the non-Muslim world (whether Jewish, Christian, or "pagan"), Muslim extremists will continue their acts of violence, finding justification for their deeds in a particular reading of Qur'anic verses.

THE CHRISTIAN RESPONSE TO TERRORISM

The one word that might be said to characterize the life of Jesus was the word *compassion*. In Matthew's words: "When [Jesus] saw the

18. Bukhari, *Sahih*, IV, LII, chap. 152, no. 261, 162.

crowds, he had compassion for them, because they were harassed and helpless, like sheep without a shepherd" (Matt. 9:36). Wherever terrorism occurs and whatever form it takes, the Christian response should, first of all, be one of compassion. Compassion for the victims of the violence and especially for the families of the victims, husbands, wives, mothers, fathers, brothers, sisters, sons, daughters—the pain produced by violence stretches out in ever-widening circles, like stirred-up waves on the waters of a placid lake. Violence is a storm, striking without warning, hurting at random.

But, strangely, compassion also for those who are responsible for violence, those who are so filled with hatred that they can willfully cause fellow human beings to suffer. The lives of such people are twisted and tortured; they are no longer men and women as their Creator intended them to be. Indeed, all killers put themselves into a category apart: they have killed, and the stain of their crime is indelible. Maybe they paused before they committed themselves to the act, but once acted out, the future is fixed. As Thomas Carlyle expressed it:

> From the purpose of a crime to the act of crime there is an abyss; wonderful to think of. The finger lies on the pistol; but the man is not yet a murderer: nay, his whole nature staggering at such consummation, is there not a confused pause rather—one last instant of possibility for him? Not yet a murderer; it is at the mercy of light trifles the most fixed idea may not yet become unfixed. One slight twitch of a muscle, the death-flash bursts; and he is it, and will for all eternity be it—and earth has become a penal Tartarus for him.[19]

Compassion also for those politicians who must shoulder the responsibility of responding to terrorism, a response that will, in all probability, lead to further loss of life, further violence. It may be that some politicians can take such decisions and still sleep quietly in their beds; it must be that many cannot.

But compassion is meaningless unless it is expressed in action. Prayers are all very well but may be used as an alternative to action. There is always something that can be done in situations of terrorist attack: letters to be written, money to be contributed, even the offer of particular skills where they are relevant. And sometimes governments need to be goaded into action that their peoples cannot initiate: those embarrassingly abundant food stocks opened up and sent to the hungry, the expertise of the military made available. Much can be done,

19. Thomas Carlyle, *The French Revolution: A History* (New York: Random House, Modern Library, [1934]), 492.

but little will be done unless Christians demand that compassion is expressed in concrete action.

Second, Christians should open their eyes to the real world, the world beyond pop stars and perfumes, the real world of pain that Paul was talking about when he wrote to the church at Rome:

> For the creation waits with eager longing for the revealing of the children of God; for the creation was subjected to futility, not of its own will but by the will of the one who subjected it, in hope that the creation itself will be set free from its bondage to decay and will obtain the freedom of the glory of the children of God. We know that the whole creation has been groaning in labor pains until now; and not only the creation, but we ourselves, who have the first fruits of the Spirit, groan inwardly. (Rom. 8:19–23)

Paul sees a magnificent picture: a world of pain and futility looking to its one hope, the appearing on the scene of the children of God, filled with compassion and a burning desire to see violence ended and the kingdom of God established. The term *kingdom of God* must not be equated with the rule of the church, which has too often been tainted by the same greed and ambition as secular governments. God's kingdom comes when violence ends, when justice is established, when the good things the earth produces so bountifully are shared equally, when clean water and sufficient food and a safe home are no longer the perquisites of the few, but the common experience of all.

A potential problem arises as Christians insist that they have a responsibility to share with the Muslim world their understanding and experience of Jesus. Islam already respects Jesus, but according to Christianity, Jesus is so much more than the Qur'an admits. During the persecution years in Mecca, Muhammad sent many of his followers to Ethiopia for refuge. So the Ethiopian church learned of the new religious movement across the Red Sea, in Arabia. On their part the refugees heard of the Christian gospel. Some of them became Christians, among them Ubaydullah bin Jahsh. He returned to Arabia, and according to Ibn Ishaq, he used to say to those who still followed Muhammad: "We can now see, but you are still blinking."[20] He used an Arabic word as though describing a puppy trying to open its eyes. Muhammad had opened closed eyes to see the majesty of the One God. But he needed revelation to get his eyes and his followers' eyes fully open. However, the Ethiopian church did not send teachers to Mecca. If they had done so, the history of the world might have been quite different.[21]

20. Guillaume, *Life of Muhammad*, 527f.
21. Trimingham, *Islam in Ethiopia*, 45f.

The Christian and Violence

If total pacifism is the counsel of perfection for individual Christians in the real world, it is difficult, if not impossible, to attain it. In Britain during World War 2 those who had conscientious objection to fighting were often allowed to take up noncombatant duties. Some went into the coal mines, but of course they were merely making it possible for the military to continue the fight, while they were attempting to avoid direct involvement in the war. Some chose to go to prison, but there they were fed and maintained through the efforts of the rest of society, which was *not* pacifist. Here is the problem identified by J. D. G. Dunn as "quietism," the tendency of Christians, and especially evangelical Christians, to distance themselves from politics and the decisions of the politicians.[22] The stance is seen, for example, in the early Bonhoeffer,[23] later executed for his part in the plot to assassinate Hitler. But *should* Christians involve themselves in warfare?

From the time of Tertullian (who lived toward the end of the second century) Christians have struggled with the question of their involvement in the violent actions of their governments. In *War and Christian Ethics*, A. F. Holmes outlines the views of Tertullian, Augustine, Luther, and others on the issue of war and pacifism.[24] Reinhold Niebuhr, writing in 1948, just after the end of World War 2, rejected pacifism as an inappropriate response to evil in any real world. Of pacifists he wrote:

> They have really absorbed the Renaissance faith in the goodness of man, have rejected the Christian doctrine of original sin as an outmoded bit of pessimism, have re-interpreted the cross so that it is made to stand for the absurd idea that perfect love is guaranteed a simple victory over the world.[25]

While Christians may well disagree over Niebuhr's verdict on pacifism, they will not disagree about a more fundamental conflict and the Christian involvement in it: the spiritual conflict. Behind every evil deed there is an evil power. While this is phrased in a specifically Christian way, it is remarkable that extreme cases of violence, aggression, torture, and terrorism are regularly designated "evil," even by those who make no overt pretense at a religious faith. The concept of

22. See Dunn's comments on Rom. 13:1–7, in *Romans 9–16*, Word Biblical Commentary 38B (Dallas: Word, 1988).

23. See L. L. Rasmussen, *Dietrich Bonhoeffer: Reality and Resistance*, Studies in Christian Ethics (Nashville: Abingdon, 1972).

24. A. F. Holmes, ed., *War and Christian Ethics* (Grand Rapids: Baker, 1975).

25. Ibid., 303–4.

evil goes beyond the recognition of actions that cause suffering, to a judgment of those actions in terms of good and evil.

The statement that evil powers lie behind evil deeds must be clearly differentiated from the proposition made by some that non-Christian religions are merely inventions and tools of some devil. That proposition is to be rejected. But still Christians do recognize the existence of two kingdoms pitched against one another. Jesus himself spoke of these two kingdoms when he was accused of using the powers of evil: "*Every kingdom* divided against itself becomes a desert, and house falls on house. If Satan also is divided against himself, how will *his kingdom* stand? . . . But if it is by the finger of God that I cast out the demons, then *the kingdom of God* has come to you" (Luke 11:17–20, italics added).

The concepts of a "devil" and "demons" raise all sorts of problems mainly because of the mental images they conjure up. As the arch-tempter Screwtape says to his junior tempter in C. S. Lewis's *Screwtape Letters*, "The fact that 'devils' are predominantly comic figures will help you. If any faint suspicion of your existence begins to arise in his mind, suggest to him a picture of something in red tights, and persuade him that since he cannot believe in that, . . . he therefore cannot believe in you."[26]

It is the second kingdom, however it might be perceived, that rejoices over destruction and is opposed to God's plan for bringing in his kingdom. It thus becomes the focus of Christian warfare. Paul, writing to the church at Ephesus, warned: "We are not fighting against human beings, but against the wicked spiritual forces in the heavenly world, the rulers, authorities, and cosmic powers of this dark age" (Eph. 6:12 TEV). The Christian is committed to the view that in this aspect of "warfare" the weapons to be deployed are not missiles and helicopter gunships, not mines and Kalashnikovs; instead, they are spiritual weapons, among which perhaps the most potent is prayer. The Christian response to this aspect of terrorism ought not to be more violence, but a peacemaking response (cf. Matt. 5:9).

A MUSLIM RESPONSE TO TERRORISM

There are two things that the Muslim world might do in responding to terrorism from within its own community. The first is to disown terrorist violence. Although many Muslim leaders have been quick to distance themselves from violence, especially after the September 11

---

26. C. S. Lewis, *Screwtape Letters* (New York: Macmillan, 1943), 40. There are many editions of this book.

attacks on America, few indeed have gone so far as to express anything remotely authoritative by way of condemnation, as discussed at
length in the previous chapter. But it would be a great step forward
for the Islamic world and for the understanding of Muslims everywhere to have a fatwa (decree) widely endorsed by Muslim leaders,
based on a rigorous and holistic examination of the Shari'a law, and
formally, unambiguously, and permanently rejecting the use of violence of the type seen on September 11, 2001.[27]

But there is a second step that Muslims might consider. The Sardar
"fatwa" cited in the previous chapter is weak because it is not clear
that it has any Qur'anic support. Nor is this surprising, since in the
present state of Muslim hermeneutics, verses of the Qur'an could be
quoted *supporting* violence. What is needed is for Muslim scholars en
masse (rather than comparatively small numbers of moderates) to engage with developments in the world of linguistics dealing with the interpretation and understanding of texts. Qur'anic verses that clearly
advocate violence and those that demean women[28] could then be put
back into their original context, from which they have been wrenched.

For example, it is generally admitted that the Qur'anic verses ap-
proving of polygamy related to the period immediately after the hijra,
when the nascent movement had lost men in the fighting with the
Meccans, leaving widows without protectors and young women without prospective husbands. Pragmatically it must be admitted that in
such a situation polygamy made good sense. So the *meaning* of such
verses in their original context is clear, but the *significance* of such
verses for today might be quite different.

In current linguistic thinking the *meaning* of a text must be determined by reference to the wording of the text, the related text around
it, and the historical context within which the text was produced. That
exercise produces the meaning of the text for the original readers of it,
the meaning intended by the writer. Then after determining the meaning of the text in its original setting, the readers must decide on the *significance* of the text for themselves.[29] To give a biblical example, Paul

27. Harvard University professor Roy Mottahedeh makes a similar call, arguing that
the Shari'a provides ample ingredients for such a pronouncement (Alan Cooperman,
"Scholars Plan to Show How Attacks Violated Islamic Law," *Washington Post*, January
20, 2002). At the same time, Christian leaders worldwide could issue a parallel decree/
fatwa as a mark of inter-religious cooperation.

28. Space limitations prevent discussing the thorny issue of the status accorded
women under Islamic law. Many commentators think this issue calls for a revised
Qur'anic hermeneutic similar to that applied to jihad.

29. See Peter Cotterell and Max Turner, *Linguistics and Biblical Interpretation* (London: SPCK, 1989), chap. 2, esp. 2.1.9, "Meaning and Significance."

makes reference to widows' pensions and says: "Let a widow be put on the list if she is not less than sixty years old and has been married only once. . . . But refuse to put younger widows on the list" (1 Tim. 5:9–11). The meaning of these words is quite clear. But what is the significance of this verse for churches today? Does it mean that every church should set up a pension fund for its older widows? This would be so only if the real-life context today were the same as the context within which Paul wrote. *Then* there were no state pensions for widows, no insurance policies. *Now* there are. And yet it is still true that widows (and widowers) might be in need of assistance beyond their pensions. The significance of the passage is that the church should ensure that the needs of its older and more vulnerable members are properly cared for.

This hermeneutical principle, distinguishing between meaning and significance, could be applied by Islamic scholars to deal with the problem of having a major world religion locked into the thought patterns, and especially the law systems, of the eighth century. The Qur'anic punishment for theft is well-known: "As to the thief, male or female, cut off his or her hands: a punishment by way of example, from Allah, for their crime. . . . But if the thief repents after his crime, and amends his conduct, Allah turneth to him in forgiveness" (Sura 5:38–39). The *meaning* of these verses is quite clear. Unfortunately, that meaning has also been taken as its permanent *significance* through succeeding centuries. In countries where Shari'a law is practiced, the hands of thieves are still struck off.[30] But it seems that there are two principles embedded in the verses that could guide us to a different significance. First of all, the amputation discourages and impedes the thief from further stealing. Second, the punishment is an example to others who might be tempted to steal. Both principles are today served by imprisonment, a punishment not practiced in the Arabia of Muhammad's day.

It might prove difficult to persuade conservative Muslims of the validity of a new hermeneutic, especially if such a suggestion were to come from outside the Islamic fold. However, some new approach (other than abrogation of Qur'anic passages) is required to enable Islam to move forward with a Shari'a law for the new millennium. In fact, this is the essence of the arguments of moderate Muslim scholars (Makiya, Majeed, Sardar) discussed in the previous chapter. Furthermore, the Muslim scholar Fazlur Rahman (1919–88) also offered a significant contribution in this regard. On the one hand, he criticized

30. In Ethiopia in the 1930s, before her conversion to Christianity, Ha'da Shi'fa had her hand struck off in the Jimma marketplace for theft. She was, in fact, the first Christian in Jimma, and she was one of the informants for F. P. Cotterell, *Born at Midnight* (Chicago: Moody, 1970).

the Mu'tazila for raising reason to a level with the revelation of the Qur'an, and for raising it above Tradition. But he applauded their injection of reason into the formulation of Muslim belief in general and into the interpretation of the Qur'an in particular. He carefully distinguished reason from mere rationalism, and (without using linguistic terminology or even being aware of it) proposed a distinction between the meaning of any Qur'anic passage (as determined by a study of the text of the Qur'an and the conditions under which it had been produced) and its significance for the Islamic world today.[31]

The Issue of the Ulama

The way forward for Islam into the twenty-first century is complicated by the influence of an authoritarian class of clerical leaders, the ulama. The Nigerian Muslim author Alhaji Adeleke Dirisu Ajijola argues for the need to address "the problem of the ulama":

> Many of the "ulama" do not have the ability to interpret the principles and law of Islam in the light of changing conditions. . . . They are obsessed with the past and addicted to uncritical acceptance and blind imitation of ancient dead Muslim jurists' views. . . . Because of deficiencies in their education they are incapable of leading and guiding modern Muslims in any spheres of life.[32]

Their role is best seen in Iran and in Afghanistan, where obscurantist views were put forward as normative, and where, correspondingly, repressive laws and practices were established. In Afghanistan, under the rule of the Taliban from 1996 until 2001, men were required to be bearded and women were banned from both work and education. In Iran, Ayatollah Khomeini consistently taught that Muslims should live holistically; that they should follow the sunna, the pathway of the prophet; and that since only the jurists could authoritatively interpret the texts that establish sunna, only the jurists were qualified to lead the affairs of the nation. It has been estimated that of one thousand senior administrative posts in the country, some six hundred were given to the *sayyed*, those who claimed direct descent from Muhammad. Other positions of authority were filled through a blunt nepotism that put at least fifty of Khomeini's own relatives in power. The power of the clerics was, therefore, almost absolute.[33]

---

31. See Fazlur Rahman, *Islam* (London: Weidenfeld and Nicolson, 1966), 87–90.

32. Alhaji Adeleke Dirisu Ajijola, "The Problem of 'Ulama,'" in *Liberal Islam: A Sourcebook*, ed. Charles Kurzman (New York: Oxford University Press, 1998), 239–40.

33. A. Ehteshami in an obituary assessment of the achievements of Ayatollah Khomeini, in the *Independent* (London), June 5, 1989.

The consequences were predictable. Khomeini's own view of open trials, defense lawyers, and proper procedures was that they were merely a reflection of "the Western sickness among us" and that criminals should not be tried: they should be killed.[34] The details of the consequences of such views, as given by Shaul Bakhash and by organizations such as Amnesty International, make horrific reading. Amnesty noted 2,946 executions in a single year; the left-wing Mujahidin opposition listed 7,746 deaths from June 1981 to September 1983.[35] Writing in the wider context of developments in Islam, and yet highly relevant to the Iranian revolution, Esposito commented:

> If we ask ourselves how it was that a movement which at the beginning was revolutionary, progressive, and modern, could be turned into an agent of intellectual petrification and social stagnation, our reflection will lead us to two factors which were not present in Islam originally, but which appeared together during the ages of the decline of Islamic civilization and became so firmly rooted that people imagined them to be among the fundamental principles of Islamic religion. The first was the appearance of a caste (the ulama) which monopolized the explanation of religion, claiming that it alone had the right to speak in the name of religion. . . . The second factor was the conviction of this caste that any laws, decisions, and solutions found in earlier religious sources were binding doctrines whose observance was obligatory, and which could not be modified or changed in any respects, whether they dealt with matters of doctrine or touched on affairs of daily life. . . .
>
> The majority of ulama continue to maintain that they alone possess the requisite religious learning and thus ought to be the ultimate authority in determining what the law is or should be. The Ayatollah Khomeini took this argument one step further. He asserted that since an Islamic state is one that is governed by the Sharia and since the ulama are the experts in law, government by the jurist-scholar is the best form of government prior to the return of the Hidden Imam.[36]

Clearly, then, any reformation in Islamic thinking along the lines of that called for by many moderate Islamic thinkers would need to address not only the threat posed by radical Islamist activists, but also the stranglehold on authority held by the group of traditionalist conservative clergy who are entrenched in positions of religious power at various levels throughout the Muslim world. This latter challenge, though difficult, is not insurmountable, given that some voices of moderation are being heard increasingly within the ulama

34. Shaul Bakhash, *The Reign of the Ayatollahs* (London: Tauris, 1985), 56–63.
35. Ibid., 221.
36. Esposito, *Islam: The Straight Path*, 233.

fraternity, from clerics such as Yusuf al-Qaradawi, who speaks out against extremism:

> [One] characteristic of extremism is the overburdening of others without regard for time and place—applying Islamic principles to people in non-Muslim countries or to people who have only recently converted to Islam, as well as to Muslims who are newly devout. . . . [Another] characteristic of extremism manifests itself in harshness in the treatment of people, roughness in the manner of approach, and crudeness in calling people to Islam, all of which are contrary to the teachings of the Qur'an and sunna.[37]

The Case of Iraq

The regime of Iraq's Saddam Hussein has presented a different face of extremism: the brutalizing of its own Muslim people and the wider threat of its weapons of mass destruction.

As we write, the outcome of the March 2003 American-led, preemptive strike on Iraq's leadership is uncertain, but the events leading up to it and the arguments used to justify it will long be debated. The French determination to veto any second United Nations motion intended to authorize such a strike was claimed to have left the American coalition with only two options: to revert to yet more negotiations or to proceed under the authority of the United Nations Resolution 1441. The British attorney general ruled that the resolution was, of itself, sufficient authorization for an attack on Iraq.

In the post–Saddam Hussein period, a major issue is the establishment of a democratic society embracing three disparate groups: the Sunni Arab minority, the large Shi'a majority in the south, and the northern Sunni Kurds. The Kurdish problem is complicated by the concerns of Turkey and by the 1970 promise of the Iraqi regime to grant the Kurds autonomy.

37. Qaradawi, "Extremism," 200–201.

CONCLUSIONS

If they implement historical shari'a, Muslims cannot exercise their right to self-determination without violating the rights of others.

'Abdullahi Ahmed An-Na'im[1]

There is a need to encourage and initiate audacious, free, productive thinking on Islam today.

Mohamed Arkoun[2]

Islam emerged out of the Arabian peninsula from a people divided by almost everything except the Arabic language. The faith was given expression by a man who was able to see the absurdity of that mixture of superstition, idolatry, animism, and polytheism that gripped his people, and to see beyond that to the grandeur of tawhid, "One God." But more than that: this one man had the tenacity to hold on to his beliefs through years of increasing persecution, and had the ability to gain such a measure of devotion from his followers that they, too, could hold on.

Although he was a man of the people, Muhammad was still able to clothe his ideas in the literary forms of his day, often employing startling and vivid imagery, resulting in a poetry that lent itself to memorization, so that after his death much of it could be gathered together for later generations to ponder.

His system of theology was uncluttered by the abstruse; that would be added later by the ulama and by the Traditions, especially as they were brought together, codified, and given an authority over everyday life that Muhammad could scarcely have imagined, enduring even into the twenty-first century. And it is a system that built a bridge

1. 'Abdullahi Ahmed An-Na'im, *"Shari'a* and Basic Human Rights Concerns," in *Liberal Islam: A Sourcebook*, ed. Charles Kurzman (New York: Oxford University Press, 1998), 222.
2. Arkoun, "Rethinking Islam Today," 205.

from the traditional practices of the past, retaining a sufficient core to allow his followers to sense it as still an Arab religion. The Ka'ba is still there, and pilgrimage, and the Arabic language, together with a book directed to the Arab peoples. No foreign hand can be seen to have imposed this new faith on the Arab world: it carries an indelible Arab stamp and has come to be seen as a gift from Allah particularly for the Arab peoples but ultimately for the world beyond.

Muhammad's many abilities were demonstrated in the comparatively brief time in which he led his growing community. The Constitution of Madina and the Treaty of Hudaybiyya testify to his ability as a political administrator. The battles and raids in which he freely participated or which he directed testify to his courage, his strategic skills, and his innovations, amusingly railed against by his enemies as unfair and un-Arabic. And there was his early concern, even during the difficult Meccan period, for the poor and powerless, the oppressed urban orphans (of whom he had been one), and for widows, and his willingness to give to women at least *more* rights than they had previously enjoyed.

But this recognition of quite positive aspects of Islam and its prophet cannot be allowed to conceal another side, a side entirely understandable in its context, but a side that sits uncomfortably with twenty-first-century ethical expectations. There can be no doubt that Islam was cradled in violence, and that Muhammad, through the twenty-six or twenty-seven raids in which he personally participated, came to serve for some Muslims as a role model for violence. Justification for violence thus has found its way into the pages of the Qur'an, alongside the more generous passages promoting peace. This ambivalence of the Qur'an on the question of violence has been used to encourage and justify the violence of those extremists who have arisen from time to time in the long history of Islam, beginning with the Kharijis and represented most recently by Osama bin Laden's al-Qa'ida terrorist network.

Inevitably throughout its history, Islam has impacted Christianity. The two have much in common, and indeed there is every reason to suppose that Muhammad believed that he was simply giving to the Arab world what Jesus had brought to the Greek-speaking Gentile world and Moses to the Jewish people. But Muhammad seems to have had little access to the Christian Scriptures and had a limited understanding of its theology, of its carefully phrased Greek and Latin formulas that recognized a Trinitarian theology but asserted tawhid as emphatically as did Muhammad. The consequence was a denial of two of the fundamentals of Christian belief, one theological and the other historical: Christ's deity and his crucifixion.

Nor was that all. Encountering the Jewish and Christian Scriptures only orally, Muhammad was unable to distinguish between canonical Scripture and legendary accretions. Through the Qur'an, both alike were invested with the authority of Islamic scripture, and both Jews and Christians were not slow in pointing out the discrepancies between their Scriptures and the Qur'an. This in turn led to the Qur'anic accusation that Jews and Christians had allowed their Scriptures to become corrupt or, worse, had knowingly corrupted them in favor of their respective theologies—an accusation that has never been justified.

Being so closely related, the three great monotheistic religions have repeatedly clashed over their competing claims, not least over the city of Jerusalem, sacred to all three. These clashes led to the Crusades, to the present impasse in the Middle East, and hence to at least some part of the bitterness that has poisoned relationships between Muslims, Jews, and Christians ever since.

In recent years the bitterness felt by many Muslims from many parts of the world has been seen to focus on such political issues as the demand for a homeland for the Palestinian people or alleged American aggression in various parts of the world. Yet in fact the violence threatened by Islamist radicals against the West and the divisions within Islam itself ultimately owe more to the ambiguities of the Islamic scripture than to modern political issues. As is clear from diverse statements by Muslims, both moderate and radical, the Qur'an and Hadith are inconsistent in certain aspects of teaching, especially in the matter of the means for spreading Islam and for dealing with non-Muslim minorities.

In contact with the economically sophisticated and technologically advanced Western world, Islam has divided into three strong streams of thought. The first may be described as liberal and moderate: it seeks to modernize Islam and to re-present Muhammad in terms that could be appreciated and accepted by the non-Muslim world. The second, that of the radical Islamist, seeks to re-create in today's world the Islam of the seventh century. The destiny of Islam is to overcome all other religions and be installed as the world religion, and its victory is to be hastened, if necessary, by violence and terrorism. The third group is uncomfortably caught in the middle. The traditionalist masses wish to take their place as equal partners in the modern world under the guidance of their religious leaders, the ulama, as history moves on. And yet this third group is aware that the scriptures of Islam, read literally, more readily lend support to the Islamist radicals than they do to the modernizing liberals.

The way forward for Islam seems to lie in accepting for the Qur'an and Hadith a hermeneutic, a system of interpretation, that will allow their *meaning*, intended by Muhammad for specific situations in the seventh century and not for unimagined situations thirteen hundred years later, to be interpreted for the modern world by identifying the present *significance*. As we saw in previous discussion, this is essentially what modernizing Muslims are attempting to do, but there is still a long way to go in translating the efforts of the intellectual elite into a mass movement, whereby the tradition-bound masses are equipped to undertake such a task of interpretation for the modern day. The Indonesian Muslim scholar Masykuri Abdillah describes one of the dilemmas facing Muslim moderate intellectuals in the following terms:

> On the one hand, they demand freedom of thought and expression in order to support creative thinking, on the other hand their ideas are limited by Islamic teaching. This is the opposite to secular intellectuals who have hardly any limits to their thinking. It is correct to state that in Islamic history there was no conflict between faith and the sciences, as has occurred, for instance, within the Christian church.[3]

This is a path that Christianity has trodden. Much of the Christian community has long recognized the responsibility of the individual Christian to read, to understand, and to interpret Scripture without the interposition of a cleric. For the Muslim masses the door to *ijtihad* (personal interpretation of the Qur'an) has been closed, bolted, and barred by the traditionalist ulama for centuries. The Indonesian scholar Nurcholish Madjid expresses this clearly: "What has happened now is that the umma [Muslim community] has lost its creativity in this temporal life to the extent that it leaves the impression that it has decided not to act rather than [risk making a] mistake. In other words it has lost the spirit of ijtihad."[4]

What is required is widespread use of an ijtihad that is forward-looking, one that will have the courage to face up to certain anachronisms in the sacred texts and be more selective in applying these texts to the modern day, and one that can impress itself upon vast numbers

---

3. Masykuri Abdillah, *Responses of Indonesian Muslim Intellectuals to the Concept of Democracy (1966–1993)* (Hamburg: Abera, 1997), 235.

4. Nurcholish Madjid, "The Necessity of Renewing Islamic Thought and Reinvigorating Religious Understanding," in *Liberal Islam: A Sourcebook*, ed. Charles Kurzman (New York: Oxford University Press, 1998), 286.

of Muslims around the world. In this way a new age might dawn for Islam, not an age in which it would be absorbed into other religions, but an age in which it could move among other religions without threat either to them or from them.

The suggestion that the gates of ijtihad should be opened once again is not new, nor is it an innovative Western device aimed at undermining Islam in general and the ulama in particular. Muhammad Iqbal (1877–1938) criticized the ulama, saying that they halted "the dynamic process that originally produced Islamic law and instead were content to merely perpetuate established traditions." Although Iqbal would not go so far as to suggest restoring the principle of the responsibility of *individual* Muslims to interpret the Qur'an for themselves, he suggested that Islam should open the gates of ijtihad through representative national assemblies.[5] It is clear that he did not envisage those assemblies being dominated by the ulama.

Any move toward a substantial reinterpretation of the Qur'anic text, emphasizing some elements and demoting others, would almost certainly be opposed by many of the Shari'a-bound ulama. And here is a further challenge for Islam. Too many of the ulama throughout the Muslim world are educated within a narrow framework of disciplines and are little involved with contemporary scholarship. Inevitably this leads to a suspicion of it and ultimately to an unthinking rejection of it. Providing a generously educated ulama is a major challenge; yet as the world shrinks geographically and as technology breaks down the barriers to international communication, the essential isolation of the ulama must come to an end. The June 2002 ordinance of the Pakistani government in bringing the network of madrasa schools within mainstream educational systems and monitoring mechanisms is a step in the right direction and hints at what might be done in the wider Muslim world to provide a more open education for Islam's potential leaders.

Nevertheless, there is a further problem, and arguably a more difficult challenge. The radical Islamist has to be persuaded not merely logically but also emotionally that the way of peace and nonviolence is Qur'anic and Islamic. The fact is that radicalism appears heroic, especially to many young Muslims. It is exciting and attractive, an activism in comparison with the apparent pacifism of any middle way. Radicalism demands sacrifice, and to the young idealist the upward way, the hard way, has to be the right way. It is true that this is all emotion rather than logic, but the masses tend to be swayed by emotion and repelled by cold logic and intellectualizing. It can be no easy

5. John Esposito, "Contemporary Islam," in *The Oxford History of Islam*, ed. J. L. Esposito (Oxford: Oxford University Press, 1999), 649.

task for the moderates to persuade and convince the radicals that violence and terrorism are, in the end, counterproductive, and that the way of peace, the way of *salaam*, is the right pathway, a true sunna, for Islam today.

The widespread promotion of a forward-looking ijtihad could resolve the problem posed for the non-Muslim world by specific aspects of Shari'a law, such as the punishments prescribed for theft and immorality. It could remove certain aspects of legal discrimination against women. It could deal with Islamic law's disregard for the Universal Declaration of Human Rights, with its assertion of the right to freedom of religion; the United Nations cannot indefinitely ignore such disregard. The Sudanese-American Muslim scholar 'Abdullahi Ahmed An-Na'im addresses this issue: "By granting women and non-Muslims a lower status and sanctioning discriminatory treatment against them, shari'a denies women and non-Muslims the same degree of honor and human dignity it guarantees to Muslim men."[6] He foresees the demise of Shari'a law: "Current efforts to implement the public law of shari'a will fail because they are harmful to the best interests of Islam and the Muslims. These efforts will fail because the public law of shari'a is fundamentally inconsistent with the realities of modern life."[7]

The non-Muslim world may be able to wage war on terrorism and even to assist in the search for a solution to the Palestinian question. The issue of American military bases in Muslim lands also can be addressed. But these and other related matters, even if resolved, would be mere palliatives in the search for peace. The hard decisions and the crucial decisions need to be taken by Muslims and by them alone.

Islam stands at the crossroads. It has reached its present intersection not along a single route, but along several divergent roads: the Sunni road, the Shi'a road, the Sufi road, the road taken by the masses, the road of Folk Islam, the Khariji road, the modernizing road. In the words of Professor James Beverley of Tyndale Seminary in Toronto:

> The tensions [Islam] has been facing for centuries have risen to the surface. Is Islam a religion of peace? Does it believe in human rights? Can it find a way to be a part of the human community without violently insisting on its own way? We hear so many differing accounts of Islam today precisely because Muslims are in the midst of a struggle for the soul of Islam.[8]

6. An-Na'im, "*Shari'a* and Basic Human Rights Concerns," 224.
7. Ibid., 238.
8. James A. Beverley, "Is Islam a Religion of Peace?" *Christianity Today* 46.1 (January 7, 2002): 42.

SELECT BIBLIOGRAPHY

The following list includes published volumes and articles appearing in journals. Internet-based resources and newspaper articles are not listed here. Their details are available in the footnotes to each chapter.

Abdillah, Masykuri. *Responses of Indonesian Muslim Intellectuals to the Concept of Democracy (1966–1993)*. Hamburg: Abera, 1997.

Achtemeier, P. J. *1 Peter*. Hermeneia. Minneapolis: Fortress, 1996.

Ahmed, Akbar S. *Living Islam: From Samarkand to Stornoway*. London: BBC Books, 1993.

Ajijola, Alhaji Adeleke Dirisu. "The Problem of 'Ulama.'" In *Liberal Islam: A Sourcebook*, ed. Charles Kurzman. New York: Oxford University Press, 1998.

Alexander, Y., and M. Swetnam. *Usama bin Laden's al-Qaida: Profile of a Terrorist Network*. Ardsley, N.Y.: Transnational Publishers, 2001.

Ali, Abdullah Yusuf. *The Meaning of the Holy Qur'an*. 8th ed. Beltsville, Md.: Amana, 1996.

Ali, Syed Ameer. *The Spirit of Islam*. London: Chatto and Windus, 1984.

An-Na'im, 'Abdullahi Ahmed. "*Shari'a* and Basic Human Rights Concerns." In *Liberal Islam: A Sourcebook*, ed. Charles Kurzman. New York: Oxford University Press, 1998.

Arkoun, Mohamed. "Rethinking Islam Today." In *Liberal Islam: A Sourcebook*, ed. Charles Kurzman. New York: Oxford University Press, 1998.

Atkinson, James. *The Great Light*. Exeter: Paternoster, 1968.

Ayubi, N. *Political Islam*. London: Routledge, 1991.

Azzam, Salem, ed. *Islam and Contemporary Society*. London: Longmans, 1982.

Bakhash, Shaul. *The Reign of the Ayatollahs*. London: Taurus, 1985.

Barraclough, Geoffrey. *The Medieval Papacy*. London: Thames and Hudson, 1968.

Barrett, David. *World Christian Encyclopedia*. Nairobi, Oxford, and New York: Oxford University Press, 1982.

Bennett, Clinton. *In Search of Muhammad*. London and New York: Cassell, 1998.

Blankinship, Khalid Yahya. *The End of the Jihad State*. New York: State University of New York Press, 1994.

Bradshaw, Bruce. *Change across Cultures*. Grand Rapids: Baker, 2002.

Browne, Edward G. *A Literary History of Persia*. 4 vols. Cambridge: Cambridge University Press, 1902–24.

Brundage, James. *The Crusades: A Documentary History*. Milwaukee, Wis.: Marquette University Press, 1962.

Bukhari, Muhammad ibn Ismail. *Sahih al-Bukhari*. Ed. and trans. Muhammad Muhsin Kahn. Gujranwala: Dar Ahya Us-Sunnah, 1973–.

Burnett, David. *Unearthly Powers*. Eastbourne: MARC, 1988.

Carlyle, Thomas. *The French Revolution: A History*. New York: Random House, Modern Library, [1934].

Chakmakjian, Hagop A. *Armenian Christology and Evangelization of Islam*. Leiden: Brill, 1965.

Chapman, Colin. "Living through the 900th Anniversary of the First Crusade: To Apologise or Not to Apologise?" *The Faith to Faith Newsletter* 1 (November 1998): 1–3.

Churchill, Randolph S., and Winston S. Churchill. *The Six Day War*. London: Heinemann, 1967.

Churchill, Winston. *Great Contemporaries*. London: Fontana, 1937.

Cohen, Joshua, Martha Nussbaum, and Matthew Howard, eds. *Is Multiculturalism Bad for Women?* Princeton: Princeton University Press, 1999.

Cotterell, F. Peter. *Born at Midnight*. Chicago: Moody, 1970.

———. "The Gospel of Barnabas." *Vox Evangelica* 10 (1977): 43–47.

———. *Mission and Meaninglessness*. London: SPCK, 1990.

Cotterell, Peter, and Max Turner. *Linguistics and Biblical Interpretation*. London: SPCK, 1989.

Cragg, Kenneth. *The Event of the Qur'an*. London: Allen and Unwin, 1971.

———. *Islamic Surveys 3: Counsels in Contemporary Islam*. Edinburgh: Edinburgh University Press, 1965.

Cranfield, C. E. B. *A Critical and Exegetical Commentary on the Epistle to the Romans*. 2 vols. International Critical Commentary. Edinburgh: Clark, 1975–79.

Creasy, Edward. *The Fifteen Decisive Battles of the World*. 13th ed. London: Richard Bentley, 1863.

Crombie, Kevin. *For the Love of Zion*. London: Hodder and Stoughton, 1991.

Crone, Patricia. *Meccan Trade and the Rise of Islam*. Princeton: Princeton University Press, 1987.

Crone, Patricia, and Michael Cook. *Hagarism*. Cambridge and London: Cambridge University Press, 1977.

Daniel, Norman. *Islam and the West*. 2d ed. Oxford: One World, 1993.

Davis, R. H. C. *A History of Medieval Europe*. London: Longman, 1957.

Davis, William Stearns, ed. *Readings in Ancient History: Illustrative Extracts from the Sources,* vol. 2, *Rome and the West.* Boston: Allyn and Bacon, 1912–13.

Doi, Abdur Rahman I. *Shari'ah: The Islamic Law.* London: Ta Ha Publishers, 1984.

Dubnov, Simon. *History of the Jews.* Vol. 3. London: Thomas Yoseloff, 1969.

Esposito, John L. *Islam: The Straight Path.* 3d ed. New York and Oxford: Oxford University Press, 1998.

———, ed. *The Oxford History of Islam.* Oxford: Oxford University Press, 1999.

Firestone, Reuven. *Jihad: The Origin of Holy War in Islam.* Oxford and New York: Oxford University Press, 1999.

———. *Journeys in Holy Lands.* New York: New York State University Press, 1990.

Frend, W. H. C. *The Rise of Christianity.* Philadelphia: Fortress, 1984.

Gibb, H. A. R. *Modern Trends in Islam.* Chicago: University of Chicago Press, 1947.

Gibb, H. A. R., and J. H. Kramers, eds. *Shorter Encyclopaedia of Islam.* Leiden: Brill, 1953.

Gilchrist, John. *The Qur'an, the Scripture of Islam.* Mondeor, South Africa: MERCSA, 1995.

Goitein, Shlomo Dov. "The Jews under Islam 6th–16th centuries." In *The Jewish World: Revelation, Prophecy, and History,* ed. Elie Kedouri. London: Thames and Hudson, 1979.

Goldziher, Ignaz. *Muslim Studies.* Vol. 2. London: Allen and Unwin, 1971.

Green, Lynn. *The Reconciliation Walk: Defusing the Bitter Legacy of the Crusades.* YWAM, Procla Media Productions, 1995. Videocassette.

Griffiths, M. C. "Thomas Valpy French." In *Mission and Meaning,* ed. A. Billington and A. Lane. Exeter: Paternoster, 1995.

Guillaume, Alfred. *Islam.* 2d ed. Harmondsworth: Penguin, 1956.

———, trans. *The Life of Muhammad: A Translation of Ishaq's Sirat Rasul Allah.* London and New York: Oxford University Press, 1955.

Gunaratna, Rohan. *Inside Al Qaeda: Global Network of Terror.* London: Hurst, 2002.

Guthrie, Donald. *New Testament Introduction.* 4th ed. Leicester: Apollos; Downers Grove, Ill.: InterVarsity, 1990.

Hallam, Elizabeth, ed. *Chronicles of the Crusades: Eye-Witness Accounts of the Wars between Christianity and Islam.* London: Weidenfeld and Nicolson, 1989.

Halliday, Fred. *Two Hours That Shook the World: September 11, 2001: Causes and Consequences.* London: Saqi Books, 2002.

Hawting, G. R. *The First Dynasty of Islam.* 2d ed. London: Routledge, 2000.

———. "John Wansbrough, Islam, and Monotheism." In *The Quest for the Historical Muhammad.* New York: Prometheus, 2000.

Henderson, Ernest F. *Select Historical Documents of the Middle Ages.* London: George Bell and Sons, 1910.

Hillenbrand, Carole. *The Crusades: Islamic Perspectives.* Edinburgh: Edinburgh University Press, 1999.

Hitti, Philip K. *The Arabs: A Short History.* London: Macmillan, 1968.

———. *History of the Arabs.* 10th ed. London: Macmillan, 1970.

Holmes, A. F. *War and Christian Ethics.* Grand Rapids: Baker, 1975.

Humphreys, R. Stephen. *Islamic History.* Rev. ed. London: Tauris, 1991.

Ibn 'Abd-el-Hakem. *History of the Conquest of Spain.* Trans. John Harris Jones. Göttingen: W. Fr. Kaestner, 1858.

Inalcik, Halil, "The Rise of the Ottoman Empire." In *The Cambridge History of Islam,* vol. 1, ed. P. M. Holt, Ann K. S. Lambton, and Bernard Lewis. Cambridge: Cambridge University Press. 1970.

Islamophobia: A Challenge for Us All. London: Runnymede Trust, 1997.

Joinville, Jean. "The Life of Saint Louis." In *Chronicles of the Crusades,* trans. M. R. B. Shaw. Harmondsworth: Penguin, 1963.

Kaegi, Walter E. *Byzantium and the Early Islamic Conquests.* Cambridge: Cambridge University Press, 1992.

Kenny, Joseph. "The Sources of Radical Movements in Islam." *Skepticos* 1 (1990): 19–22.

Kerr, David. "Islamic Da'wa and Christian Mission: Towards a Comparative Analysis." *International Review of Mission* 79, issue 353 (April 2000).

Khan, Muhammad Zafrulla. *Deliverance from the Cross.* Southfields: London Mosque, 1978.

Kramers, J. H., H. A. R. Gibb, and E. Lévi-Provencal, eds. *The Encyclopaedia of Islam.* New ed. Leiden: Brill, 1960–.

Kurzman, Charles, ed. *Liberal Islam: A Sourcebook.* New York: Oxford University Press, 1998.

Lapidus, Ira M. *A History of Islamic Societies.* Cambridge: Cambridge University Press, 1988.

Laqueur, Walter, ed. *The Israel-Arab Reader.* Expanded ed. New York: Bantam, 1969.

Latourette, K. S. *A History of the Expansion of Christianity.* 7 vols. Grand Rapids: Zondervan, 1970.

Lawler, Philip. "The Looming Showdown." *Catholic World Report* 11.9 (October 2001).

Lewis, Bernard. *The Arabs in History.* 5th ed. London: Hutchinson University Library, 1970.

Lewis, Bernard, ed. and trans. *Islam from the Prophet Muhammad to the Capture of Constantinople.* New York: Harper and Row, 1974; reprint, New York: Oxford University Press, 1987.

Lewis, C. S. *Screwtape Letters.* New York: Macmillan, 1943.

Lewis, I. M. *Religion in Context: Cults and Charisma.* London and New York: Cambridge University Press, 1986.

Lietzmann, Hans. *The Founding of the Church Universal.* 3d ed. London: Lutterworth, 1953.

Lings, Martin. *Muhammad: His Life Based on the Earliest Sources.* New York: Inner Traditions International, 1983.

Madjid, Nurcholish. "The Necessity of Renewing Islamic Thought and Reinvigorating Religious Understanding." In *Liberal Islam: A Sourcebook,* ed. Charles Kurzman. New York: Oxford University Press, 1998.

Mallouhi, Christine A. *Waging Peace on Islam.* London: Monarch, 2000.

Marcus, Jacob. *The Jew in the Medieval World: A Sourcebook, 315–1791.* New York: JPS, 1938.

Martin, R. C., R. Woodward, and D. S. Atmaja. *Defenders of Reason in Islam.* Oxford: One World, 1997.

Melissenos, Makarios, "The Chronicle of the Siege of Constantinople, April 2 to May 29, 1453." In *The Fall of the Byzantine Empire,* trans. Marios Philippides. Amherst, Mass.: University of Massachusetts Press, 1980.

Moucarry, Chawkat. *Faith to Faith.* Leicester: Inter-Varsity, 2001.

Musk, Bill. *The Unseen Face of Islam.* Eastbourne: MARC, 1989.

Muslim. *Sahih Muslim.* Ed. Abdul Hamid Siddiqi. Lahore: Sh. Muhammad Ashraf, 1980.

Nasr, Seyyed Hossein. *Islamic Life and Thought.* London: Allen and Unwin, 1981.

Nazir-Ali, Michael. *Islam: A Christian Perspective.* Exeter: Paternoster, 1983.

Neill, Stephen. *Crises of Belief.* London: Hodder and Stoughton, 1984.

———. *A History of Christian Missions.* 2d ed. London: Penguin, 1986.

———. *Salvation Tomorrow.* Nashville: Abingdon, 1976.

Nicholson, Helen J. *Chronicle of the Third Crusade: A Translation of the Itinerarium Peregrinorum et Gesta Regis Ricardi.* Aldershot: Ashgate, 1997.

Niebuhr, Reinhold. "Why the Church Is Not Pacifist." In *War and Christian Ethics,* ed. A. F. Holmes. Grand Rapids: Baker, 1975.

Norwich, John Julian. *Byzantium: The Early Centuries.* London: Viking, 1988.

Okin, Susan. "Reply." In *Is Multiculturalism Bad for Women?* ed. Joshua Cohen, Martha Nussbaum, and Matthew Howard. Princeton: Princeton University Press, 1999.

Oussoren, A. H. *William Carey.* Leiden: Suthoff, 1945.

Parrinder, Geoffrey. *Jesus in the Qur'an.* London: Sheldon, 1965.

Peers, E. A. *Fool of Love.* London: SCM, 1946.

Powers, David S. "The Exegetical Genre Nasikh al-Qur'an wa Mansukhuhu." In *Approaches to the History of the Interpretation of the Qur'an,* ed. Andrew Rippin. Oxford: Clarendon, 1988.

Qaradawi, Yusuf al-. "Extremism." In *Liberal Islam: A Sourcebook,* ed. Charles Kurzman. New York: Oxford University Press, 1998.

Qutb, Sayyid. *Milestones.* Indianapolis: American Trust, 1985; New Delhi: Naushaba, 1995.

Ragg, Lonsdale, and Laura Ragg. *The Gospel of Barnabas.* London: Oxford University Press, 1907.

Rahim, Muhammad Ata ur-. *Jesus: A Prophet of Islam.* 2d ed. London: MWH Publishers, 1979.

Rahman, Fazlur. *Islam.* London: Weidenfeld and Nicolson, 1966.

Rasmussen, L. L. *Dietrich Bonhoeffer: Reality and Resistance.* Studies in Christian Ethics. Nashville: Abingdon, 1972.

Rauf, Muhammad Abdul. *The Islamic Tradition*. Niles, Ill.: Argus, 1978.

Redgate, A. E. *The Armenians*. Oxford: Blackwell, 2000.

Reeves, Donald, ed. *The Church and the State*. London: Hodder and Stoughton, 1984.

Richard, Jean. *The Crusades, c. 1071–c. 1291*. Cambridge: Cambridge University Press, 1999.

Riddell, Peter G. "The Diverse Voices of Political Islam in Post-Suharto Indonesia." *Islam and Christian-Muslim Relations* 13.1 (January 2002): 65–84.

———. "From Qur'an to Contemporary Politics: Hamas and the Role of Sacred Scripture." In *Fundamentalisms*, ed. C. H. Partridge. Carlisle: Paternoster, 2001.

———. "Islamic Perspectives on Globalisation." *St. Mark's Review* (2003).

Riley-Smith, Louise, and Jonathan Riley-Smith. *The Crusades: Idea and Reality, 1095–1274*. London: Edward Arnold, 1981.

Rippin, Andrew. *Muslims: Their Religious Beliefs and Practices*. 2d ed. London: Routledge, 2001.

Rippin, Andrew, and Jan Knappert, eds. *Textual Sources for the Study of Islam*. Chicago: University of Chicago Press, 1986.

Rodinson, Maxime. *Mohammed*. Harmondsworth: Penguin, 1971.

Ruthven, Malise. *Islam in the World*. 2d ed. London: Penguin, 2000.

Sambur, Bilal. "The Insider/Outsider Problem in the Study of Islam." *The Islamic Quarterly* 46.1 (2002): 95–106.

Seale, Patrick. *The Struggle for Syria*. London: Oxford University Press, 1965.

Senior, Donald, and Carol Stuhlmueller. *The Biblical Foundations for Mission*. London: SCM, 1983.

Siberry, Elizabeth. *Criticism of Crusading, 1095–1274*. Oxford: Clarendon, 1985.

Siddiqi, Muhammad Zubayr. *Hadith Literature*. Cambridge: Islamic Texts Society, 1993.

Sleeman, J. F. "Usury and Interest." In *A Dictionary of Christian Ethics*, ed. John Macquarrie. London: SCM, 1967.

Smith, Ian, "God and Economics." In *God and Culture*, ed. D. A. Carson and J. D. Woodbridge. Carlisle: Paternoster; Grand Rapids: Eerdmans, 1993.

Smith, Jane. "Islam and Christendom: Historical, Cultural, and Religious Interaction from the Seventh to the Fifteenth Centuries." In *The Oxford History of Islam*, ed. J. L. Esposito. Oxford: Oxford University Press, 1999.

Smith, Mary. *Baba of Karo*. London: Faber and Faber, 1954.

Sox, David. *The Gospel of Barnabas*. London: Allen and Unwin, 1984.

Stokey, Robert W. *America and the Arab States: An Uneasy Encounter*. New York: John Wiley and Sons, 1975.

Talal, Hassan bin. "Towards a World with 10,000 Cultures." *Discourse* 1 (August 2000).

Trimingham, J. S. *Islam in Ethiopia*. London: Oxford University Press, 1952.

Ullmann, W. *The Growth of Papal Government in the Middle Ages*. London: Methuen, 1965.

Villehardouin, Geoffrey de. "The Conquest of Constantinople." In *Chronicles of the Crusades,* trans. M. R. B. Shaw. Harmondsworth: Penguin, 1963.

Wahono, S. Wismoady. "Christian Mission in Asia: The Colonial Past and Challenges for Today." *International Review of Mission* 87, issue 345 (April 1998).

Wakf, Aisha Bawany, ed. *The Gospel of Barnabas.* Karachi: Ashram Publications, 1976.

Watt, W. Montgomery. *Early Islam.* Edinburgh: Edinburgh University Press, 1990.

———. *The Majesty That Was Islam.* London: Sidgwick and Jackson, 1974.

———. *Muhammad: Prophet and Statesman.* London: Oxford University Press, 1961.

———. *Muslim-Christian Encounters.* London and New York: Routledge, 1991.

Watt, W. Montgomery, ed. *Bell's Introduction to the Qur'an.* Edinburgh: Edinburgh University Press, 1970.

The Westophobia Report: Anti-Western and Anti-Christian Stereotyping in British Muslim Publications. Occasional Paper, no. 1. London: London Bible College Centre for Islamic Studies, 1999.

Woodberry, J. Dudley. "Terrorism, Islam, and Mission: Reflections of a Guest in Muslim Lands." *International Bulletin of Missionary Research* 26.1 (January 2002).

World Population Prospects. New York: United Nations, 1997.

Ye'or, Bat. *The Dhimmi: Jews and Christians under Islam.* Rutherford, N.J.: Fairleigh Dickinson University Press; London and Toronto: Associated University Presses, 1985.

———. *Islam and Dhimmitude: Where Civilizations Collide.* Translated by Miriam Kochan and David Littman. Cranbury, N.J.: Associated University Presses; Lancaster, U.K.: Gazelle Book Services, 2002.

Yusseff, M. A. *The Dead Sea Scrolls, the Gospel of Barnabas, and the New Testament.* Indianapolis: American Trust, 1985.

INDEX